Environ'd With Eternity

God, Poems, and Plants
in
Sixteenth and Seventeenth Century
England

Charlotte F. Otten

Coronado Press   1985

Set in 10 on twelve point Souvenir

Published in the United States of America
by
Coronado Press
Box 3232
Lawrence, Kansas 66044

To Bob

This study, which draws upon so many primary sources, could not have been completed without the use of research libraries. I should like to express my thanks to the officials and assistants of the Reading Room, the North Library, and the Manuscript Department of the British Library (London) for permitting me to use their rich collections; to Michigan State University Special Collections for extending to me so many courtesies over the years; and to the Rare Book Collections of the following libraries: Harvard, Yale, Princeton, Chicago, and Michigan (Ann Arbor).

Down the years there have been generous scholars who were willing to answer questions. I wish to thank Blanche Henrey (British Museum, Natural History) for supplying me with information from her vast knowledge of botanical illustration; Dr. Charles Webster (Wellcome Unit for the History of Medicine, Oxford) for elucidating a complex issue from his researches in the Hartlib Papers; Muriel A. Arber for a lengthy reply to a question arising from her mother's book *Herbals;* and Mr. F. White (Curator of the Claridge Druce Herbarium, Department of Botany, Oxford) for opening to me the Bobart Herbarium and sharing with me his botanic expertise.

Research funds for this study came from a number of sources. I wish to thank Grand Valley State Colleges, Allendale, Michigan, for two research grants; the Calvin Foundation (Calvin Alumni Association) for a summer travel grant; Calvin College for a sabbatical leave; and the American Council of Learned Societies for a grant-in-aid.

I owe to the late Lawrence Babb of Michigan State University a large debt of gratitude; I only regret that he did not live to see the publication of the book which he originally suggested that I write. I thank Frank L. Huntley of the University of Michigan for his early confidence in me, and for his continuing interest.

To my children I owe a debt of gratitude for their constant encouragement and inspiration. And to my husband I owe the largest debt of all — for he not only facilitated my work but felicitates my life.

Charlotte F. Otten
Calvin College

Acknowledgment is made for permission to reprint from the following: Donald Davie, from "In the Stopping Train" and "Observances," permission of the author. Norman Nicholson, "The Burning Bush," from *Five Rivers*, permission of Faber and Faber. The following journals have granted permission to quote from my articles which originally appeared in them in altered form: "Milton's Haemony," *English Literary Renaissance*, Winter 1975, pp. 81-95. "Donne's *Elegie upon the untimely death of the incomparable Prince Henry*," *Explicator*, Vol. 33, No. 7, March, 1975 (Article 59). "Garlanding the Dead: The Epicedial Garland in *Lycidas*," *Milton Studies*, XVI, 1982. "Ophelia's 'Long Purples' or 'Dead Men's Fingers,' " *Shakespeare Quarterly*, Summer 1979, pp. 397-402.

CONTENTS

List of Illustrations

PREFACE

When the terraculturalists[1] of the sixteenth and seventeenth centuries took to writing books about the vegetable creation, they began with God, and they put their studies in the perspective of Heaven. Their ebullient prefaces show them revelling in the beneficence of a Creator whom they regarded as the Husbandman of the Universe. They believed that "the Great Design" had originated with Him in Heaven and that this design had been conceived in Eternity and impressed upon Time. From making order out of cosmic chaos to planting a garden eastward in Eden for His image-bearer to live and work in, the God of the universe had found nothing too mundane for His concern and care:

> The Excellency of Husbandry appeareth partly by its Antiquity, as we esteem Things to be the more Admirable, the more Ancient, and the nearer they come to God, the First Being of all Beings; for as all Things nearer the Centre move more strongly, so all Excellency appears most evidently the nearer . . . to the Great Majesty, the Almighty Husbandiser, God himself . . . God was the Original and Pattern of all Husbandry, and First Contriver of the Great Design, to bring that odd Mass, and Chaos of Confusion,

unto so vast an Improvement, as all the World admires and
subsists on: And having given Man such a Pattern, both for
Precept and Precedent for his Encouragement, he made
him Lord of all until he fell . . .[2]

"Until he fell" — these words echoed in their ears as a warning.
There were those of their contemporaries who feared that studying
and working in the vegetable creation would reproduce the first sin:
the worship of the created instead of the Creator. The terraculturalists recognized the constant danger to fallen man of embracing
the transitory rather than the Eternal. But as gardeners who planted
gardens and fruit trees, as farmers who raised vegetable and grain
crops, as herbalists who grew herbs, did field botany, and practiced
medicine, they had seen "the Great Design" with their own eyes, and
had touched it with their own hands. Their study of the vegetable
creation had not deflected their attention from the Creator but had
drawn their gaze upward to Him. "It was the sin of the Heathen,"
Robert Sharrock, Fellow of New College, Oxford, and Fellow of the
Royal Society, had observed, "that they did not rise in their mindes
from the contemplation of the beauty of the creatures, to consider
how such lineaments could be made, and to glorifie thereby the
wisdome of the Maker."[3]

To ignore the Creator in the study of the vegetable creation was a
danger to be reckoned with, but there were those who adduced even
stronger arguments against the study of Nature. They saw the study
of Nature as a direct route to atheism. To them Sir Thomas Pope
Blount, a spirited writer-collector of materials on natural history,
replied, vigorously denouncing those who refused to study God's
creation for fear of becoming atheists:

It was certainly the Design of the great Architect, that his
Creatures should afford not only Necessaries and Accom-
modations to our Animal part, but also Instructions to our
Intellectual. Every Flower of the Field, every Fibre of a
Plant, every Particle of an Insect, carries with it the Impress
of Ethics or Divinity. The deeper insight any Man hath into
the Affairs of *Nature*, the more he discovers of the
Accurateness, and Art, that is in the Contexture of Things:
For the Works of God, are not like the Compositions of
Fancy, or the Tricks of Juglers, that will not bear a clear

> Light, or strict Scrutiny; but their Exactness receives
> advantage from the severest Inspection; and he admires
> most, that knows most. How unreasonable (then) are those
> Men, who will not herein allow us the use of our *Rational*
> *Faculties,* but with great Fury and Zeal declaim against the
> Study of *Nature,* as a thing most dangerous and pernicious;
> telling us, that too strict an Enquiry into the Works of
> *Nature,* does often terminate in a Spirit of Atheism . . .[4]

In addition to those who were wary of being beguiled by the
vegetable creation, and to those who were certain that the study of
the vegetable creation was a road to repudiation of the Creator,
there were those who found dabbling in the *concept* of Nature more
inspiring than dibbling in the earth. The terraculturalists admitted
that terraculture was often considered a "beastly and beggarly
occupation" and was "by many accounted a base and mean Study."[5]
In this hostile climate, Blount could only respond with sarcasm to
those who thought terraculture beneath their dignity:

> . . . another sort of Men . . . who pretend to be wiser and
> more knowing than the rest of Mankind: These, I know, will
> be able to smile at, and despise many of the Subjects here
> treated of, as mean and trifling. What! Entertain such brave
> Heros, such mighty Dons, with an insipid Discourse of
> Plants . . .[6]

But the terracultural writers were not intimidated by the fearful,
nor by the "brave and mighty." They had the Triune God on their
side. And they were surrounded by a cloud of terracultural
witnesses: the history of the world lay before them in the figures of
prestigious gardeners, both Christian and pagan. In their inspiriting
prefaces they urged all men to become as they were — husbandmen. Their books, with that remarkable blend of the richly
philosophical and the intensely practical, were designed to convince
the reader of the values of terraculture and to provide accurate
guides to the practice of the profession. One had only to "take up
and read." And then do likewise.

Terracultural literature is a large body of writing which emerges as
a wide-ranging and substantial genre. It is an index to the aesthetic,
horticultural, agricultural, scientific, philosophical, and theological
thought of the day. It includes:

1) *Garden books,* which describe, among other things, horticulture, pomoculture, viticulture, landscape architecture, and which frequently articulate an aesthetic theory as well as a philosophy of nature.
2) *Herbals,* which describe the botanical, medical, pharmaceutical, horticultural, magico-medical, and aesthetic properties of plants.
3) *Itineraries* of early botanists, which include data collected in the field.
4) *Descriptions* of orchards, of kitchen, cottage, physic/ botanic, pleasure gardens by herbalists, gardeners, historians, travellers, poets.
5) *Floristic* books.
6) *Agricultural manuals.*
7) *Regional natural histories; herbaria.*
8) *Natural Philosophy.*
9) *Iconography.*

In short, as one garden writer declared, it is all that is "excellent, amiable, desirable, medicinable, physical, profitable, and mystical." It is a genre whose neglect results not only in a serious underestimation of the effect that garden literature had on the age itself —sometimes reflecting, sometimes shaping the thought — but also in a diminution of the sensibilities and a hardening of the affective responses of the reader of the poetry of those centuries. The observations of Stephen Switzer (a garden writer) show how brisk was the commerce between poetry and gardening:

> But altho' things were in this terrible Combustion, we must not omit the famous Mr. *John Milton,* one of *Cromwell's* Secretaries; who, by his excellent and never-to-be parallell'd Poem of *Paradise Lost,* has particularly distinguish'd *Gard'ning,* by taking that for his Theme; and shews, that tho' his Eyes depriv'd him of the Benefit of seeing, yet His Mind was wonderfully mov'd with the Philosophy, Innocence, and Beauty of this Employ, his Books, tho' mix'd with other Subjects, being a kind of a Philosophical Body of *Gard'ning,* as well as Divinity. Happy Man! had his Pen been employed on no other Subject.[7]

For poets, as well as for terraculturalists, plants were an

immediate as well as a mediate form of knowledge:

> All things here shew him heaven . . .
>> trees, herbs, flowres, all
> Strive upwards stil, and point him the way home.[8]

In Nature, they saw Grace, and in Grace, Nature. The vegetable creation (and the books about it) showed the presence of the "human face divine"; in the smells of plants an ontology was revealed; and in the loveliness and energy of plants, the Paradise of Adam and Eve and the Paradise-to-come was evidenced. Poetic references to Paradise and to all subsequent Paradises, and descriptions of all the vast creation of vegetable strength and beauty, supported the growth of the kind of natural spiritual knowledge which originally had given Adam's life such dignity and joy. Traherne's felicity consisted in rediscovering in poetry the original simplicity of Adam, whose delights were natural:

> All Bliss
> Consists in this,
> To do as *Adam* did.[9]

For the sixteenth and seventeenth centuries, the vegetable creation was the meeting ground of Nature and Grace. Plants and poems witnessed to the presence of God in the Garden of Eden, of the Risen Lord in the Garden of the Resurrection, and of the redeemed creation in the Garden of Eternity.

Today we are baffled by the intimacy between God and His vegetable creation which the sixteenth and seventeenth centuries found so comfortingly instructive; we are profoundly embarrassed by the sixteenth and seventeenth century poets who shared with terraculturalists a love for plants; and we are scarcely able to understand, or endure, except by straining, the implications of Vaughan's faith that "th' herb he treads knows much, much more."[10] We do understand when the twentieth-century poet Donald Davie asks, "What's all this about flowers?" With three and more centuries separating today's poets and scientists from both the poetry and the terraculture of those centuries, the interdependence of plants and poems in their spiritual natural environment can be understood only by going back to both the terraculture and the poetry. Davie mourns that loss while he attempts to discover why he cannot feel the lack of the sense of loss:

What's all this about flowers?
They have an importance he can't
explain, or else their names have.

* * *

Love *them?* Love flowers? Love,
love . . . the word is hopeless:
gratitude, maybe, pity . . .

Pitiful, the flowers.
He turns that around in his head:
what on earth can it mean?

Flowers, it seems, are important.
And he can name them all,
identify hardly any.[11]

My book cannot replace the histories of gardening with their lavish illustrations of gardens; nor can it serve as a history of terraculture; nor is it an "influence study" tracing the allusions in the poetry back to the terracultural writings. It does not attempt to cover all the poems that speak of plants; nor does it claim to be the final statement on the relationship between poems and plants. It is designed to show the philosophical and theological basis for terraculture, to point out the values of terraculture, to introduce the reader to the world's most illustrious terraculturalists, to acquaint the reader with terracultural practices and information that are no longer common knowledge, to reveal the human shape perceived by poets and terraculturalists in the vegetable creation, to identify the ontology of smells in plants and poems, and to share in the vision of a Paradisal eschatology. Like those early terracultural books and poems, it should engage the mind and heart of the reader by bringing him not only the intensity of the library and laboratory but also the fragrance of the field and garden, "interwoven in so beautiful a manner that [like Thomas More's garden] it appeared like tapestry woven by Nature herself."

NOTES

To Preface

1 The word *terraculture* was first used in 1702 by T. Snow in *Apopiroscopy*. Although it is an unfamiliar term for modern readers, it has the advantage of being comprehensive and avoids the problems raised by such terms as *botany, agriculture, horticulture, gardening, husbandry,* all of which are restricted by specialization.

2 Leonard Meager, *The mystery of husbandry* (London, 1697), pp. 1-2; see also Walter Blith, *The English improover* (London, 1649), p. 3, which is the original statement from which Meager (or his printer) borrowed. I have chosen Meager's statement to show the persistence of this belief.

3 *The history of the propagation & improvement of vegetables* (Oxford, 1660), p. 139.

4 *A natural history* (London, 1693), *Preface.*

5 T. Snow, *Apopiroscopy* (London, 1702), p. 3.

6 *A natural history, Preface.*

7 Stephen Switzer, *The nobleman, gentleman, and gardener's recreation* (London, 1715), p. 39.

8 Henry Vaughan, "The Tempest," *The Complete Poetry of Henry Vaughan,* ed. French Fogle (New York, 1964), 11. 25-28.

9 Thomas Traherne, "The Apostacy," *Centuries, Poems, and Thanksgivings,* ed. H.M. Margoliouth (Oxford, 1958), II, 96, 11. 37-39.

10 Vaughan, "The Constellation," l. 28.

11 *In the Stopping Train* (Manchester, 1977), pp. 25-26.

CHAPTER ONE

VEGETABLE PHILOSOPHY

Incomparable are the works of the eternal God, the Creator of all things that live, move, or have any being . . . the innumerable company of Vegetables spread over the face of the earth, do participate, draw and contract into their several natures, the operations of the teeming womb of the Earth . . . [1]

I

Terraculture sprouted very few atheists. The Triune God, of whose presence in all aspects of terraculture the terracultural writers were certain, was the source and the inspiration of terraculture, the foundation on which it was built.

The Triune God — the terracultural writers referred to Him as "the Almighty Husbandiser" and as "the first Husbandman" — created the vegetable world for man; planted a garden in Eden; and gave to Adam a pre-lapsarian and post-lapsarian terracultural mandate.

The Incarnate God — they referred to Him as "a husbandman and the son of a husbandman" — husbandised on the sin-blasted earth; provided the sacrifice to atone for the Original Sin which had blighted the vegetable creation; delighted in the beauties of flowers; validated, even recommended, gardening as an activity fit for the God-Man, and hence for His redeemed sons and heirs, by appearing as a gardener after His Resurrection; and was Himself the mystical reality of all Paradise gardens.

The Holy Ghost instilled in man original vegetable knowledge; kept this knowledge alive in man after the Fall; and enabled man, through the practice of terraculture, to restore terraculture to its prestigious position among the professions.

The terraculturists believed and therefore they wrote. Without God, there would have been very few books on gardening, agriculture, botany. Had these writer-practitioners not been able to discover the incomprehensible power and wise benevolence of God in His vegetable creation, in all likelihood they would not have practiced the terracultural profession with such zealous confidence nor written about it with such confident zeal. God was their reason for engaging in terraculture and for writing about it.

In this chapter I shall look with the terracultural writers at the godliness of terraculture and at the trinity of terracultural activity.

II

God as the Creator was recognized by virtually all these sixteenth and seventeenth century writers. Whether they were obscure gardeners, farmers, herbalists, gardeners to royalty, or members of the Royal Society; whether they lived in the middle of the sixteenth century or in the earlier part of the eighteenth; whether they were Puritans or Anglicans, Roundheads or Royalists[2] — all began with the Creator. They admired Him, rejoicing that His goodness was mirrored in His world. Their prefaces show a remarkable uniformity in praising the Creator: they wrote so that God might be glorified. Stephen Blake, for example, in his practical little quarto volume on the garden of pleasure, the physical garden, and the kitchen garden (1664), felt sure that as an image-bearer of the Creator he was commissioned to reveal the goodness of God in the vegetable creation:

> Reason at the first set my understanding awork, to know to
> what end I was made, presently the Word told me, and
> Reason confirmed it, that I was made to set forth the
> greatnesse and the goodnesse of God in his wonderfull
> works he hath set before me, and unless I should blind my
> eyes by winking at the light of Nature, I could not chuse but
> see the wisdome of a Creator in forming the whole Creation
> . . .[3]

An earlier writer, Leonard Mascall, translated his vegetable
experience into a psalm of praise to the Creator. He rejoiced that the
vegetable creation not only reveals the divine imprint but that those
who touch seeds and soil, plants and fruits, touch the Hand of God.
He rapturized when he saw that among all the sciences there is none

> that more doth refresh ye vital spirits of men, nor more
> engender admiration in the effects of Nature . . . then is the
> skill of Planting and Graffying, the which not onely wee mny
> (sic) see with our eies, but also feele in our hands the secrete
> works of Nature: yea, nothing more discouereth vnto vs the
> great and incomprehensible worke of God, that of one little
> Pepin seede, Nutte, or small Plant, may come the selfe same
> herbe or tree, and to bring forth infinite of the same fruite,
> which also doth shine & shew foorth it selfe vnto vs,
> especially in the Spring time, by their diuersitie of shootes,
> blossomes and buddes, in diuers kinde of Naturee, by the
> goodnesse and mightie power of the great Lord and
> Creatour towards his people, in such things as commeth
> forth of the natural Earth, to nourisht, (sic) to sustaine, and
> maintaine our liues.[4]

André Mollet, a prestigious landscape-architect of the seventeenth century who came from a family of Royal gardeners, engaged
in gardening in France, England, Holland, and Sweden. In a lavish
folio volume, Le jardin de plaisir (1651), he shared with the reader his
gardening expertise and his experience of the continuing presence
of the Creator in Nature:

> Wie es dem lieben Gott gefallen sich den Menschen
> gleichsam als in einem Spiegel zu offenbahren/durch allerley
> würckungen der Natur/sonderlich aber in der lebendigen
> Krafft der Erdgewächse/und des Ackerbawes/wobey eine

unendliche Zahl unbegreifflicher Wunder/so wol an den
Bäumen/und derselben Früchten/als der wunderbarlichen
Verenderung der Blumen/Tugend der Kräuter/und Ge-
wächse verspüret wird: Also ist es nicht ohne ursach
geschehen/dass von unsern ersten Vätern an/biss auff
diese unsere Zeit die fürnehmsten und grösten sich allezeit
des Ackerbawes beflissen/und damit erlustiget haben . . .
ich auch wol sagen mag/dass/dieweil diese Kunst mit also
schönen Wückungen erfüllet/und die unbegreiffliche
Weissheit des Almächtigen also eigentlich darauss zu
ersehen ist/sie mit nichten solle verachtet/oder hindan
gesetzet werden/zuvorauss weil je und allezeit Könige und
Monarchen gefunden worden . . . [5]

Stephen Switzer, natural historian and practical gardener writing
in the earliest part of the eighteenth century, was a man who had
"tasted both rough and smooth (as we plainly call it) from the best
business and books, to the meanest labours of the scythe, spade,
and wheelbarrow."[6] His short account of terraculturists who were
members of the Royal Society (Dr. Grew, Mr. Boyle, Dr. Beale, Dr.
Woodward, Mr. Ray, et al.), shows that for these scientific terraculturists the Creator is at the heart of the scientific study of the
vegetable world:

. . . And when they came to make those Inferences which
are or ought to be the Result of every virtuous Man's
Labour and Practice; as they studied it on purpose to
demonstrate the Being of a God infinitely Wise, Powerful,
and Good, so they always concluded their Speculations in
this or the like Phrase, *(b) O Lord, how manifold are thy
Works? In Wisdom hast thou made them all: the Earth is
full of thy Riches.*
And altho' Vegetation is in some respects accounted the
meanest part of the Creation, yet from thence the poorest
Person may argue, *If this Tree or Plant cann't be made by
the most curious Artist amongst us,* how is it possible that
*Chance or the fortuitous Concourse of Atoms should jump
together in its Formation, or of the Earth on which it
germinates and flourishes;* and from thence will revolve that
there must be an Almighty Power that not only made, but

also still governs these creeping Vegetables as well as the procerest Cedars in Libanus; and conclude in the Words of the Psalmist, (c) All thy Works shall praise thee, O Lord, and thy Saints shall bless thee: they shall speak of thy Kingdom, and talk of thy Power, to make known to the Sons of Men his mighty Acts, and the glorious Majesty of his Kingdom. Thy Kingdom, O Lord, is an everlasting Kingdom, and thy Dominion endureth throughout all Generation.[7]

III

The Lord God planted a garden eastward in Eden (Genesis 2:8)

The terracultural writers moved from the wide vistas of the whole earth with its magnificent vegetable creation to the most beautiful garden ever planted: Paradise. They focused on Paradise because they believed that in a garden — more than in any other place — and in gardening — more than in any other vocation — the blessedness of the Edenic pre-lapsarian state could be recaptured:

> 'Tis in the quiet Enjoyment of Rural Delights, the refreshing and odoriferous Breezes of Garden Air, that the Deluge of Vapours and those Terrors of Hypocondriasm, which croud and oppress the Head, are dispell'd, and that divine kind of Halitus there drawn, perspiring the organs of the Body, which regulates the precipitate Palpitation of the Heart, and the irregular Pulsation of the whole Machine: 'Tis there Reason, Judgment, and Hands are so busily employed, as to leave no Room for vile Thoughts to interrupt their sweet Retirement: And 'tis from the Admiration of these that the Soul is elevated to unlimited Heights above, and modell'd and prepar'd for the sweet Reception and happy Enjoyment of Felicities, the durablest as well as happiest that Omniscience has created . . . [8]

The high expectations for gardening sprang from their vision of God as the prototype of all gardeners and His Paradise as the archetype for all gardens. When they recalled that act of highest love which prompted the Creator to become the Gardener-Architect of the earthly home of His image-bearer, with Heaven as His model for earth,[9] they rejoiced that the Gardener-Architect of Eden had commissioned them as gardener-architects and that His Paradise served as the model for their paradises. Because they caught glimpses of the Great Original Gardener and of Paradise in their own activities and gardens, they were moved to write about gardening, urging their readers to share in that activity where the divine had stooped to the human in order that the human could share in the divine.

William Lawson, author of the first gardening book to appear in the north of England (1618), found the celestial in the terrestrial, Paradise in orchards, and gardeners godlike in gardening:

> But comfortable delight, with content, is the good of every thing, and the patterne of heaven . . . The very workes of, and in an Orchard and Garden, are better then the ease and rest of and from other labours. When God had made man after his owne Image, in a perfect state, and would have him to represent himself in authority, tranquillity, and pleasure upon the earth, he placed him in *Paradise*. What was *Paradise?* but a Garden and Orchard of trees and hearbs, full of pleasure? and nothing there but delights. The gods of the earth, resembling the great God of heaven in authority, Majesty, and abundance of all things, wherein is their most delight? and whither doe they withdraw themselves . . . whither? but into their Orchards?[10]

So ecstatic did these writers become when they wrote about orchards that the seedsman and pomologist Stephen Switzer borrowed unblushingly from Milton's poetic description of Paradise for his account of the actual aesthetic, physical, and religious qualities of contemporary gardens:

> And indeed, if Fruit-Trees had no other Advantage attending them than to look upon them, how pleasurable would *that* be? Since there is no flowering Shrub excells, if equals, that of a Peach or Apple-Tree in Bloom. The tender enammell'd Blossoms, verdant Foliage, with such a glorious Embroidery of Festoons and Fruitages, wafting their Odours on every Blast of Wind: And at last bowing down their laden Branches, ready to yield their pregnant Offspring into the Hands of their laborious Planter and Owner.

Indeed a well contriv'd Fruit-Garden is an Epitome of
Paradise it self, where the Mind of Man is in its highest
Raptures, and where the Souls of the Virtuous enjoy the
utmost Pleasures they are susceptible of in this sublunary
State. For there the happy Planter is cooling and refreshing
himself with *Scooping the brimming Stream* of those
nectarous Juices . . . [11]

Their ecstasy had deep roots: God's goodness is the ground of His
Being and the very substance from which all goodness springs. Their
ecstasy sprang from the firm knowledge that the Good of the
universe had shared His goodness with His first creatures in
Paradise and that this goodness — metaphysical rather than ethical
— could best be received in a garden of fruit trees. Why is a garden of
fruit trees such a place? Ralph Austen, famous planter of thousands
of fruit trees for the common good at Oxford, in addressing himself
to this question, described Eden as a place of godlike pleasures:

God, who is wisdome it selfe, saw that a *Garden of Fruit-
trees* was the meetest place upon all the Earth, for *Adam* to
dwell in, even in his state of perfection: And therein assigned
him *an imployment* for his greater delight, and pleasure . . .

*God planted a Fruit-garden; That is . . . He caused a
parcell of ground to bring forth Plants and Trees most
exquisite and usefull for man, and enriched that place with
more fruit-fulnesse and beauty, then any other part of the
Earth, and called it* EDEN, *that is, a place of
Pleasures.* [12]

Austen did not construe *pleasure* as a hedonistic post-lapsarian
pursuit but defined *pleasure* as "the Good of every thing, and a
patterne of Heaven."[13] Although Austen was careful to distinguish
between the unsullied pleasures of Eden and the tarnished pleasures
of post-Eden, he did insist that an orchard remained the supreme
place of pleasures — ie., of goodness — on earth: for body, mind,
and spirit. He saw at the pinnacle of pleasures the fruit trees, that
"bring us nearer the Creator, climbing up by them, as by steps, or
staires, till we ascend to the highest good.[14] For Austen, then, the
orchard was the place where the gardener (whose heart had been
made receptive by the redeeming grace of God) meets the Good and
where the gardener is prepared for His eternal Good.

But Paradise was more than an orchard, and Paradise and paradisiacal activities were not restricted to orchards and landscape gardens. God's goodness in planting a garden eastward in Eden (which included forest trees) was extended to arboriculture and to arboriculturists. John Evelyn, who responded to England's crucial need for good timber by writing his *Sylva* (1664), chided his country for "the sensible and notorious decay of her Wooden-walls" and the "im-politick diminution of . . . Timber."[15] In an introductory complimentary poem to Evelyn, John Beale (a fellow member of the Royal Society) praised Evelyn for imitating the Original Sylvan Gardener. What gave Beale and Evelyn a common vision and commitment was the belief that in propagating and perpetuating forest trees, the arboriculturist is permitted to recapitulate the work of God Himself:

> *Progredere,* O Soecli Cultor *memorande futuri,*
> *Felix* Horticolam *sic imitere* Deum.[16]

In the mind and hands of the agriculturist and experimenter Walter Blith, there was a vivid sense of the "agriculture in Eden" and the "Eden in English agriculture." He saw that God the Original Husbandman had, in the Great Design of Creation, made Paradise a place of abundant food production and had included Adam in the Great Design by commissioning him as Husbandman of Eden:

> God was the Originall, and first Husbandman, the pattern of all Husbandry, and first projector of that great designe, to bring that old Masse and Chaos of confusion unto so vast an Improvement, as all the world admires, and subsists from. And having given man such a Patterne both for precept and president for his incouragement, he makes him Lord of all untill the fall . . . [17]

Although the problem of executing the Pattern of Husbandry in the Great Design was complicated by the Fall, Adam remained a commissioned husbandman with the command to "till the Earth, and improve it"[18]; his progeny of husbandmen inherited this commission. The way to "improve" England was to take the road back to Eden and to the Fall. Realist that he was, Blith knew that the difficulty in making England an agricultural Eden lay in the sinful heart of the husbandman, who might in pride forget the Original Husbandman and ascribe to himself the powers of production, and in the recalcitrant earth, which would spit up thorns and thistles rather than bring forth fruits and grains. If the husbandman, however, would acknowledge the First Husbandman, "omnifying him above all, and in all," then a blessing would be *"upon the head of him that Tilleth Corn, and the* thoughts of the diligent bring abundance."[19] In terraculture the agriculturist could achieve "the best progresse for perfection . . . of any Art, Mysterie, or Calling practised and held forth in England . . . [20] The impulse to experiment for increased grain production so that England might become a fruitful field, not remain a barren land, came from the conviction that the Great Husbandman had "Himself experimented."[21] If the heart and mind were firmly fixed on the Great Husbandman; if the commitment to make the land fruitful as Eden was based on the knowledge that agriculture was the "divinely ordained" first profession; then, the husbandman could be restored to his original place in the Great Design and "this very Nation might be made the paradise of the World."[22]

For most of these terracultural writers, the road forward was really the way back: to the Triune God, to creation, to Paradise. Although the road was frequently a rough one, and the labor on it arduous, it was not a commitment to progress that impelled them but the image of restoration that upheld them.

IV

One way to reclaim terraculture was by looking to its Source-Practitioner, God the Husbandman. An additional way was to look to the practice and precedent of the Incarnate God. As the God-Man, He participated fully in the divine and the human experience. Doing His Heavenly "Father's business" meant participating with His Father in creating the vegetable world, planting the Garden, and commissioning Adam. Doing His earthly father's business meant participating in His father's occupation: terraculture. In many of the writings of the terraculturists there emerges a Christology of husbandry.

M. Conradus Heresbachius (a learned husbandman to a nobleman of Cleves), editor and collector of materials on husbandry, delighted in showing his readers that Christ was proud to be known as the Son of the illustrious Husbandman of the Universe, God the Father. Further, Heresbachius established that Christ husbanded on earth: that Christ not only shared His experiential knowledge of husbandry with His listeners but that Christ's teaching mission included instruction in terraculture:

> What should I speake of the antiquitie of it? the holy Scriptures declare husbandry to be the ancientest of all trades; and to begin with the very beginning of man . . . that the most mightie Lord himselfe did first ordaine it: for Adam and his sons were all husbandmen . . . Our Saviour Christ himself glorieth to be the son of a husbandman, & frameth his parables of planting of vines, of sheep & sheepheards: moreover, as it is in Luke, our Lord seemeth to be a teacher of husbandry, where he sheweth, that trees are to be digged & dunged, that they may prosper the better . . . [23]

According to Thomas Newton, Christ did not hesitate to inject terracultural wisdom into His spiritual teaching. Newton was the poet, theologian, naturalist who recognized that for many of his sixteenth century contemporaries Christ's spiritual teaching was inaccessible because they were "rawe" in their understanding of the "Metaphors, Resemblances and Comparisons, that is ignorant of the nature of herbs & plants, from whence these Similitudes be taken . . . [24] In an effort to make available to his readers the natural knowledge necessary for spiritual understanding, he translated Lemnius's *An Herbal for the Bible*. His was an enthusiastic endorsement of the values of terracultural knowledge: citing precedents — prophets and kings whose terracultural knowledge enhanced their Scriptural writings — he focused especially on Christ and His Apostles, whose terracultural knowledge made their teaching ministry so effective:

> Seeing therefore each one of the Prophets (among whom, many were kings, and descended of roiall blood) have discoursed of these things, and inserted the same into their writings: seeing likewise our Saviour Iesus Christ and his Apostles have practised the same, and shewed forth the like kinde of doctrine: I thought my labour should be well bestowed, if briefly and by the waie, I should in this treatise shew what store of excellent learning, profound wisedome, hidden knowledge, and exact skill of nature; what zeale likewise of aduancing true religion, and of banishing all

idolatrie and superstition there rested in those men that by
diuine inspiration haue left and deliuered vnto vs such
woorthie and wholesome matters, and such surpassing
knowledge, by drawing into their bookes (for the greater
ornament and setting out of their speech) the whole store
and furniture of Nature.[25]

Terracultural knowledge, then, was indispensable for understanding
Christ's teaching and for maintaining "true religion and undefiled."
Christ practiced terraculture and taught it. He also saved it from the
ravages of sin. If Christ had not died on the cross, the vegetable
creation would have continued under sin's curse. Because He gave
Himself to atone for sin, the vegetable creation was redeemed; it
could, therefore, be reclaimed and restored. So argued Walter Blith,
who looked to Christ not so much as gardener but as Saviour of
gardens and gardeners. Although Blith's deep concern for the
hungry moved him to spend himself and his funds on technical
improvements in agriculture, the motivation for the experiments
arose from the belief that Christ had ransomed the whole creation.
Blith turned to Christ, the Source of all healing, even for specific
diseases of crops:

> For Blasting is one of a Kingdomes Curses, And therefore
> to Prescribe naturall absolute Unfailing Remedie in all
> Places, and at all Times, is beyond my Skill, yet one
> Unfailing remedy there is . . . it is the Removall of all Causes
> or Occasions of Barrennesse whatever, and that is Sinne,
> the Root that brings forth all: First brought forth the Curse,
> and ever since the Fruite thereof: The onely Cure thereof is
> Our Lord Jesus set upon the Pole, he must damne this
> Curse for us, and in us; and we by looking up to him, and our
> Application of himselfe to us, Mourning over him, and
> humbling our Soules before him; Hereby must we be made
> Sensible of the Removall hereof, by which, and by no other
> means it is Removable.[26]

Blith, however, who promoted the common good through agriculture, did not ally himself with the Diggers or Levellers, whose land
reforms were based on an urgent millennial eschatology:

> Although I indeavour so mainly to work my Improvement
> out of the Belly of the Earth, yet am I neither of the Diggers

mind, nor shall I imitate their practice, for though the poor
are or ought to have advantage upon the Commons, yet I
question whether they as a society gathered together from
all parts of the Nation could claim a right to any particular
Common . . . Nor shall I countenance the Level principles
of Parity or Equality, which they seem to urge from the
begining, till I see the heads of Families and Tribes, Judges
and Governors, Lords and Princes of whole Countries,
blotted out of the First or succeeding generation; unless
they bring us to the new Jerusalem, or bring it down to us,
when we shall not need to trouble our selves about greater
or lesser or any distinction of person, places, or estates, any
more . . . [27]

With his feet firmly placed in the present, Blith experimented as
though in the presence of the Christ whose redemptive act had given
to agricultural experimentation an exciting immediacy. Looking
down at the earth, however, Blith did not blot out the facts: that crop
diseases remained to plague the farmer; that the earth was
frequently uncooperative; that the weather was often destructive;
that the farmer could be incompetent or inept. Then it was that Blith
gazed into the future: there the vision of Christ's Second Coming
heartened him, for Christ would restore the earth to its creational
fruitfulness and man would again be the perfect husbandman. It is
this Christology that informed his appeal to the soldiers to abandon
fighting and to take up farming:

> . . . humbly pray you study how to serve your present
> generation in extolling Gods glory, endeavoring the Common-
> good, and in the interim abandon privacy of Spirit.
> Remember Christs Counsell, view the promised Land, and
> rejoyce to think of that day when your swords shall be
> turned into Ploughshares, your Speares into pruning-
> hooks, and Christ only be exalted in the Earth, and you
> brought back again to sit under your vines and figtrees,
> eating the fruit of your own labours, and injoy one another in
> Peace; which once accomplished, here is cut out work for
> you, some to till the Lands, and others to feed the Cattell, as
> from the beginning, so will this be the lasting Improvement.
> Then will the God of Peace keep them in perfect Peace,

>   whose mindes are stayed on him, And Emanuell will breake
>   in pieces all that gather against Him . . . [28]

John Ray, one of the most distinguished English botanists of the
late seventeenth century who made substantial contributions to
systematic botany, inherited from Christ the delight in the beauties
of flowers. The more Ray grew in botanic knowledge, the more his
eyes were opened to the Divine Wisdom, the Divine Benignity, and
to the "great design of Providence" in the vegetable creation. Field
botany became for him a quest — for both botanic knowledge and
for beauty. In his botanic excursions into the fields of England,
Germany, Italy, and France, he shared in the joys of his Savior, who
while walking through the fields of Palestine, had remarked on the
glories of flowers:

>   such is the beauty and lustre of some Flowers, that our
>   Savior saith of the Lillies of the Field . . . that *Solomon in all
>   his glory was not arrayed like one of these.* And it is
>   observ'd by *Spigelius* That the Art of the most skillful
>   Painter cannot so mingle and temper his Colours, as exactly
>   to imitate or counterfeit the native ones of the Flowers of
>   *Vegetables.*[29]

Much earlier, the continental florilegist and bulb exporter Emanuel Sweert, in addressing the readers of his *Florilegium* (1612),
viewed human life in the context of floral life because Christ had
done so:

>   . . . wie gross dagegen Gottes Barmhertzigkeit sey/dass er
>   uns nichtswürdigen Creaturen so mancherley schöne/
>   herzliche und wunderbare Geschöpffe der Blumen zu
>   Erquickung mittheilen. Und geben uns dieselbigen zu
>   erkennen/ dass dess Menschen Leben nicht anders sey
>   dann wie eine Blume dess Feldes/welche alssbald ver-
>   welcket/und gleichwol nach Christi unders Lieben Hey-
>   lands selbst Zeugniss/herzlicher ist/weder der König
>   Salomon in seiner grösseste Herzligkeit je gewesen:
>   Dadurch wir dann zu Lob und Preiss seiner Göttlichen
>   Güte aufferweckt und ermahnet werden.[30]

Christ's recognition of the beauties of plants and of their
significant relationship to human life was the spiritual base of

Sweert's commitment to floriculture. He hoped that those who purchased his bulbs would also place floriculture on this firm Christological foundation.

The terraculturists were not unique in perceiving Christ as gardener. For centuries Christ as gardener had captivated the imagination of the Church: this is the "Mistaken Gardener" appearing after His resurrection to Mary Magdalene in the "Noli me tangere" scene. Christian iconography abounds with illustrations of Christ as gardener. Before 1400 there are at least six hundred recorded instances, and the Renaissance occurrences are count-less. He appears on altars, ivory book covers, in Biblical illustrations; in choirs, stalls, windows; in sculpture, paintings, illuminations, engravings, woodcuts, metalcuts. Sometimes he wears a gardener's cap or cowl, frequently a halo. He is always equipped with a gardener's tool — hoe, spade, shovel, dibble — and sometimes he has a watering can.[31] Since Christ as post-resurrection gardener was so much a part of their environment, it was natural for the terracultural writers to embrace Him as their gardener, loving Him because His halo did not prevent Him from holding the tools of their trade. They could hardly have found a better endorsement for gardening than this: that the Resurrected Christ, his earthly mission completed, made Himself look so much like a gardener that Mary misidentified Him, "supposing him to be the gardener" (John 20:15). No shame, then, in being a gardener. Only a reflected glory. (FIGURE 1)

This reflected glory shines in Ralph Austen's observations on orchards, making them almost iconographic; his flourishing orchard had more in it than met the physical eye. As Austen walked in his Oxford orchard, he saw "Our Saviour [who] had the custom of walking in a garden-John 18.1"[32] and heard "Our Saviour [who] used the similitude of the vine to express the condition of his Church-John 15.1"[33] As Austen meditated in his garden, he remembered original sin, which had taken place in a garden of fruit trees, but, looking beyond sin, he saw Christ on the cross and rejoiced in God's "infinite and boundless mercy."[34] It was in the orchard that Austen and the orchardist-reader could best "give Him Love & Praise."[35] Finally, as Austen stopped to look at a fruit tree, he recognized that a "Fruit-tree beares the figure and resemblance of our Saviour Christ in the description of Spirituall Paradise-Revel. 22.2 and 2.7."[36] For Austen, the purest physical environment, a garden of fruit trees,

Figure 1.

CHRIST APPEARING TO MARY MAGDALENE; South German.
From the National Gallery of Art, Washington; Rosenwald
Collection.

provided the purest spiritual environment, a place for meeting Christ, the Savior of the world: as He walked in gardens, as He discoursed of gardens, as He opened eyes to the spiritual garden awaiting those who love Him.

V

All knowledge comes from the Holy Ghost, the Enlightener of mankind. At creation, unwilling to leave Adam in the darkness of ignorance when He placed him in the "garden of Eden to dress it and keep it" (Genesis 2:15), He illumined Adam, giving him the natural knowledge essential for joyous living in Nature. This illumination was perpetual: it enabled Adam's capacity for joy to be expanded as his natural knowledge grew. As the Holy Ghost would not leave Adam in darkness at creation, so He would not abandon man to the forces of destruction after the Fall. He did not permit the vegetable creation to destroy itself nor vegetable knowledge in the mind and heart of man to die, since without the vegetable world — and without knowledge of the vegetable world — human life could not continue on the earth.

Standing in the lucid theological tradition which affirms God's continuing care of the universe and of mankind, the terracultural writers turned to the Holy Ghost for natural knowledge and insight.[37] They asked Him to illumine them when they wrote terracultural books. They asked Him to use their terracultural books for enlightening their readers and to inspire those readers to activities in the vegetable world. They asked Him to guide their efforts when they planted gardens and when they labored to detect the medicinal properties of plants for the alleviation of human suffering. They asked Him to inspirit all who spent themselves in the struggle to make the earth fruitful and vegetable knowledge prevail.

John Parkinson's *Paradisi in sole Paradisus Terrestris* (1629), which describes three kinds of gardens — Pleasure, Kitchen, and Orchard — is a lovely book filled with delightful graces. Its courteous bearing and its godly humility show the writer to be filled with the Spirit of God. The descriptions of plants exude the fragrance of a gardener whose life is a sweet smelling sacrifice to God. Parkinson went to his immediate and ultimate Source, using such terms as *inspired* and *natural knowledge* to show his indebtedness, as a son of Adam, to the Holy Ghost. Although Parkinson did not single out the

Holy Ghost from the other Persons in the Trinity, his references are to the work clearly attributed traditionally to the Third Person of the Trinity.

> . . . the Creator of Heauen and Earth, at the beginning when he created Adam, inspired him with the knowledge of all natural things (which successiuely descended to Noah afterwardes, and to his Posterity) . . . And although Adam lost the place for his transgression, yet he lost not the naturall knowledge, nore vse of them . . . [38]

Parkinson's description of the work of the Holy Ghost in initiating, sustaining, and enlarging vegetable knowledge in man, constituted a plea for his readers to plant gardens and/or to study plants. From Adam to Parkinson to Parkinson's readers, the unbroken continuity of the work of the Holy Ghost was apparent. It is the Holy Ghost who made gardens and botany possible: by supplying the inspiration and wisdom necessary for establishing gardens and the perspicacity for studying plants, and by giving man the sensitivity to delight in them as well as the skill to use them.

Parkinson's recognition of the Triune God in his monumental botanic study *Theatrum Botanicum* (1640) constituted an acknowledgment of man's role in the dissemination of vegetable knowledge as the instrument of God for good:

> And now unto God Almighty *Triuno,* and *Vno in Trinitate,* who I hope hath beene at the beginning of this Worke, and holpen me through all the passages thereof, notwithstanding the *multa discrimina rerum mortalium,* whereof I have felt my part, to bring it to the end, for the benefit of others . . . be given all the praise, honour, and glory, for I am but (like the Bee, that workes out waxe and hony for others, not his owne good:) his instrument to accomplish it, receiving all from Him. *Amen.*[39]

The Enlightener of mankind did not limit vegetable knowledge to those in the Judaeo-Christian tradition: He supplied vegetable knowledge to both pagan and Christian. The surgeon George Baker, in his tribute to Gerard, thanked God for the universality of His illuminating power:

> And although it be necessarie for man to learne and know all sciences, yet neuerthelesse the knowledge of naturall

philosophie ought to be preferred, as being the most necessarie . . . The first inuentor of this knowledge was *Chiron* the Centaure, of great renowne, sonne to *Saturne* and *Phillyre:* and others say that it was inuented of *Apollo:* & others of *Esculape* his son; esteeming that so excellent a science could neuer proceed but from the gods immortall, and that it was impossible for man to finde out the nature of Plants, if the great worker, which is God, had not first instructed and taught him. For, as *Pliny* saith, if any thinke that these things haue bin inuented by man, he is vngratefull for the workes of God.[40]

Baker also stressed the fact that the Holy Ghost is so involved in the distribution of vegetable knowledge that He stirs the spirit of princes to contribute money for the publication of books on the vegetable creation:

. . . *Matthiolus* did write . . . how I should finish so great a charge, which I had neuer carried out, but that by Gods stirring vp of the renowned Emperour *Ferdinando* of famous memorie, and the excellent Princes had not helped mee with great sums of money . . .[41]

According to the translator of *The Grete Herball* (1526), the Holy Ghost gave gifts of wisdom and love to all those who discerned the pharmaceutical properties of plants for the benefit of mankind:

Wherfore brotherly love compelleth me to wryte thrugh ye gyftes of the holy gost shewynge and enformynge how man may be holpen with grene herbes of the gardyn and wedys of ye feldys as well as by costly receptes of the potycarys prepayred.[42]

Since the Holy Ghost so generously distributes the gift of vegetable knowledge, the readers of the *Herball* must accept the responsibility for making this knowledge available to all:

O ye worthy reders or practicyens to whome this noble volume is present I beseche yow take intellygence and beholde ye workes and operacyons of almyghty god which hath endewed his symple creature mankynde with the graces of ye holy goost to have parfyte knowlege and understandynge of the vertue of all maner of herbes and trees in this booke comprehendyd.[43]

The Holy Ghost, Giver of vegetable knowledge, is the One who established terraculture in the early days of creation and who continued to attest to the antiquity, nobility, and utility of the profession:

> Terreculture [or the Tillage of the Earth] is the most *Ancient,* most *Noble,* and most *Useful,* of all Practical *Sciences.*
>
> *As for its Antiquity,* it is almost coaevous with the World it self, for we find it practised by *Adam* . . . and by his Sons . . . and afterwards by several of the *Patriarchs,* and particularly by *Noah . . .*
>
> *As for the Nobility of this Science,* (tho' it be by many, accounted a base and mean Study; yet I say) besides that *Adam,* and several of the *Patriarch's,* scorned not the Study and Practice of it . . . the *Holy-Ghost* himself, has been pleased to Honour this Science; not only in appointing *Adam* the Practise of it, even when he was in *Paradice,* Gen. 2.15. But also in the History of the First *Monarchs* of the World, from *Adam* to *Noah;* there is nothing of their Actions mention'd, but only That they lived so long, and taught their Posterity Husbandry, &tc.
>
> As to the Utillity of *Terraeculture,* it must be acknowledged by all, to be the most useful of all Humane *Sciences;* and that, without which (since the uphappy *Fall* of our First *Parents,* and the *Curse* upon the Earth, consequent thereupon) none in *City* or *Country* could subsist, unless they would be content to live like *Brutes.*[44]

The terracultural books do not end with a description of the work of the Holy Ghost but, rather, they begin there — with His warm breath that gives life to the earth and to those who work it.

NOTES

Chapter One

[1] Stephen Blake, *The compleat gardeners practice* (London, 1664), *Preface.*

[2] Although the terracultural writers were separated by time, place, and even by politics and religion, their statements of praise to the Creator are remarkably similar; cf. Heresbachius's *Four bookes of Husbandry* (London, 1577) translated into English by Barnabe Googe (1540-1594), the Oxbridge scholar and poet who spent time at Court; and by the renewer, correcter, and enlarger of this work, Gervase Markham (1568?-1637), Captain under the Earl of Essex in Ireland; *The grete herball* (London, 1526) by an unknown author; *The Herball* (London, 1597) by John Gerard (1545-1612), gardener and examiner for admission to the Barber-Surgeons Company; and Gerard's *Herball* (London, 1633) enlarged by Thomas Johnson (1595/1597-1644), a Royalist who died in 1644 as the result of wounds; books on modern methods in agriculture (London, 1649, 1652) by the parliamentarian soldier Walter Blith (fl. 1649); and on orchards by John Beale (1603-1682?), famous orchardist and Chaplain to Charles II; and books on botany showing remarkable advances in classification, histology, and physiology by John Ray (1627-1705), deacon and priest who refused to subscribe to the Bartholomew Act of 1662 and who therefore participated in lay communion with the established church.

[3] *The compleat gardeners practice, Preface.* The terracultural writers did not want to suffer the torments of the wicked and unprofitable servant who hid his talent: see Hugh Platt, *Floraes Paradise* (London, 1608): "Having out of mine owne particular experience, as also by long conference with diverse gentlemen of good skill and practice, in the altering, multiplying, enlarging, planting, and transplanting, of sundry sorts of fruites & flowers, at length obtained a pretty volume of experimentall observations in this kinde: And not knowing the length of my dayes, nay, assuredly knowing that they are drawing to their periode, I am willing to unfolde my Napkin, and to deliuer my poore talent abroad . . ., *To the studious and well-affected reader;* and William Lawson, *A new orchard and garden,* 3rd ed. (London, 1638), " . . . I of my meere & sole experience, without respect to any former written treatisé gathered these rules, & set them downe in writing, not daring to hide the least talent given me of my Lord and Master in Heaven," *Preface;* and Moses Cook, *The manner of raising, ordering, and improving forrest-trees* (London, 1676), "I have not bushelled my Light, and have set it to the Publick view . . . to thy benefit and pleasure . . . if the Lord permit, some other piece of service, farther to direct thee in the Truth," *Preface.*

[4] *The country-mans new art of planting and graffing* (London, 1652), *Dedicatory epistle.* Mascall's book, which is a translation from the French, with additions, first appeared about 1569; its popularity is attested to by its frequent reprinting, the last edition having appeared in 1656.

[5] *Der lust-garten* (Stockholm, 1651), *To the reader.* The first English edition was published in London (1670) under the title *The garden of pleasure.*

[6] *The nobleman, gentleman, and gardener's recreation* (London, 1715), pp. vii-viii.

[7] Switzer, p. 48; *(b)* Psalm 104.24; *(c)* Psalm 105.10, 11, 12, 13. John Dixon Hunt and

Peter Willis's statement that garden writing of this period "reveals a characteristic Enlightenment bias and a post-Restoration mistrust of any religious argument" (*The Genius of the Place* [New York, 1975], p. 88) finds very little support in either the practical or theoretical writings of the terraculturists. As late as 1783, William Curtis, the famous naturalist, called to mind that "as philosophers, we may admire, and contemplate the beautiful works of an Almighty Being," *A catalogue of the British, medicinal, culinary, and agricultural plants cultivated in the London botanic garden* (London, 1783), p. 10.

[8] Switzer, p. iv. It is a commonplace in Renaissance terracultural writing that there is a direct relationship between the body's physiological environment and soul's ability to delight in and ascend to God: the rural setting promotes body health and thus spiritual comfort.

[9] For the theological counterpart of this view, see Jospeh E. Duncan's account in *Milton's Earthly Paradise* (Minneapolis, 1972), pp. 247-257.

[10] *A new orchard and garden*, 3rd ed., p. 69.

[11] *The practical fruit-gardener*, 2nd ed. (London, 1763), p. 3; Milton's description of, Paradise reads: "to thir Supper Fruits they fell,/Nectarine Fruits which the compliant boughs/Yielded them, side-long as they sat recline/On the soft downy Bank damaskt with flow'rs:/The savory pulp they chew, and in the rind/Still as they thirsted scoop the brimming stream," *Paradise Lost*, IV. 331-336, in *John Milton: Complete Poems and Major Prose*, ed. Merritt Y. Hughes (New York, 1957). All subsequent references to Milton's poetry are to this text.

[12] *A treatise of fruit-trees*, 2nd ed., 3rd impression (Oxford, 1665), pp. 22-24.

[13] *A treatise of fruit-trees*, p. 62.

[14] *The spiritual use of an orchard or garden of fruit trees* (Oxford, 1657), p. x; repr. London, 1847. Ralph Austen's contributions to pomology were so significant that Anthony Lawrence and John Beale wrote to Henry Oldenburg, Secretary to the Royal Society (in *Nurseries, orchards, profitable gardens, and vineyards encouraged* [London, 1677]), urging that Austen's work be recognized by the Royal Society. Lawrence and Beale cited Austen's books, his contributions to the science of pomology, his contributions to the health of scholars and of the entire nation, and the monument raised to Austen at Oxford in Roman letters of gold upon black marble, pp. 5-7.

[15] London, 1664, p. 1

[16] Amico charisimo Johanni Evelyno Armerigo, è Societate Regali Londini. J. Beale, S.P.D. In Sylvam.

[17] *The English improover* (London, 1649), p. 3.

[18] *The English improover*, p. 3.

[19] *The English improover*, p. 4.

[20] *The English improover*, *To the reader.*

[21] *The English improover*, p. 9.

[22] *The English improover improved*, 3rd impression (London, 1652). *To the honorable society of the houses of court and universities.*

[23] *The whole art of hvsbandry*, enlarged by Gervase Markham, p. 7.

[24] *An herbal for the Bible*, trans. Thomas Newton (London, 1587), p. 223.

[25] P. 9.

[26] *The English improover*, p. 94.

[27] *The English improover improved, The epistle to the reader.*

[28] *The English improover improved, To the honorable souldiery of these nations of England Scotland & Ireland.*

[29] *The wisdom of God manifested in the works of creation*, 3rd ed. (London, 1701), pp. 119-120.

[30] Francofurti, 1612, *To the reader.*

[31] I am indebted to Dr. Rosalie Green, Director of the Index of Christian Art, Princeton University, for the information that there are more than 600 examples of "Noli me tangere" before 1400 recorded in the Index. For a representative list, see Engelbert Kirschbaum, *Lexicon der Christlichen Ikonographie* (Rom, Freiburg, Basel, Wien, 1970), "Gärtner," cols. 81-82. To mention a few: the oldest known example is on an ivory book cover at Bamberg (end of the 11th century, Library at Würzburg) where Christ holds a spade in his left hand; Christ appears with cap and spade in the window of the Lower Church, S. Francesco, Assisi (1315/30); in the choir of Liebfrauenkirche zu Oberwesel (c. 1330); and Dürer's small woodcut (1511).

[32] *A treatise of fruit-trees*, p. 26.

[33] *A treatise of fruit-trees*, p. 27.

[34] *A treatise of fruit-trees*, p. 57.

[35] *A treatise of fruit-trees*, p. 58.

[36] *A treatise of fruit-trees*, p. 29.

[37] Lambert Daneau, working within the Augustinian framework (*The wonderful workmanship of the world*, trans. Thomas Twyne [London, 1578]), gives a clear picture of the work of the Holy Ghost: "Why the spirite of God was vpon this mole, and matter . . . the creation of the world might bee understoode, not only to bee the woorke of the Father, and of the Sunne, but also of the holy ghost, who is likewise in person distinct from them twaine . . . the Spirite of God, had also his owne proper function and office, openly and distinctly in the creation of this world . . . the almightie spirite of God, which susteineth and quickneth all thinges by his diuine power, by whom that huge and unprofitable mole of earth and water, subsisted, flourished, was quickened, was susteined, was reteined, and as I may saye, made aliue . . . the Spirite of God had giuen a lyuely force vnto that greate mole, not onely by whiche it should exist, susteine, and as it were beare vp it selfe: but also that it ingraffed, engendred, & raised vp in it a certeine vertue, where by it should afterwarde waxe hot, as it were, to conceiue, and to bringe foorth," pp. 53-54. It is interesting to note the persistence of this belief: in 1877 the poet Gerard M. Hopkins ("God's Grandeur") took comfort in the fact that, although the world is smudged and smeared, "the Holy Ghost over the bent/World broods with warm breast and with ah! bright wings."

[38] *Paradisus* (London, 1629), *To the courteous reader.*

[39] London, 1640, p. 1671.

[40] In Gerard's *Herball* (Johnson, London, 1633), *To the reader.*

[41] *Herball, To the reader.*

[42] London, 1526, *Introduction.*

[43] *The grete herball;* this appears before the Index.

[44] T. Snow, *Apopiroscopy* (London, 1702), p. 3.

CHAPTER TWO

THE VALUES OF TERRACULTURE

And where as they saye that a booke of wedes or grasse . . .
is a righte unmete gift for such a Prince as all men confesse
you to be/I aunswere that if the noble Poet Virgil sayd well
and truelye:

> *Si canimus syluas, syluae sunt consule dignae,*
> I maye also iustelye saye/
> *Si canimus plantas, plantae sunt principe dignae.*

For the knowledge of herbes/trees and shrubbes/is not
onelye verye delectable for a Princis minde/but profitable
for all the bodies of the Princis hole Realme both to preserue
men from sicknes/sorrowe and payne that commeth there-
by/and from poison and death . . .[1]

I

With the hope that they would encourage enlistment in the active
ranks of terraculture, the terraculturists wrote to move men and

women from their homes, scholars from their libraries, kings and queens from their palaces, to the fields surrounding them. Building on the foundation of a vegetable philosophy that assigned to terraculture the highest place in divine and human life, they outlined the values of the oldest profession in the world and described the contributions of the world's most prestigious terraculturists. If their joy-inducing statements on the values of terraculture, and their rapturous accounts of the heroes of terraculture, sometimes approached the ecstasies of the writer of Hebrews 11 on the heroes of faith, it was their unassailable faith in terraculture that enabled them to experience, while working with dibble and dung, the felicity of those who took up the profession most able to restore their friendship with God and their kinship with Adam. In this chapter I shall discuss the values of terraculture which they articulated, and in the next I shall look at those figures whom John Evelyn called the "hortulan saints."

II

"The Handes of God"

Within the broad area of terraculture, the climate was particularly friendly to the study of botanic medicine. Along with the housewife, who was expected to be a practical pharmacist, the herb-woman a field botanist,[3] the apothecary and physician trained dispensers of botanic medicine, there were poets, clergymen, and men of property whose commitment to the values of botanic medicine made them easy and articulate travellers in the world of plants. They felt comfortable there because they knew they were walking in their "Father's world." The poet-clergyman George Herbert, for example, urged his fellow priests to cultivate herb gardens as the God-given, inexpensive defense against disease:

> In the knowledge of simples, wherein the manifold wise-
> dome of God is wonderfully to be seen, one thing would be
> carefully observed; which is, to know what herbs may be
> used in stead of drugs of the same nature, and to make the
> garden the shop: For home-bred medicines are both more

easie for the Parsons purse, and more familiar for all mens bodyes. So, where the Apothecary useth either for loosing, Rubarb, or for binding, Bolearmena, the Parson useth damask or white Roses for the one, and plantaine, shepherds purse, knot-grasse for the other, and that with better successe . . . Accordingly, for salves, his wife seeks not the city, but preferrs her garden and fields before all outlandish gums. And surely hyssope, valerian, mercury, adders tongue, yerrow, melilot and Saint *Johns* wort made into a salve; And Elder, camomill, mallowes, comphrey and smallage made into a Poultis, have done great and rare cures.[4]

Herbert's poetry, redolent of herbs,

> Farewell deare flowers, sweetly your time ye spent,
> Fit, while ye liv'd, for smell or ornament,
>   And after death for cures[5]

was impatient of botanic stupidity,

>   . . . in ev'ry path
> He treads down that which doth befriend him
> When sicknesse makes him pale and wan.[6]

His brother, Edward Lord Herbert of Cherbury, found so much value in botanic medicine that he organized field excursions, giving specific instructions on proper equipment and plant identification:

I conceive it is a fine study and worthy a gentleman to be a good botanic, that so he may know the nature of all herbs and plants, being our fellow-creatures and made for the use of man; for which purpose it will be fit for him to cull out of some good herbal all the icones together, with the descriptions of them and to lay by themselves all such as grow in England, and afterwards to select again such as usually grow by the highway-side, in meadows, by rivers, or in marshes, or in cornfields, or in dry and mountainous places, or on rocks, walls, or in shady places, such as grow by the seaside; for this being done, and the said icones being ordinarily carried by themselves or by their servants one may presently find out every herb he meets withal, especially if the said flowers be truly coloured . . .[7]

Among the early scientists who contributed to English medical
botany was a man of fervent conviction, William Turner (c. 1508-
1568). Coming to medical botany by way of theology, medicine, and
herbalizing, he found in the Bible his authorization for the study of
the vegetable creation:

> . . . there be many noble and excellent artes & sciences,
> which no man douteth, but that almyghty God the author of
> all goodnes hath gyuen vnto vs by the handes of the Hethen,
> as necessary vnto the vse of Mankynd: yet is there none
> among them all, whych is so openly commended by the
> verdit of any holy writer in the Bible, as is ye knowlege of
> plantes, herbes, and trees, and of Phisick. I do not
> remember, that I have red anye expressed commendation
> of Grammer, Logick, Philosophie, naturall or morall,
> Astronomie, Arithmetyke, Geometry, Cosmographie,
> Musycke, Perspectiue or any other such lyke science. But I
> rede amonge the commendatyons and prayses of kyng
> Salomon, that he was sene in herbes shrubbes and trees,
> and so perfectly that he disputed wysely of them from the
> hyghest to the lowest, that is from the Cedre tre in mount
> Liban vnto Hysop that groweth furth of the wall. If the
> knowledge of Herbes, shrubbes, and trees, which is not the
> lest necessary thynge vnto the knowlege of Phisicke were
> greatly commendable, it shulde neuer haue bene set among
> Salomons commendacyons, and amongest the syngular
> giftes of God. Therefor whereas Salomon was commended
> for the knowledge of Herbes, the same knowledge of herbes
> was expressedly ynough commended there also.[8]

For Turner, the immediate value to be found in the study of plants
was a dramatic one: the knowledge of the medical properties of
plants could prevent murder. The ultimate value was the other side
of prevention: proper identification of plants, knowledge of their
properties, and experience in prescribing them, could sustain and
preserve life. Turner's life-long quest, pursued in the large context of
theology and botany, was to preserve the life of the creatures God
had created to live forever. Because the value of life itself was
enhanced by Turner's Protestant reading of the Scriptures, he was
fearless and aggressive in preaching both the values of botanizing for

health and of studying the Scriptures for salvation. Salvific plants and efficacious grace combined to heal the whole human being, who, by the Fall, was alienated from God and hence from health. Turner's militant involvement in both areas was highly visible: As a theologian, his castigation of his Romish opponents brought him in and out of the Deanery at Wells, but his theological exiles to the Continent put him in touch with Continental botanists and with Continental plants and medical preparations. From his excursions into fields, gardens, and libraries came the *Herbal* (in installments, but complete in 1568). Turner's commitment to putting botanical information into the vernacular was as unshakeable as his commitment to making the Bible available in the vernacular; the accessibility of materials which had previously been guarded by professionals would open the door to investigation, discovery, and knowledge (not to erroneous, private interpretation in theology and botany, as charged). His theological books were banned in England; his *Herbal* was pejoratively described as "a booke of wedes or grasses." Yet, paradoxically, his critics considered the *Herbal* a dangerous, if not lethal weapon, in the hands of the uneducated. To these critics Turner hurled a reply, insisting, first, that the ancient, most esteemed writers on botanic medicine had, without hesitation, placed botanico-medical information in the hands of anyone who could read; and, second, that lack of botanico-medical information could cause murder as frequently as could information in the hands of those who lacked both formal medical education, and skill in reading Pliny, Galen, and Dioscorides. He deplored the fact that many an apothecary

> putteth . . . many a good man by ignorance in ieopardy of his life, or marreth good medicines to the great dishonestie both of the Phisician and of Goddes worthy creatures when as by hauyng an herball in English all these euelles myght be auoyded . . . Dyd Dioscorides and Galene gyue occasion . . of murther . . If they gaue no occasyon of murther: then gyue I none . . .[9]

The ultimate value — the preservation of life through the use of death-forestalling, life-giving plants — was his spur to assiduous study and indefatigable botanizing. His contributions include not only the identification of 238 native plants (his identifications were noted by the Continental botanist Jean Bauhin in *Historia plan-tarum universalis* in 1650-51) but also an awareness of structure and an appreciation of form that go beyond plant identification. Finally, it was his unique vision of God, man, and salvation that led him to explore the vegetable creation and brought him to areas undreamed of by the medieval herbalists.[10]

Many physicians, apothecaries, and herbalists dedicated them-selves to finding ways of improving health. Not all who practised botanic medicine became botanists. For the physician Philip Barrough, the study of nature was important for health's sake; but it was more than a utilitarian concern that shaped his outlook on the value of studying nature. Barrough had a vision of restoration: By study and experiment he hoped to discover the means of recap-turing the perfect physico-spiritual health which Adam and Eve had possessed in Paradise. This high value, restoration to wholeness, prompted him to write *The method of phisicke* (1583):

> . . . there is no meanes by vvich a man can approach neerer unto the perfection of that nature vvhich he first enioyed, and then lost by his fall, then by the painfull indagation of the secretes of nature, or anie vvay, vvhereby he may more truely glorifie his maker, then in his life time vvith his tongue to communicate that knovvledge vvhich he hath by his industrie acheiued . . . vvhat can be more excellent then to be able to maintaine & kepe in order that best vvorkman-ship of God, & (that vvich is more) to correct, reforme & amend it . . . And seeing there is nothing giuen vnto vs of God, more acceptable then the health of the bodie, hovve honorable must vve thinke of the meanes, by vvhich it is continued and restored if it be lost?[11]

If the *Method* (a compilation of recognized medical prescriptions combined with Barrough's own experiements) did not actually reinstate Edenic health, it was effective in promoting both spiritual and physical health in England, and in the American colonies for more than one hundred years, where its prescriptions became part of the pharmacopeia.

In what was to become the most famous and long-lived of the English herbals, John Gerard, as he focused on the medicinal aspects of plants, was aware of the aesthetic and spiritual aspects as well. In the dedication to Lord Burghley, his spirit soared when he described the values of herbalizing: the senses delight in beholding the beauty of the vegetable creation, and the mind joys in glimpsing the invisible wisdom of the Creator:

> Among the manifold creatures of God . . that haue all in all ages diuersly entertained many excellent wits, and drawne them to the contemplation of the diuine wisdome, none haue prouoked mens studies more, or satisfied their desires so much as Plants haue done . . . For if delight may prouoke mens labor, what greater delight is there than to behold the earth apparelled with plants, as with a robe of embroidered worke set with Orient pearles, and garnished with great diuersitie of rare and costly iewels? If this varietie and perfection of colours may affect the eye, it is such in herbs and floures, that no *Apelles*, no *Zeuxis* euer could by any art express the like: if odours or if taste may worke satisfaction, they are both so soueraigne in plants, and so comfortable, that no confection of the Apothecaries can equall their excellent vertue. But these delights are in the outward sences: the principall delight is in the minde, singularly enriched with the knowledge of these visible things, setting forth to vs the inuisible wisedome and admirable workmanship of almighty God.[12]

This view of the aesthetic and spiritual dimensions of herbs gave birth to a deep concern for the earth itself: it must not be violated. There is a hauntingly modern sound to Gerard's account of the rape of the earth by the mining interests:

> . . . and yet this dusty mettal, or excrement of the earth (which was first deepely buried least it should be an eye-sore to grieue the corrupt heart of man) by forcible entry made into the bowels of the earth, is rather sna`ched at of man to his owne destruction, than directly sent of God, to the comfort of this life.[13]

Unlike mining, which enriched the country while it destroyed the earth, botanizing-herbalizing gave to the country "harmlesse treasure of herbes, trees, and plants, as the earth frankely without violence offereth vnto our most necessarie vses." The botanic treasures of earth are accessible; their beauty has no competitors:

Easie therefore is this treasure to be gained, and yet
pretious. The science is nobly supported by wise and Kingly
Fauorites: the subiect thereof so necessary and delectable,
that nothing can be confected either delicate for the taste,
daintie for smell, pleasant for sight, wholesome for body,
conseruatiue or restoratiue for health, but it borroweth the
relish of an herbe, the sauour of a floure, the colour of a
leafe, the iuice of a plant, or the decoction of a root.[14]

As a gardener-botanist-herbalist, Gerard exercised a protective
benevolence when he worked the soil to make it hospitable to
foreign plants "that they might liue and prosper vnder our clymat, as
in their natiue and proper countrey."[15] From Gerard's awareness of
the usefulness and beauty of the vegetable creation came a new and
valuable perception: that accompanying an enlarged capacity to
appreciate the beauty of the earth was the added responsibility of
protecting it from exploitation.

By the time that John Parkinson's herbal, *Theatrum botanicum*,
was published in 1640, he was too old to participate in field
excursions or to engage in extensive experiments with plants.
Although Parkinson had been apothecary to James I and was
Botanicus Regius Primarius in the reign of Charles I, his herbal
contributed more to the spirit of botany than to botany itself. The
values he saw in botany were exuded from the pages of his herbal:
medical formulas were permeated by a quiet joy in the vegetable
world. Like an attractive seed catalogue, its descriptions could
delight the person who had no inclination to exert physical energy
for botanizing in the fields or for reproducing terracultural glories in
a garden. His was a sedentary person's herbal, a painless, engaging
discussion of plants. Marked not by new insights into the values of
botanizing nor by advances in herbal knowledge, it was the gentlest
of introductions to vegetable utility and beauty. Like poetry, it was
itself a thing of beauty. John Speed, Doctor of Medicine at Oxford, in
his opening address to Parkinson, caught the tone and saw the value
of the herbal:

You have built us a Botanicke Theater; with such excellent
skill and advantage to the Spectator; that at one view he
commands the prospect of both Hemisphers; and all their
vegetables in the pride of beauty, ranged in their proper

orders, decking the Hils, Plaines, Valleyes, Medowes, Woods, and Bankes, with such a world of shapes and colours, so delightfull to the eye, so winning upon the rationall Soule which feeds on rarieties! that we cannot hope for a more compleate Paradise upon earth . . .[16]

William Coles, a famous herbalist in his day, assimilated the values cited by his predecessors — prevention of murder, preservation of life (both human and vegetable), and the perception of beauty — and articulated an even higher value: the ascent to a kind of mystical-spiritual state. When Coles botanized in the fields of England and in the Oxford Botanical Garden, he found himself transported by plants into the rapturous Edenic state of Adam and into the ecstasy granted to those who rise by the senses to the contemplation of God. If the mystical route to Eden and to Heaven was paved by plants, it is not surprising that for Coles the study of botany was more valuable than the study of the other sciences. Coles wanted the readers of his books, *The art of simpling* (1656) and *Adam in Eden* (1657), to botanize so that they, with him, could see the vegetable creation through the eyes of Adam, unclouded by the depressing mists of sin. This value, the recapitulation of the mystical-spiritual Adamic state, made Coles an inspired student of botany, and his utterances on herbalizing quasi-mystical:

To make thee truly sensible of that happinesse which Mankind lost by the Fall of *Adam,* is to render thee an exact *Botanick,* by the knowledge of so incomparable a Science as the Art of *Simpling,* to re-instate thee into another *Eden,* or, *A Garden of Paradise:* For if We rightly consider the Addresses of this Divine Contemplation of Herbs and Plants, with what alluring Steps and Paces the Study of them directs Us to an admiration of the Supream Wisdome, we cannot but even from these inferiour things arrive somewhat near unto a heavenly Contentment; a content-ment indeed next to that Blessednesse of Fruition, which is onely in the other World . . . amongst all these transitory Entertainments of our Lives, there is none more suitable to the mind of man then this; for I dare boldly assert, that if there be any one that is become so much an Herbarist, as to be delighted with the pleasant Aspects of Nature, so as to

have walked a few turns in her solitary Places, traced her
Allies, viewed her severall imbroidered Beds, recreated and
feasted himself with her Fragrances, the harmlesse delights
of her Fields and Gardens; He it is, that hath embraced one
of the greatest of our terrestriall Felicities. Hence it is, that
Emperours, Princes, Heroes, and Persons of the most
generous Qualifications, have trod on their Scepters,
sleighted their Thrones, cast away their Purples, and laid
aside all other Exuberancies of State, to Court their Mother
Earth in her own Dressings; Such Beauties there are to be
discerned in Flowers, such Curiosities of Features to be
found in Plants. When God Almighty would have *Adam* to
partake of a perfection of happinesse, even then when he
stood innocent, he could find none greater under the Sun
then to place him in a Garden . . . the best Hours of my life
being spent in the Fields and in Physick Gardens, more
especially in that Famous One at *Oxford,* where I made it a
great part of my study to be experienced in this laudable art
of Simpling . . . The truth is though it be necessary for a man
to know and learne all Sciences, neverthelesse, the knowledge of naturall Philosophy ought to be most esteemed . . .
what fairer objects are there for the sight then these painted
Braveries? what Odours can ravish the sense of smelling
more than those of flowers? If the sensuality of the Taste
hath delighted him, what can be more acceptable then the
luxurious deliciousnesse of Fruits: And for that high
concernment we all seek after, Health, what hath the great
preserver of all things rendered more soveraigne then the
vertues of Herbs and Plants . . .[17]

With the prospect of Eden beckoning him, Coles directed
considerable botanic energy to alleviating the miseries of human life.
It was his sensitivity to the raptures of the mystical spiritual Edenic
state that caused him to be concerned for those whose tortured
mental state prevented them from experiencing mystical spiritual
joys. Seeking to restore the mentally disturbed to their senses and to
composure, Coles urged his readers to turn with him to the
vegetable world and to find in it the healing power for mental disease.
For Coles, the violation of the earth was not accomplished by the
mining interests but by all those who "goe the way to put out their

owne Eyes, by trampling upon that which should preserve
them . . . [18] No wonder that Coles saw higher value in studying the
vegetable creation than in divinity; and that those who were healed
through herbal medicine looked upon the hands of the herbalist as
"the handes of God":

> . . . Students in the Herbarary Art are as profitable
> Members as any other, for besides that they are Trumpets
> of Gods glory, setting forth it selfe so wonderfully in those
> Vegetables, they are also by some, called the Handes of
> God, because they are his Instruments to apply those things
> unto Mankind, that he hath Created for their preservation.
> And in this respect, Physick may be said to be more
> effectuall then Divinity it selfe, for though the Charmer or
> Preacher charme never so wisely, yet if the Auditor be not
> compos mentis, but like the Deafe Adder, he will lose his
> labour. But such are the Powerfull vertues of Herbs
> administred by a skillfull Professor, that they will even
> restore those that have lost their Sense, and so not only
> make them capable of good Counsell and wholesome
> instruction, but cause both mind and body to resume their
> pristine Integrity.[19]

The medical botanists found that the study of the plant world had
values reaching into Heaven. The cultivation and study of plants
drew William Coles from the medical properties of plants to the
landscape of Eden and to the prospect of Heaven: It was the
experience and promise of transcendence that assured him of the
value of studying plants. Even in the act of administering botanic
medicine, human hands were transformed into the "handes of God."

For the distinguished physician and student of plant anatomy
Nehemiah Grew, it was the experience of transfiguration that gave
value to his botanic studies. The transfiguration occurred in the field
or laboratory while scrutinizing the anatomy of a plant, not on the
mountain top of mystical experience. His eyes were not drawn to
Heaven but to the plant, for there the plant turned into a godly thing
(but not into God):

> Wherefore Nature and the Causes and Reasons of things
> duly contemplated, naturally lead us unto God, and is one
> way of securing our veneration of Him; giving us not only a

general demonstration of his *Being;* but a particular one of
most of the several *Qualifications* thereof. For all *Goodness, Proportion, Order, Truth,* or whatever else is excellent and amiable in the *Creatures,* it is the demonstration of
the like in God . . . [20]

Grew, who expressed some uneasiness about spending time with
plants rather than with patients, justified to himself and to the world
the study of botany. The reason that he could devote his energies to
plants was that he could detect the Creator's imprint in His
handiwork: the more intensely Grew studied plants, the higher the
visibility of the Creator. The visibility of the Creator did not lead
Grew, however, into metaphysical mistakes; he was too sophisti-
cated to think that the Creator's attributes were inherent in plants.
Grew's explorations into the nature of Nature and the nature of God
led him to write *Cosmologia sacra* (1701), illuminating *An idea of a
phytological history propounded* (1673) and preventing the botanist
from working in his own shadow. Grew's articulation of the
transfigurative value of botany made it possible for him to make a
real contribution to botany and to the experience of the botanist.

Not all the medical botanists attempted to define the nature of
Nature or the nature of God, but for all of them the value of botanic
investigation could be epitomized in the elegiac couplet on the title
page of Gerard's *Herball:*

Excideret ne tibi diuini muneris Author,
Praesentem monstrat quae libet herba Deum.[21]
So that He who is the source of divine goodness will not
escape your notice.
Any plant at all indicates the presence of God.

This couplet, like the botanist, was under the eye of God.

III

The Matter thereof concerns Husbandry, which is the most
harmless, the most necessary, and the safest & of all others
the most profitable Industry and Humane Society; wherein
the Providence, the Power, the Wisdom and the Goodness
of God, appears unto man more eminently then in any
other way of Industry whatsoever . . . [22]

Agriculture, which occupied a large place in the world of terraculture, was the occupation of those who were narrowly rural and of those who were broadly cosmopolitan. Drawing from all walks of life, it included those who had studied at Oxford and Cambridge; who were scholars, gentlemen, physicians, clergymen, soldiers; who were theorists, experimenters, inventors, reformers; and, of those who joined the ranks later in the seventeenth century, many became members of the Royal Society. Agriculture had to do with pomoculture, viticulture, arboriculture, as well as with the cultivation of grain and vegetable crops. Its values seem obvious and material: good crops promote the physical, social, and economic health of the nation. Those who contributed most to the practical and experimental aspects of the agricultural enterprise did not wish, however, to have the agricultural enterprise circumscribed by the physical, social, and economic values, important as these were. For the agricultural writers, men of broad and humane education, agriculture also "quickened the Genius, recreated the spirits, and accuated the intellect."[23] This is what gave impetus to their experimentation, and direction to their endeavors, especially in times when the obvious and immediate — poverty and hunger —were acute. Participating in their view that agriculture was worthy of a rational man's consideration was the poet John Milton, who, in designing an ideal curriculum for students, included agricultural writings as proper reading for young intellectuals but also as "an occasion of inciting and inabling them hereafter to improve the tillage of their country, to recover the bad soil, and to remedy the wast that is made of good . . ."[24]

Since agriculture was not the domain of those who were exclusively rustic, the civilized man's concern for a prose style adequate to the subject is apparent in the agricultural books. The books are plain and eloquent, lovely and lucid, euphonious and instructive, understandable by educated and unlettered. Not arm-chair farmers who indulged lofty thoughts to the neglect of the lowly art of farming, the writers worked in the fields; experimented with seeds, fertilizers, grafts; devised methods of productive land use; designed implements. While their work led to agricultural improvement and increased production, it also led to the discovery that the practice of agriculture had values beyond physical survival; farming was, in fact, consonant with the virtuous life. Their own experience and experiments showed that in itself farming made all of life worth living.

One of the earliest contributors to the science and practice of fruit culture was the active orchardist William Lawson. For him the values lay in the multiple delights; as food for the body and for the senses, nothing could equal agriculture:

> For whereas every other pleasure commonly filles some one of our sences, and that onely, with delight, this makes all our sences, swim in pleasure and that with infinite variety joyned with no lesse commodity.[25]

What he saw was

> . . . fruit-trees of all sorts, loaden with sweet blossomes, and fruits of all tasts, operations, and colours . . . borders on every side hanging and drooping with Feberries [goose-berries], Raspberries, Barberries, Currents, and the rootes of your trees powdred with Strawberries, red, white, and greene . . . [26]

What he recognized was that the senses, functioning as "Organes, Pipes, and windowes," work on the "gentle, generous, and noble mind and refresh it."[27]

An additional value, a note only lightly touched by Lawson which swelled into a chorus by the middle of the seventeenth century, was that an orchard is a perpetual annuity — for one's heirs and one's country:

> . . . what joy may you have, that you living to such an age, shall see the blessings of God on your labors while you live, and leave behind you to heires or successors (for God will make heires) such a worke, that many ages after your death, shall record your love to their Countrey? And the rather, when you consider . . . to what length of time your worke is like to last.[28]

"Love of country" becomes the gracious but aggressive motivation for involvement in agriculture by a distinguished group of writers whose contributions were stimulated by Samuel Hartlib, the Polish merchant's son who came to England and contributed powerfully to agricultural reform. Among these writers were Gabriel Plattes, Ralph Austen, Sir Richard Weston, Robert Child, Arnold

Boate, Walter Blith, Cressy Dymock, John Beale, and Robert Sharrock.[29] Mainly Puritan in outlook and commitment, they abhorred "base privacy of spirit" and regarded agriculture as "the sinnewes and marrow that holds together the joynts of common good."[30] They attacked poverty, unemployment, unproductive land, in order to bring health and prosperity to the nation. They emphasized wealth, employment, and productivity, but they did not dichotomize *material* and *spiritual*, *economic* and *religious*, *secular* and *sacred*. It was a vocation metaphysic (not a work ethic) that gave them their brilliant vision of England being turned into a Rehoboth, a new world, or a Paradise. Theirs was not a secular pursuit with religious motivation [31] but a world-and-life view that saw no antithesis between *secular* and *religious* simply because *secular* did not exist in a world created by God. No matter what their perspective — whether from the heights of agricultural success or from the depths of barren failure — they knew that God had not abandoned His world, that nothing was separated from His love, and that the vegetable world especially proved it. Agriculture revealed the miracle of the growth of a seed, the mystery of the fruitfulness of the land, the beauty of the fertile earth, the godliness of the profits and pleasures of the enterprise. In their view — and in God's, they believed — all work is a vocation; they therefore made no distinction between *menial* and *noble* work. Agriculture, which had generally been regarded as fretfully earthy and particularly subject to mortality, now took on immortality, so that even the commercial aspects of fruit-farming had eternal value: ". . . this adventure is, without dispute, sure of a reward in heaven . . . alwayes acknowledged to deserve everlasting Monuments of glory."[32] Since they considered the value of agriculture neither secular nor terminal (it was tinged with God's glory in this life and unfading in the life to come), they endeavored to involve all levels of society in agriculture. They addressed their books to people as widely separated socially, politically, and economically as Cromwell; the Council of State; the Nobility and Gentry; the Honorable Society of the house of Court and Universities; the Souldiery of England, Scotland, and Ireland; The Husbandman, Farmer, or Tenant; the Cottager, Labourer, or meanest Commoner. They urged local parishes to disseminate writings on agricultural improvement. They made proposals for the establishment of agricultural colleges for "the advancement and encrease of *publique plenty* and wellfare."[33] They attempted to influence legislation for the improvement of rural conditions, even for making plantations of trees compulsory.[34] Trying to elevate agriculture to its rightful position in the professions, they were expansive in their articulation of its values.

Walter Blith, Captain in Cromwell's army, was dedicated to the welfare of the Republic. Seeing agriculture as a major contributor to national strength and to spiritual identity, his indefatigable efforts to attract his countrymen to this productive, peaceful occupation were inspired by his "pure love to Mankind."[35] In the pages of his books, illustrations of farm machinery brought forth anticipations of the day when *"Emmanuell* will break in pieces all that gather against him";[36] diagnoses on diseases and the reasons for crop failure evoked reflections on the causes of spiritual death. In *The English improover* (1649) and in *The English improover improoved* (1652), the values of agriculture were similarly juxtaposed:

— Agriculture provides employment for the poor and soldiers, and, hence, gives liberty to those who were formerly dependent on others for food and sustenance; it also realigns vocational priorities for maximum participation in the great design of God.

— Agriculture preserves estates from self-destruction through neglect; it also enables the present generation to extol God's glory by working for the common good.

— Agriculture improves productivity through experiment and practice and thus makes the nation Rehoboth, a new world, even the "paradise of the World"; it also corrects the proud and unteachable spirit "which banes and poysons the very plenty of our Nation."

— Agriculture opens the door for a "more facile and readier approach unto profits"; it also brings agriculturists into closer proximity to God because they are engaged in the primary profession.[37]

The most elaborately rigorous statement of the values of fruit cultivation was made by Ralph Austen of Oxford. Subsumed under four Humane Arguments in *A treatise of fruit-trees*, the values were expanded in Arguments Three and Four, "Profit and Pleasure."

While to modern eyes Profit goes about in capitalistic dress, and Pleasure wears sensual clothes, for Austen they were "King and Queen of the world," to be shared for the common good and to be used as "helps and furtherances unto God." The profits, to the estate and to the body, are in the fruit itself and in its by-products (cider, perry, wine), both of which nourish and refresh the spirits, keep the body from superfluous humours, and counteract diseases. When Austen spoke of the profits to the body, i.e., health and long life, he thought of the pure air created in an orchard by fruit trees. With air pollution as menacing to health in Austen's world as it is today, pure air emerged as a valuable commodity.[38]

These pomological promoters of health and longevity also improved spiritual health. Translating physical stimuli into spiritual profits, Austen counted the ways in which fruit trees touch the senses:

— birds and boughes and leaves singing or whistling: *Ear;*

— cool fruits cooling the body externally and internally: *Touch;*

— trees "bespangled, and gorgeously apparelled with green Leaves, Blooms, and goodly Fruits, as with a rich Robe of imbroidered work, or hanging with some pretious and costly Jewels or Pearls": *Sight;*

— sweet and cool fragrances: *Smell;*

— relieving hot infirmities and thus keeping the spirits in equal temper: *Taste.*

Along with physical and spiritual health, fruit trees promoted mental health by creating the environment for hope, joy, admiration, knowledge, and meditation. Here Austen carefully delineated the characteristics of each: *Hope* (quoting Bacon) is "as a Leaf-joy which may be beaten out to a great extension, like gold"; *Joy,* a "clear, shining, beautiful affection rising some degree higher than Hope," is settled, habitual, and renewable; *Admiration,* higher than Hope and Joy, defines one's response to God, the Creator of orchards; the *Knowledge* which is imparted by fruit trees is natural, moral, and spiritual; and *Meditation* raises the affections of the spirit into a "spiritual temper" capable of meditating upon sin and on redemption.

Finally, the highest value combined both Profit and Pleasure: in sharing the values and the products of agriculture with his fellow-man, the orchardist gave the Giver His own gifts.[39]

Through books such as John Evelyn's *Sylva,* the nation became aware of the devastation of the forests and of the need for arbori-culture. In the dedication to Charles II of the second edition of the *Sylva* (1670), Evelyn observed that as a direct result of the first edition, England had been enriched by two million trees.[40] Moses Cooke, gardener to the Earl of Essex, spent his life raising forest trees, planting woods, walks, avenues, and hedges, and creating stunning gardens at Cassiobury Park. In a startling comparison between the values of reading books on divinity and on arbori-culture, Cooke argued that arboriculture was more edifying and more unifying: "Books of Disputes in Divinity . . . tend more to make our Differences the greater, than any wayes to edifie or unite us: therefore if your Genius leads you to read such Books, this is not for your Fancy."[41] Writing because "the Gifts of God are improved by communicating and Knowledge thriveth as Ingenuity is improved and communicated," Cooke believed that the values of arbori-culture lay in their contribution to the health of man, to the adoration of the Creator and the concomitant gift of tranquillity of spirit. But he also believed that apart from the values to the arboriculturist, man had a duty to the vegetable creation: to "take care of those which are tender, and want the more care, lest they should be lost." The value had a negative threatening side: "those that are Wasters and wilfull Spoylers of Trees and Plants without just Reason so to doe, have seldom prospered in this World . . ."[42]

Timothy Nourse, an Oxford man and noted preacher, turned to agriculture when his conversion to Roman Catholicism deprived him of his fellowship. In agriculture he found the kind of employment that "may most properly be call'd a *Recreation,* not only from the Refreshment it gives to the Mind, but from the *Restauration of Nature,* which may be lookt upon as a *New Creation* of things; when from Nothing, or from something next to Nothing, we become the Instruments of producing, or of restoring them in such Perfection."[43]

Nourse did not revel in the power over Nature that participation in agriculture conferred. Rather, he rejoiced in the grace conferred upon the agriculturist by God to transform the sin-cursed earth into a fruitful field. The value lay in the wonder of it — that man should be given the power to create restoration or to restore creation.

Stephen Switzer's seventy-one page apologia for agriculture ended with the truculent statement that only those with "base, ungenerous Thoughts" would eschew agriculture. In a last effort to persuade his readers of the value of agriculture, he recommended it as the employment most suitable as preparation for dying:

> . . . 'tis thus doing, thus Planting, Dressing, and Busying themselves, that all wise and intelligent Persons would be found, when Death, that King of Terrors shall close their Eyes, and they themselves be obliged to bid an Eternal Farewel to these and all other Sublunary Pleasures.[44]

If agriculture did not raise its readers to "a glimpse of bliss," the reluctant ones might be persuaded by its final value: it contributed to the *ars moriendi*.

IV

> . . . he is welcome to enter, that is the least Lover of Flowers; but those that think the Divertisement too easie or effeminate, preferring a piece of Bacon or Cabbage, before Natures choicest Dishes, advantag'd by Art is welcomer (if possible) to stay out; and indeed is forbid Reading or Censuring what he understands not, or hath no Affection for.[45]

Who would argue for a rose? or prove the value of a flower? Not a poet. Flowers were made for poetry. A poet could roam the fields and gardens of Nature or of memory and plant flowers lavishly in the fertile ground of poetry; there flowers needed no excuse for being. For the poet, primroses were to adorn the hill of ecstatic love; flowers of "sad embroidery" were to mourn the death of a friend; roses of exquisite fragrance were to evoke the amorous linguistics of young love; the life-cycle of flowers was to mirror the poet's shrivelling and greening. The values of flowers were limited only by the poet's imagination and floristic experience.

But many of the terraculturists who decided to set aside land for flowers and Pleasure Gardens rather than for medical purposes or food crops felt that a defense of flower-gardens was necessary. Horticultural values had to be articulated if ornamental plants were to make equal claims for soil-rights with, say, potatoes or peaches. There was, of course, the obvious argument-from-beauty: by their form, fragrance, and color, flowers could defend their right to co-exist with utility plants. Although this argument seemed irrefutable, it had its detractors when it was applied only to horticulture. For had not the medical botanists recognized flowers of indescribable beauty which could also heal the sick? and had not the agriculturists planted orchards of unsurpassed loveliness which could also feed the hungry? Why then flower gardens, horticulture, and florilegia? Those who were involved in the Pleasure Garden — in promoting, expanding, and advancing it — were pressed to translate their floristic commitment into discernible and discrete values.

John Parkinson's *Paradisi in sole paradisus terrestris* (1629), although it contains descriptions of kitchen and orchard gardens in addition to the Pleasure Garden, is generally considered the first floristic book published in England.[46] Parkinson wrote because of the inadequacy of earlier books, which he described as "but handfulls snatched from the plentifull Treasury of Nature." He argued that from flowers

> we may draw matter at all times not only to magnifie the Creator that hath giuen them such diuersities of formes, sents and colours, that the most cunning Worke-man cannot imitate, and such vertues and properties, that although wee know many, yet many more lye hidden and vnknowne, but many good instructions also to ourselues . . .[47]

Parkinson's first argument — a richly religious one —implied that to neglect the floral creation is to close an avenue of praise to the Creator. Along this aesthetico-spiritual avenue, a florist could travel, alone or in community, delighting in the forms, scents, and colors of flowers, and, by increasing horticultural knowledge, enlarge the capacity to magnify God. A community of florists (which amounted almost to a subculture) shared Parkinson's horticultural commitment and outlook, enlivening one another's experiences and adding to one another's floral collections. On the pages of the *Paradisus* appear the names of Parkinson's fellow-travellers and collectors —merchants, botanists, professional gardeners, home gardeners, many of whom wear Parkinson's tag "a worthy lover of faire flowers": Nicholas Lete, Master Bradshawe, John Witte, Master Ralph Tuggie, Mistris Thomasin Tunstall, Vincent Sion, John de Franqueuille, George Wilmer, Richard Barnesley, Guillaume Boel, Humfrey Packington, John Goodier, John Tradescant, Sir Thomas Hanmer, Thomas Johnson, and many others. They gathered information, seeds, bulbs, plants, from all over England and foreign lands: from Constantinople, Italy, Spain, France, Holland, West Indies, Sardinia, Germany, Hungary, Portugal, Greece, Cape of Good Hope, the River of Canada where the French plantation in America is seated, and Lord Wotton's garden at Canterbury. In connection with the "out-landish" flowers from foreign lands, Parkinson warned his readers "to bee as carefull whom they trust with the planting and replanting of their fine flowers, as they would be with so many Jewels."[48] So lovely a route was this for Parkinson, that when he took to writing about the medicinal properties of plants (1640), he mourned the loss of his *Paradisus*: "From a Paradise of pleasant Flowers, I am fallen (*Adam* like) to a world of profitable Herbes and Plants . . . "[49]

   Parkinson's second argument for the value of horticulture was an ethical one. Expatiating on the instructive values of flowers, Parkinson divided this value into two aspects — moral and civil. As a moral analogue for human life:

> That as many herbes and flowers with their fragrant sweete smels doe comfort, and as it were reuiue the spirits, and perfume a whole house; euen so much men as liue vertuously, labouring to doe good and profit the Church of God and the Common wealth by their paines or penne, doe as it were send forth a pleasing sauour of sweet instructions,
> not only to that time wherein they liue, are fresh, but being drye, withered and dead, cease not in all after ages to doe as much or more.[50]

In his elaboration of the moral analogue, Parkinson added several points of comparison between floral life and human life: Those plants that are gloriously beautiful but that stink can be correctives to judgments that humans make on other humans; those lilies that grow among thorns can turn the human eye to sources of human beauty hitherto unexplored; those plants that are withered or blasted can marvelously concentrate the mind on human frailty; and the susceptibility of all plants to change and decay serves to remind humans of the mutability of states as well as of persons.

As a civil influence on human life: The beautiful forms of flowers have such a powerful humanizing effect on the beholder that "he is not humane, that is not allured with this obiect"; the cultivation of floristic beauty is not so time-devouring as to prevent even kings from engaging in it, with time left for deliberation on weighty civil affairs; and horticulture is an "Instructer in the verity of the genuine Plants of the Ancients, and a Correcter of . . errours."[51]

Beauty and Goodness, an ancient inseparable pair, blithely co-habited in Parkinson's *Paradisus*. Parkinson's wisdom in seeing that flowers could provide a guide for human life — a guide that revealed the ethico-aesthetic aspects of human life and that shaped a florist's perceptions of his garden — gave to horticulturists an incentive to engage in this profession. And besides, from horticulture would spring the finests flowers and the finest humans.

One of the most distinguished horticulturists of the seventeenth century, John Rea, wrote *Flora: seu, de florum cultura* (1665), for those who "are taken with the alluring Charms of this lovely Recreation."[52] His forty years as a planter brought him recognition from the community of terraculturists, including Sir Thomas Hanmer (author of a manuscript garden book, 1659), Samuel Hartlib,[53] and Samuel Gilbert, Rea's son-in-law. His book contains no formal list of values because he would "not attempt to celebrate so sublime a subject as this in hand, since all the Flowers that are to be found in Rhetorick, hold no comparison with those of the Garden . . . "[54] His dedicatory poems to Lady Gerrard of Gerrards Bromley, Mris Trever Hanmer, Lady Hanmer (wife of Sir Thomas), and to the Ladies, show him as a "lowly wise" man capable of detecting the essence of each flower:

> For see the Auriculaes come forth,
> Adorn'd with Dies of much more worth,
> And fair Eyes twinckling on each stem,
> The Heavenly Bear shines not like them.[55]

The absence of a formal statement of values in no way implies a failure on Rea's part to recognize or admit values. For the values, Rea looked to the flowers themselves, in whose presence artificial rhetoric could only spoil the natural eloquence of Nature. Rea believed that the value of horticulture lay in the emotional commitment it could evoke from the horticulturist: it demanded love. Apart from love it could do nothing:

> . . . it is Knowledge that begets Affection, and Affection increaseth Knowledge. Love was the Inventer, and is still the Maintainer, of every noble Science. It is chiefly that which hath made my Flowers and Trees to flourish . . . and hath brought me to the knowledge I now have in Plants and Planting: for indeed it is impossible for any man to have any considerable Collection of noble Plants to prosper, unless he love them: for neither the goodness of the Soil, nor the advantage of the Situation, will do it, without the Masters affection: it is that which animates, and renders them strong and vigorous . . .[56]

The effects of this animating love were to be observed rather than articulated: on the flowers and on the lovers of flowers.

For John Worlidge, author of *Systema agriculturae* (1669) and *Systema agriculturae* (1677), terraculture was a science whose "several Branches and Streams of pleasure and delight" could provide the "highest and most absolute Content" on earth.[57] To support this belief, he compared gardens with other inanimate objects of delight and with other works of art. From the comparisons the values emerged. No other inanimate objects could compete with a Garden, which is "the only compleat and permanent inanimate object of delight the World affords, ever complying with our various and mutable Minds, feeding us, and supplying our Fancies with daily Novels."[58] And no other work of art was so perpetually renewable as was a Garden:

> All curious pieces of Architecture, Limning, Painting,
> or whatever else that seem pleasant to the eye or

other senses at first sight or apprehension, at length become dull by too long acquaintance with them. But the pleasures of a *Garden* are every day renewed with the approaching Aurora.[59]

Abounding in enthusiasm for flower gardening, Worlidge was eager to show his readers that the values which he found in horticulture could be seen all over England:

Neither is there a noble or pleasant seat in England but hath its gardens for pleasure and delight; scarce an ingenious citizen that by his confinement to a shop, being denied the priviledge of having a real garden, but hath his boxes, pots, or other receptacles for flowers, plants, &c . . . there is scarce a cottage in most of the southern parts of England but hath its proportionable garden, so great a delight do most of men take in it . . .[60]

Worlidge's guide was itself (with the addition of "The gardeners monthly directions" found in later editions) a provider of "Rural pleasures and oblectations" which could be renewed *"ad infinitum."*[61]

Samuel Gilbert's *The florists vade-mecum* (1682), a handy one-shilling pocket companion for "all Lovers of Flowers," looked deceptively simple. Inexpensive and practical, it gave season-by-season instructions for planting flowers, as it testified to the Providence of God, in season and out of season. But a value emerged from Gilbert's little book that at first glance may seem simple and sentimentally moralistic. It is based on a complex and richly ambiguous perception of the double nature of a garden. In the last chapter of his book, Gilbert sat in the Summer House gazing at the garden and reflecting on gardens and on their value for gardeners. Although his eyes remained below, entranced by the garden, they also, in company with his thoughts, ascended to Heaven. There he saw the garden in a new light: he saw the garden as garden, but he also saw man's life metamorphosed into a garden:

Here may we sit, and each his time purloin,
And see our Art, with Madam Nature joyn;
And how the Jewels that adorn the skies,
Or what shines brighter, Ladies beateous Eies

Can't be compar'd to Flora's Mantle, that
She throwes on earth, and Mortals wonder at;
Embroider'd Tellus doth her Glory sing
As vvell as Birds at the approach of Spring,
And vve vvith ravisht eies, see Flora smile,
Whilst chirping Musick doth our Ears beguile:
Feel softest dovvn, in tender buds of Roses,
Arabian smells in her perfumed posies . . .
But when this sensual-banquet we have done,
On winged thoughts sore higher than the Sun;
And then contemplate how the three in One
All mortal actions view from his bright throne.
And thence resolve, our Selves as Gardens keep;
Pluck up the weeds of sin, soon as they peep.
His Graces be our flowers; for wat'ring pots
Our Eie, oft letting fall repentant drops;
That cause those flow'rs encrease, and give occasion
For our removal to a new Plantation.
Each day concluding, with account made even,
To have no Walks, but those that lead to Heaven;
Such as in Gardens innocence employ,
That vertues raise, so vices must destroy.
Then Gard'ner of Universe, his powers
Pluck not as weeds, but take us up as Flowers.[62]

It was a brilliant illumination, not a rhetorical trick, that enabled Gilbert to see the garden as garden and man's life as garden, with no loss to either. From the heights of Heavenly contemplation, Gilbert did not shuffle between actual garden and metaphoric garden; indeed, there he saw the garden in its true nature, capable of being both at once, while each was each. Since Gilbert did not press himself to make rigid distinctions between the two gardens, he could use the ambiguity to reveal rather than to conceal, to disclose rather than to hide, the true nature of both gardens. He claimed what no other horticulturist had claimed: that a garden had a double reality. In this double reality (not a duality) lay the value of horticulture: as the gardener cultivated the actual garden he cultivated the garden of his life. Gilbert's sight became insight when he saw that in God, the "Gard'ner of Universe," the double reality — garden as garden and man's life as garden — is fully realized.

NOTES

Chapter Two

[1] William Turner, *The first and seconde partes of the herbal* (Collen, 1568), *To Elizabeth I.*

[2] William Coles, *Adam in Eden* (London, 1657), *Dedication.*

[3] According to William Derham, *Mem.*, p. 37 (as cited by Charles E. Raven, *John Ray* [Cambridge, 1950], p. 9), the eminent botanist John Ray was first introduced to plants by his mother, a well-known herb-woman.

[4] *A priest to the temple, The Works of George Herbert,* ed. F.E. Hutchinson (Oxford, 1967), pp. 261-262. The theologian Joseph Mede, "when he and others were walking in the Fields or in the Colledge-Garden . . . would take occasion to speak of the Beauty, Signature, useful Vertues and Properties of the Plants then in view: For he was a curious Florist, an accurate Herbalist, throughly vers'd in the Book of Nature," "The Author's Life," in *The Works of Joseph Mede,* 3rd ed. (London, 1672).

[5] "Life," *Works,* p. 94.

[6] "Man," *Works,* p. 92. John Donne observed in a sermon, "We tread upon many herbs negligently in the field, but when we see them in an Apothecaries shop, we begin to think that there is some vertue in them," *XXVI Sermons* (London, 1661), 8, p. 111. Milton's *Comus* speaks of the "Shepherd Lad" whose "leather'n scrip" contained "simples of a thousand names" and of the most potent of plants, haemony, which was apt to be trod on by the dull swain with "clouted shoon" (11. 634-635). Earlier, the historian William Harrison, regretting the failure of English-men to use native herbs, had remarked, ". . . we tread those herbes vnder our feet, whose forces if we knew . . . we wold honor and haue in reuerence," *Harrison's Description of England,* ed. from the *First Two editions of Holinshed's Chronicle, A.D. 1577, 1587,* by Frederick J. Furnivall (London, 1877), pp. 323-327 *passim.*

[7] *Autobiography,* ed. S.L. Lee (London, 1886), pp. 57-59.

[8] *A new herball* (1551), *To the Duke of Summerset.*

[9] *A new herball* (1551), *To the Duke of Summerset.*

[10] For a detailed study of Turner's life and contribution to botany, see Charles E. Raven, *English Naturalists from Neckam to Ray* (Cambridge, 1947), pp. 48-137, and Blanche Henrey, *British Botanical and Horticultural Literature Before 1800* (London, 1975), I, 21-27.

[11] London, 1583, *Preface.*

[12] *Herball* (1633), *To Lord Burghley.*

[13] *Herball* (1633), *To the Readers.*

[14] *Herball, To the Readers.*

[15] *Herball, To Lord Burghley.*

[16] London, 1640, *Opening Address.*

[17] Adam in Eden (London, 1657), To the Reader.

[18] The art of simpling (London, 1656), Preface.

[19] Adam in Eden, Dedication. One of the most popular books on botanic medicine was The English physitian by the astrologer-physician Nicholas Culpeper, first published in 1652 and subsequently into the twentieth century; Culpeper found both medical and theological value in studying plants. See also William Westmacott's A Scripture herbal (1694), which showed how important the study of plants was for understanding the Holy Scriptures.

[20] An idea of a phytological history propounded (London, 1673), p. 99.

[21] Herball, 1633.

[22] Samuel Hartlib, The reformed husband-man (London, 1651), To the Reader.

[23] John Worlidge, Systema agriculturae (London, 1669), Preface.

[24] "Of Education," Complete Prose Works of John Milton (New Haven, 1959), II, 389.

[25] A new orchard and garden, 3rd ed. (London, 1638), p. 70.

[26] A new orchard, p. 71.

[27] A new orchard, p. 73.

[28] A new orchard, p. 74. See also Leonard Meager, The new art of gardening, 2nd ed. (London, 1732), where fruit trees are regarded as "lasting monuments" to enrich posterity, B; and John Beale, Herefordshire orchards (London, 1657), where all those who made land productive are called "hearty patriots," and C.M. is singled out as one who "hath metamorphosed his wilderness to be like the Orchards of Alcinous; herein also a hearty patriot," pp. 37-39.

[29] For the definitive study of Puritan husbandry, see Charles Webster, The Great Instauration (London, 1975), pp. 468-483. For a general history of husbandry see G.E. Fussell, The Old English Farming Books from Fitzherbert to Tull 1523-1730 (London, 1947).

[30] The English improover improved, 3rd impression (London, 1652), To the Industrious Reader; in 1639 Gabriel Plattes in A discovery of infinite treasure (London) had said, ". . . Husbandry is the very nerve and sinew, which holdeth together all the joynts of a Monarchy," Preface, and Blith had echoed this in The English improover, 1649: ". . . Good Husbandrie is the Sinew or Marrow, holding together the Joynts of Monarchie," Epistle to the Ingenious Reader.

[31] In Webster's view, the Puritan perspective was "ethical," and "religious in motivation, but it had the capacity to develop a largely secular expression," The Great Instauration, pp. 506-507.

[32] Beale, Herefordshire orchards, p. 40.

[33] Cressy Dymock, An essay for advancement of husbandry learning (London, 1651), p. 6.

[34] See "Fruit Trees and Timber," in Webster, The Great Instauration, Appendix VI, where an unsigned petition (reproduced from Sheffield University Library, Hartlib Papers LXVI 22) is attributed to Ralph Austen, who refers to Mr. Samuel Hartlib's Legacie of husbandry, A designe for plentie, and Bread for the poore, pp. 546-548.

[35] The English improover improved (London, 1652), To Cromwell.

[36] The English improover improved, To the Reader.

[37] Opening epistles (1649, 1652), passim.

[38] Austen was not alone in this view of the value of fruit trees for pure air: John Evelyn described Londoners of 1661 as "pursu'd and haunted by that infernal smoake" and suggested trees to meliorate the air, *Fumifugium* (London, 1661), *Epistolary address*.

[39] Ralph Austen, *A treatise of fruit-trees* (Oxford, 1653), pp. 40-74 *passim*. Throughout his discussion, Austen frequently referred to Sir Francis Bacon's contributions to pomology. For a similar view on the value of agriculture for the totality of life, see I. van der Groen, *Den Nederlandtsen hovenier* (Amsterdam, 1669), which stated that agriculture is "das Lustigste/Vortheiligste/Gesundeste/ja mannschmahl auch wol das seeligste Leben/dass der Mensch wünschen kan . . .," *B¹*. On the contribution of cider to longevity, see Francis Drope, *A short and sure guid* (Oxford, 1672), where Edward Drope in the *Preface* remarked that eight men dancing at a wake in Herefordshire had a total age of 800 years, which longevity they attributed to drinking cider.

[40] *The Diary of John Evelyn . . .* ed. E.S. de Beer (Oxford, 1955), 3, 541.

[41] *The manner of raising, ordering, and improving forrest-trees* (London, 1676), *To the Courteous Reader*.

[42] *The manner, To the Courteous Reader*. In 1649 Walter Blith in his address to Parliament *(The English improover)* had deplored the felling and destroying of the "gallant Timber" of the Kingdom and urged legislation for reforestation.

[43] *Campania foelix* (London, 1700), pp. 2-3.

[44] *The nobleman, gentleman, and gardener's recreation* (London, 1715), p. 71.

[45] Samuel Gilbert, *The florists vade-mecum*, 3rd ed. (London, 1702), *To the Reader*.

[46] For earlier works, see Blanche Henrey, "Gardening Books," in *British Botanical and Horticultural Literature*, I, 55-69.

[47] *Paradisus, Epistle to the Reader*.

[48] *Paradisus*, p. 13.

[49] *Theatrum botanicum*, p. 1.

[50] *Paradisus, Epistle to the Reader*.

[51] *Paradisus, Epistle to the Reader*. Although Gerard's *Herball* cannot be included in the floristic literature, his discussion of violets sounds a similar note: ". . . for floures through their beautie, variety of colour, and exquisite forme, do bring to a liberall and gentle manly minde, the remembrance of honestie, comelinesse, and all kindes of vertues. For it would be an vnseemely and filthie thing (as a certaine wise man saith) for him that doth looke vpon and handle faire and beautifull things, and who frequenteth and is conuersant in faire and beautifull places, to haue his minde not faire, but filthie and deformed," 1633, pp. 849-850.

[52] London, 1665, *To the Reader*.

[53] In a letter to Robert Boyle, Samuel Hartlib quoted one of his correspondents who described Mr. Pitt, Sir Thomas Hanmer, and Mr. Rea as "all three exquisite florists," *The Works of the Honourable Robert Boyle*, (London, 1772), 6, 119.

[54] *Flora, To the Reader*.

[55] *Flora, To the Ladies*.

[56] *Flora*, p. 1.

[57] *Systema agriculturae, Preface*.

[58] *Systema horti-culturae*, 3rd ed. (London, 1688), p. 5.

[59] *Systema horti-culturae*, p. 5.

[60] *Systema horti-culturae*, pp. 4-5.

[61] *Systema agriculturae, Preface*.

[62] *The florists vade-mecum*, 2nd ed. (London, 1693), p. 251.

CHAPTER THREE

THE HORTULAN SAINTS

It is an effect of the Divine goodness, which having condemned men to the just punishment of perpetuall labour, was pleased that they should find their consolation in their pains, and that they should, in them, meet with sweetness, which very often surpasses the bitter of them . . .[1]

I

The terracultural writers readily admitted that there were denigrators of terracultural writing who regarded it as nothing more than "a tale of a turfe, or matter for a mattocke."[2] To show that terraculture was not a contemptible business, they summoned up a host of witnesses to the dignity and glory, to the enduring, even celestial, qualities, of their earthy enterprise. Into their prefaces marched the patriarchs, monarchs, apostles, prophets of terraculture, carrying the implements of their profession: spades, pruning knives, mattocks, dibbles. Like the great Programs of Redemption in churches and cathedrals (where, in the setting of the celestial Garden of Paradise, Christ sits triumphant surrounded by apostles, prophets, kings, martyrs, bringing their wreaths to Him), the Program of Terraculture celebrated the glories of the New Creation — the restoration of the earth through the redemptive power of the Great Gardener of the Universe. First, they reclaimed the sin-infested earth:

> . . . I doe not take this earth to be worthie to bee accounted of in contemptible wise, but rather to bee helde as a soueraigne Empresse, and sole Monarch ouer earthly creatures, as wearing by best right and title, the naturall imperiall crowne: A Diuine sage, as wearing not onely the laurell, but also euery other beautifull & flowring branch . . . : A celestiall body; as one that being well viewed rounde about, will be founde for hew and ornaments incomparable: And lastly, a mother of celestiall offspring . . . For so fruitefull is this great mother of the worlde, as that . . . she conceiueth, perfiteth, and bringeth foorth most precious, seruiceable & beautifull babes . . . to containe whatsoeuer necessarie thing that might be of vse, either for the generation or nourishment of any or all the liuing things that are . . . of or from the earth is ministred matter to defende or offende; feede, or famish; cherish, or starue; make blinde, or restore sight . . . to giue, or take away light; to procure health or sicknes; foes, or friends; peace, or warre; pleasure, or paine; sorrow, or mirth; taste, or distast . . . life, or death . . . you shall cleerely see that there cannot too reuerend an estimation be had of the earth; and that it is to faile and come short of the scope of the Creatour . . . to account thereof in any base and vile manner.[3]

Second, they wrote abbreviated "universal histories" of terraculture, calling up both Christian and pagan witnesses. Their first —and most universal — witness was the first man, Adam.

II

Since Gard'ning was the first and best Vocation,
And Adam (whose all are by Procreation)

Was the first Gard'ner of the World, and ye
Are the green shoots of Him th' Original Tree;
Encourage then this innocent old Trade,
Ye Noble Souls that were from Adam made;
So shall the Gard'ners labour better bring
To his Countrey Profit, Pleasure to his King.[4]

Terraculture began in energetic leisure; the agitated distress came later. Adam, the Patriarch of Terraculture, worked in the Garden of Eden without sweat, and joyed in his fruitful labor. Described by the terraculturalists as the master of all paradisiacal arts, Adam was employed in the highest vocation available to man. The entire vegetable creation responded to his wise care: no knowledge was hidden from him. As the first botanist, herbalist, agriculturalist, gardener, he served as the model for all his descendants. When William Westmacott wrote *Theolobotonologia,* a Scripture herbal (1694), the tradition which vindicated his study of the botany of the Scriptures had at its head the world's first botanist:

Adam was the first Botanist we read of, his first Work was the Art of Simpling in the Garden of Eden . . .[5]

It was Gerard's view of Adam, the first herbalist, that impelled him to write an herbal describing both the medicinal and aesthetic properties of plants:

Talke of perfect happinesse or pleasure, and what place was so fit for that as the garden place where Adam was set to be the Herbarist?[6]

The unbroken horticultural-agricultural-pomological tradition inherited from pre-lapsarian Adam was invoked in a poetic tribute to John Tradescant the Younger, upon publication of *Musaeum Tradescantianum* (1656), by an admirer of both Tradescant and Adam:

Nor court, nor shop-crafts were thine ARTES but those
    Which *Adam* studied ere he did transgresse:
    The Wonders of the Creatures, and to dresse
The worlds great Garden . . .[7]

The patriarchal position of Adam as botanist, herbalist, agriculturalist, gardener, was threatened by the Fall but not doomed by it.

The spade (or mattock), instrument and symbol of degradation, became for Adam, through the merciful Providence of God, the instrument of relief "for the staying of his minde and hart in the middest of his pensiuenes and most greeuous calamities."[8] So significant a place did it occupy in the Program of Redemption that the picture of Adam with a spade became a ubiquitous icon in Bibles and churches, knowing few chronological or geographical bound-aries. From the woodcuts of the fifteenth century in the "Life of Christ," to the mosaics of San Marco in Venice; from the gilded sculpture of Ghiberti's doors of the Baptistery of Florence, to the spandrel carvings in the Chapter House of Salisbury Cathedral; from the four illustrated Bibles from Tours, to the Sienese triptych where Adam holds a mattock at the foot of the cross (FIGURES 2-4) and hundreds of other instances — came the familiarity and the easy reference in terracultural books to "our Grandsire *Adam*, who is commonly pictured with a Spade in his hand,"[9] without the accompanying awkwardness created by the reader's failure to recognize the scene.[10] When, in the course of time, Adam's spade could be burnished into an instrument of honor rather than dishonor, then terraculture could be reclaimed as a "princely diversion":

> By this time I hope you will think it no dishonour to follow the steps of our Grandsire *Adam*, who is pictured with a Spade in his hand, to march through the Quarters of your Garden with the like instrument . . .[11]

Adam's name lent nobility to the titles of two terracultural books: *Adam in Eden* for Coles's history of plants, fruits, herbs, and flowers (1657); and *Adam out of Eden* for Speed's agricultural manual (1659). As a terracultural icon, "Adam with a spade" took various forms in terracultural books: A spade, perched above a flourishing plant, bears the inscription "Adams toole revived" in Platt's *The nevv and admirable arte* . . . (1601); and a dignified Adam holds out a spade as the ornament of a glorious profession in Parkinson's *Theatrum botanicum* (1640).

Next to Adam stood Solomon. Although many figures — among them Adam's sons, Abraham, Noah, Saul, David, Uzziah — stood modestly in the background of sacred terracultural history,[12] Solomon "the wisest, [was] the second Husbandman or Improver of

Figure 2

Adam and Eve; German. From the National Gallery of Art,
Washington; Rosenwald Collection.

Scene 11: The expulsion from Eden.

Scene 12: Eve nursing and Adam working.

Fig. 13

Scene 13: Sacrifice of Cain and Abel.

Scene 14: Cain murders Abel.

Figure 3

Adam with a Spade, Salisbury Cathedral.

Figure 4

Ghiberti's Bronze Doors — Adam at the Gates of Paradise, Florence, Italy.

the World":[13]

> Kings, Princes, and the wisest Men of all Ages, have . . .
> taken singular Delight in this Exercise of Planting, Setting,
> Sowing, and what else is requisite in the well ordering of
> *Orchards, and Gardens,* and rejoyced to see the Fruits of
> their Labour. *Solomon* among the many Toyls of State and
> Affairs of his Kingdom, took exceeding delight in it, and to
> study the Works of Nature; so that 'tis said of him, he knew
> the Use and Virtue of all Plants, even from the Shrub to the
> Cedar; that is, from the smallest to the greatest.[14]

Unfortunately, Solomon's terracultural treatises were not extant:

> Had *Solomon* that great proficient in all sublunary experi-
> ments preserved those many volumes that he wrote in this
> kind, for the instructions of future ages, (so great was that
> spatiousnesse of mind, that God had bestowed on him) that
> he had immediately under the Deity been the greatest of
> Doctors, for the preservation of mankind . . .[15]

After Solomon, the terraculturalists boldly placed Susannah in the
ranks, the first woman to enter the sacred history of terraculture:

> . . .we have the *example* of the Mirror of Chastity, Virtuous
> *Susanna.* It was her custome to walke in a *garden,* as we see
> in the *History* vers. 7.8.[16]

In the later history were included all the people of Israel, who "(by a
speciall command from God) made use of *Arbours and shady
places,* in their great Feasts: *Nehem.* 8.14, 15."[17]

And finally, they placed Christ above the ranks in a position of
majesty, as the One from whom all terracultural lustre radiated.[18]

III

> Thus *Chiron,* for his *Skill,* was feign'd the *Son*
> Of *Saturn* and *Phillyre; Aesc'lapius* won
> A *God's* repute; Blind *Homer* magnifies
> *Italian Circe:* others, *Canonize*
> Her for a *Goddesse* . . .
> Thus, the great *Language-master, Mithridate,*
> Lives still *Adored,* for His *Cabinet*

> Of *Recipe's* and *Secrets;* welcomer
> To *Pompey,* than all else He got by th' *War:*
> *Lenaeus* famous, in the *Roman*-State,
> Because those *Jewels* He did well *Translate:*
> And *Vulgius,*for His Tract of *Simples* writ
> (Though left *Unperfect)'s venerable,* yet.
>   So *Theophrastus, Dioscorides,*
> *Galen,* and *Pliny,* wear *Immortal Baies:*
> *Rhasis* and *Mesue,* noble *Avicen,*
> Admired all, by ev'ry worthy *Pen* . . .[19]

Intermingled with the Christian hortulan saints were the pagan canonized "Hero Labourers"; and entwined with Adam's spade was the pagan "Spade crown'd with Laurels."[20] In the illustrious troops were those ancient Greek authors

> . . . who have given unto men the Rules of living well, by the knowledge of Morality; and have raised their Spirits to the search of the most hidden parts of Natural Philosophy, piercing even into the secrets of their prophane Theologie; have, at the same time, and in the same writings, taught them the Art of Tilling the Earth, and of soliciting her . . .[21]

Among the ancient botanists was Theophrastus, whose fame was so long-lived as to make him a candidate for Switzer's "Catalogue of Garden-Heroes" in 1715:

> What he wrote relating to Gard'ning was chiefly of *Botany;* and indeed it may be supposed to be the Ground-work and Foundation of all that has been writ since on that Subject. He succeeded *Aristotle,* and liv'd in his Garden; and we may guess at the great Veneration he had for Gard'ning, by the Care he took in his Will . . . of bequeathing it to his particular Friends to study in, and for the Repose of his own Bones . . .[22]

Dioscorides, who "writ not only of Plants, but *de tota materia medica,*" was venerated as the patron saint of medical botany:

> . . . to which studie hee was addicted euen from his childe-hood, which made him trauell much ground, and leade a militarie life, the better to accomplish his ends: and in this he attained to that perfection, that few or none since his time

> haue attained to, of the excellencie of his worke, which is as
> it were the foundation and ground-worke of all that hath
> been since deliuered in this nature . . . the generall method
> he obserued you may finde set forth by *Bauhine* in his
> Edition of *Matthiolus* . . .[23]

Deserving as much adulation as that given to "the greatest and
most laborious Philosophers and Heroes,"[24] the patriarchs of
planting and grafting included Cyrus, king of the Persians, who

> had no greater desire or pleasure . . . than . . . in Planting &
> Graffing . . . The Emperor *Dioclesian* . . . did leaue the
> scepter of his Empire for to remain continually in the fieldes.
> So much pleasure did he take in planting of fruit, in making
> of Orchardes & Gardens, which he did make, garnish, and
> finishe with his owne handes. The Senatours, Dictatours,
> and Consuls of the Romaynes, among all other things haue
> commended Planting and Graffing to bee one of the most
> flourishing labours in this worlde . . .
> . . . for this Art hath not onely from tyme to tyme, beene put
> in vse and practise of labour through kings and princes: but
> also it hath bene put in writing of many great and worthie
> personages, in diuers kinde of languages, as in Greke by
> Philometor, Hieron, Acheleus, Orpheus, Musceus, Homer,
> Hosiode, Constantine, Cesar: and in Latin, by Verron,
> Caton, Columella, Paladius, Virgill, Amilius Macer, and in
> the Portingall tongue by king Attalus and Mago . . . that
> after their death, the bookes of planting and graffing were
> brought to Rome, soone after the destruction of
> Carthage.[25]

And what more is there to be said of the ancient hortulan saints?
Time would fail to tell of Apollo, Lysimachus, Gentius, Nebuchad-
nezzar, Ahasuerus, Laertes, Julius and Augustus Caesar, Horace,
Seneca, Massinissa. (FIGURE 5) And of the women: the *"Phrygian
and Tyrian* Dames," of Cleopatra,[26] and of Artemisia, Queen of
Caria.[27]

IV

> But my very good Lord, that which sometime was the study
> of great Philosophers and mightie Princes, is now neglected,

Figure 5

Lyte, *A Nievve Herball*, 1578.

except it be of some few, whose spirit and wisedome hath carried them . . . to a care and studie of speciall herbes, both for the furnishing of their gardens; and the furtherance of their knowledge: among whome I may iustly affirme and publish your Honor to be one . . .[28] (FIGURE 6)

As is the way with saints, veneration gives birth to emulation. The terracultural writers, consequently, used their predecessors not so much as authorities whose pronouncements on terraculture were eternized (never to be altered or challenged), but as models for the study, investigation, and advancement of this science. Spurred on to heightened activity by these models, the writers called on their contemporaries to join the ranks of those who could help to shape England's terracultural destiny.

Looking to Susannah, Cleopatra, and Artemisia, they found contemporary women gardeners whose activities could lend immediate prestige to the vocation:

> When Men are observ'd to busie themselves in this diverting and useful Employ, 'tis no more than what is from them expected; but when by the fair and tender Sex, it has something in it that looks supernatural, something so much above the trifling Amusements of that Species of Rational Beings, that is apt to fill the Mind of the Virtuous with Admiration, and may very well retort on the dull, unactive part of Mankind, the Sluggishness of whose Lives denote a sorry, mean, and base Spiritedness of Mind; while these illustrious Heroins shine with unusual Splendor, and by their Actions perpetuate their Memories to the latest Date of Time.[29]

There were: The Duchess of Bedford; the Duchess of Beaufort, who spent two-thirds of her time in gardening; the Countess of Lindsey, who "without any regard to the rigid Inclemency of the Winter Season . . . was actually employed with Rule, Line, &c"[30]; Lady Gerrard of Gerrards Bromley; Mris Trever Hanmer; the Lady Hanmer:

> You are a Florist born and bred,
> And to a Florist married;
> Whose skill united can revive

Figure 6
John Gerard, *The Herball*, 1633.

Each tender drooping Vegetive . . .[31]

And the Lady Danvers (Magdalen Herbert) at Chelsea.[32]

They looked to Dioscorides and found an "Anglo-Dioscorides," John Gerard of contemporary *Herball* fame, in the alumni of this sacred profession ("sacrae pietatis alumni"), his brow wreathed with the everlasting crown of salvation/health:

. . . salutis
AEterna statuit frontem redimire corona.[33]

Gerard's garden, too, would live forever because of the renown of its gardener.[34]

The ranks were swelled by contemporary botanists, herbalists, physicians, horticulturalists, agriculturalists, of varying degrees of eminence. In Thomas Johnson's catalogue there were included: Brunfel, Tragus, Fuchsius, Gesner, Dodonaeus, Lobel, Clusius, Camerarius, Tabernaemontanus, Bauhine, Besler, William Turner, Henry Lyte, John Parkinson, John Gerard, George Bowles, Thomas Hickes, John Buggs, William Broad, Job Weale, Leonard Buckner, James Clarke, Robert Lorkin.[35]

On William Coles's lists there were "eminent Botanicks, in the University of *Oxford*": Mr. Steevens of Hart-Hall, Mr. Lydall, Brown, Wit, Hanley, Beeston, John Crosse the Apothecary;[36] and gardeners: Dr. How of the Physic Garden at Westminster, Master Bobart of the Physic Garden at Oxford, Master Morgan, gardener at Westminster.[37]

André Mollet's *The Garden of Pleasure* added two contemporary kings and a duke to the gardening rolls:

Lewis the Thirteenth, and the Duke of Orleans his brother . . . disdained not to change the Scepter, sometimes for the Pruning Knife . . . But, we need look no farther for Examples of a Royal Magnificency, than to what our invincible Monarch, Charles the Second, hath, with excellent choice . . . begun in his Royal Houses of St. James's, Hampton Court, and Greenwich . . .[38]

The pomologist Ralph Austen gave a position of prominence to Sir Francis Bacon[39]; and the agriculturalist Walter Blith included Bacon in his list of agriculturalists along with Markham, Gouge [sic], Sir Hugh Plats, Mr. Gabrell Plats, and Samuell Hartlip [sic].[40]

Samuel Hartlib's famous circle of saints was a heterogeneous assemblage of terraculturalists: Thomas Ducket, Robert Child, Arnold Boate, Walter Blith, Cressy Dymock, John Beale, Sir Richard Weston, Robert Sharrock, Robert Boyle, John Evelyn.[41]

Switzer's "General Catalogue of Virtuoso's in King Charles II. Time" included: Charles II; the Earl of Essex; the Lord Capel; Lord William Russel; Lord Ranelagh; Lord Weymouth; the Earl of Carlisle; Sir William Temple; Sir Thomas Browne; John Evelyn; the Members of the Royal Society; Dr. Henry Compton, Lord Bishop of London; Dr. Grew; Dr. Beale; Dr. Woodward; Dr. Pluknet; Mr. Ray; and Gardeners Rose, Cook, London, Wise, Lucre, and Field.[42]

While awarding a "Triumphall evergreene Lawrell crowne" to John Parkinson for "saving so many Citizens . . . from danger, diseases, destruction," Thomas Clayton and John Bainbridge (doctors of Physick at Oxford) celebrated the munificence of Henry Danvers, Earl of Danby, in establishing the Oxford Botanic Garden in 1621 — a garden which "once finished [will be] another Paradise."[43]

And finally, Stephen Blake, surrounded by hortulan saints whose faithfulness to terraculture had earned them an earthly crown, urged each one to view his profession in the light of Heaven so that

> . . . at his end he shall be translated into the Heaven of Heavens, before the blessed and beatifical sight of the glorious Trinity, and there receive an immortal Crown, with power to rule in unity and love, and to rest with Saints and Angels in joy and glory to all eternity.[44]

NOTES

Chapter Three

1 LeGendre, Curate of Henonville, *The manner of ordering fruit-trees*, trans. John Evelyn (?) (London, 1660), *Preface*.

2 Charles Stevens and John Liebault, *Maison rustique or The countrie farme*, trans. Richard Surflet (London, 1600), *To Sir Peregrine Bartie*. See also Sir Thomas Pope Blount, *A natural history, Preface*; T. Snow, *Apopiroscopy*, p. 3; and Henry More's comment, ". . . men dig and droyle like blinde molewarpes in the earth," Letter from More to Hartlib, 11 December 1648, *Hartlib Papers* XVII, quoted from Charles Webster, "Henry More and Descartes: Some New Sources," *British Journal for the History of Science*, 4 (1969), 365.

3 *Maison rustique, To Sir Peregrine Bartie*.

4 Moses Cooke, *The manner of raising, ordering, and improving forrest-trees*, p. 52.

5 London, 1694, *Preface*.

6 *Herball* (1597), *To the courteous and well willing readers*. See also John Parkinson, *Paradisus, To the courteous reader*.

7 London, 1656, A4r. See also Snow, *Apopiroscopy*, where terraculture is described as Adam's practise in Paradise, p. 3; and Ralph Austen, *A treatise of fruit-trees* (1657), where Adam's pomological employment in perfection is regarded as "his greater delight and pleasure: . . . as it is ancient, so it is honourable," p. 12.

8 *Maison rustique, To Jaques of Crusoll*.

9 Coles, *The art of simpling*, p. 122.

10 For a comprehensive survey of Adam as Patriarch of Terraculture, see H. Aurenhammer, "Adam und Eva bei der Arbeit," *Lexicon der Christlichen Ikonographie* (Wien, 1959-67), I, 49-50; see also Herbert L. Kessler, *The Illustrated Bibles from Tours* (Princeton, 1977), pp. 22-23; and Gertrud Schiller, *Iconography of Christian Art* (London, 1972), II, 132. In *Hamlet*, the gravedigger reflects this common association of Adam with a spade, "Come my spade. There is no ancient gentlemen but gard'ners, ditchers, and grave-makers. They hold up Adam's profession," V.i.30-32.

11 Leonard Meager, *The compleat English gardner*, now enlarged by way of *Supplement* by a lover of this princely diversion and profitable recreation (London, 1710), p. 156.

12 See Noah in the sculptured frieze at Salisbury Cathedral. See also *Maison rustique, To Jaques of Crusoll*, where there are references to these minor terraculturalists and Noah is described as "the first that planted the Vine, and made his sonnes dressers of Vines"; and Conrad Heresbachius, *The whole art of husbandry*, trans. Barnaby Googe and enlarged by Gervase Markham (London, 1631), p. 7.

13 Walter Blith, *The English improover improved*, p. 4.

14 Leonard Meager, *The new art of gardening* (London, 1697), p. 2. See also Henry

Lyte, *A nieuve herball* (London, 1578), *Epistle to the queen; An herbal for the Bible,*
trans. Thomas Newton (London, 1587), p. 3; Thomas Johnson, *To the reader* in
Gerard's *Herball* (1633); Ralph Austen, *A treatise of fruit-trees* (1653), p. 38;
Samuel Gilbert, *The florists vade-mecum, To the reader;* and Stephen Switzer,
The nobleman, gentleman, and gardener's recreation, pp. 4-5.

[15] Coles, *Adam in Eden, To the reader.*

[16] Austen, *A treatise of fruit-trees* (1657), p. 13.

[17] Austen (1657), p. 13.

[18] *An herbal for the Bible,* p. 9; Heresbachius, *The whole art of husbandry* (1631), p. 7;
and Austen, *A treatise of fruit-trees* (1657), p. 14.

[19] G. Wharton to William Coles, *Adam in Eden.*

[20] G.A. Agricola, *A philosophical treatise of husbandry and gardening,* trans. and
revised by Richard Bradley (London, 1721), *Preface.*

[21] LeGendre, *The manner of ordering fruit-trees, Preface.*

[22] Switzer, *The nobleman, gentleman, and gardener's recreation,* pp. 11-12.

[23] Thomas Johnson, To the reader in Gerard's *Herball* (1633).

[24] Switzer, *The nobleman, gentleman, and gardener's recreation, Preface.*

[25] Leonard Mascall, *A booke of the arte and maner, how to plant and graffe all sortes
of trees . . .* (London, 1572), *Epistle to Lord Sir John Pawlet.*

[26] Switzer, *The nobleman, gentleman, and gardener's recreation,* pp. 53-54.

[27] *An herbal for the Bible,* p. 2; and Coles, *The art of simpling,* p. 12.

[28] Gerard, *Herball* (1597), *To Lord Burghley.*

[29] Switzer, *The nobleman, gentleman, and gardener's recreation,* p. 55.

[30] Switzer, pp. 54-55.

[31] John Rea, *Flora: seu de florum cultura* (1665), *To the Lady Hanmer.*

[32] John Aubrey, *Brief Lives,* ed. A. Clark (Oxford, 1898), I, 75.

[33] G. Launaeus, to John Gerard, *Herball* (1597, 1633).

[34] "Sic erit aeternum hinc vt viuas, horte *Gerardi,*/Cultoris studio nobilitate tui," M.
Jacob Jhonston, to John Gerard, *Herball* (1597, 1633).

[35] Gerard's *Herball* (1633), *To the reader.*

[36] *Adam in Eden, To the reader.*

[37] *The art of simpling,* p. 12.

[38] London, 1670, *Preface to the reader.*

[39] *A treatise of fruit-trees* (1653, 1657), *passim.*

[40] *The English improover improved, To the industrious reader.*

[41] *Samuel Hartlib His Legacy of Husbandry,* 3rd ed. (London, 1655), *passim.* See also
Charles Webster, *The Great Instauration,* pp. 470-483.

[42] *The nobleman, gentleman, and gardener's recreation,* pp. 44-64 *passim.*

[43] *Theatrum botanicum* (1640), *To John Parkinson, Englands chiefest herbarist.*

[44] *The compleat gardeners practice* (London, 1664), p. 154. Blake's confident belief
that terraculture's significance is only fully realized in the perspective of eternity is

not a private belief but one shared by almost all of his fellow terraculturalists (see chapters 1 and 2).

CHAPTER FOUR
PLANTS AND POEMS

"or human face divine"[1]

I

Today the vegetable world and the human world seem strangely alien to each other. The hortulan saints have disappeared, no Divinity "irradiates" the art of gardening, and the values of terraculture no longer span earth and heaven.

Everything separates plants and poems. No literary critic studies botany to understand plants in poems; no botanist reads poetry to identify or describe plants in fields or gardens. Between botany and poetry there is a linguistic gulf: Only rarely do poets cross over into botany for scientific names of plants, or botanists into poetry for suitable nomenclature. The methods, too, of poets and botanists are basically foreign: Perception lives in one country, dissection in another. The fundamental reason for this alienation is that plants and humans no longer share in the pre-lapsarian unity of Creation or in the post-lapsarian redemption of Creation.

It was not always so. Sixteenth and seventeenth century terra-culturalists and poets believed that a kinship existed between man and vegetable — a kinship that was part of a larger conjunction and that was most intelligible in the light of Creation and Re-creation. God, in Creation, shared with man His image and made him "copartner in the Secrets of Divine Art,"[2] the "art" of the third day of Creation. In this state, man's relationship to vegetables was analogous to God's relationship to man: man exercised the same Creational care over vegetables, planting his imprint on them, as God did over man.

But the Fall intervened. The "partnership" was temporarily dissolved, and the vegetable creation suffered alienation from man as man did from God. Man's self-inflicted curse made strangers of them all.[3] Only through Christ could the "partnership" be re-instated, could man and God, man and vegetable, be reunited: "Nature, grace, physick and Divinity,/so returning to their first unity."[4] Because Christ, by acting as mediator of man, impressed His incarnational image on man and restored him to "partnership" with God, man could, by acting as mediator for vegetables, stamp his renewed image on plants and elevate them to their proper place in the universe of God's love. Two seventeenth-century poets spoke of this incarnational relationship to plants, George Herbert and Henry Vaughan, Herbert saying, "Man is the worlds high Priest; he doth present/The sacrifice for all" ("Providence") and Vaughan echoing, "Man is their high-priest, and should rise/To offer up the sacrifice" ("Christs Nativity").[5] The botanist-poet Abraham Cowley saw that as God's grace had brought salvation to man, so man's sanctified botanizing would bring restoration to plants: "It does, like Grace, the fallen Tree restore/To it's blest State of Paradise before . . . "[6]

Since vegetables shared the human condition, there was no perceived disjunction between botany and poetry, nor between the language of botany and poetry. Poets and botanists alike discerned the whole of the human anatomy in vegetables and used human structure to describe and identify vegetable structure. Hair, head, eye, ear, nose, bosom, vulva, scrotum, hand, finger, arm, knee, foot, heel, toe, joint, nerve, sinew, vein, skin, blood, appeared with regularity in the plants described by botanists and poets, who were neither crude anthropomorphists nor simple narcissists. A botanist said that "a plant is a person turned upside down" ("Planta est homo inuersus")[7]; and Abraham Cowley agreed that the plant world "contains the whole Fabrick of humane Frame."[8]

Their methods, too, were the same. The poetic method of definition by comparison was described by a botanist as his own "metaphysical" method:

> And as in *Metaphysical*, or other Contemplative Matters, when we have a distinct knowledge of the *Communities* and *Differences* of Things, we may then be able to give their true *Definitions*.[9]

In this chapter, I shall bring botanic counterparts to the plants appearing in poems, with a view to restoring plants and poems to their pre-alienation state. I risk, to be sure, the hostility of the professional botanist, who may resent the reminder of a "pre-scientific" era, and of the professional literary critic, who may resist the invasion of art by science. There can be no doubt about it, however. Plants and poems in the sixteenth and seventeenth centuries were affiliates in the realm of human experience. When the botanist Rembert Dodoens defined the *flower* of a plant as "the joy of trees and plants . . . the hope of fruits to come,"[10] he spoke scientifically and poetically. And in speaking thus, he enlarged the laboratories of dissection and the fields of perception for botanists and poets. And for us looking back.

II

"This living buried man, this quiet mandrake"[11]

Of the thousands of plants catalogued in ancient, medieval, and Renaissance science and poetry, the plant with the most illustrious (and often nefarious) history was the mandrake or mandragora. Mandrake's multiple effects on the human body and the human spirit were charted by all who came in contact with it: by physicians, botanists, Biblical commentators, and poets; and most recently by a twentieth-century pharmacologist who tested mandrake's psycho-pharmacological effects under laboratory conditions.[12] All its parts were potently active: root, leaf, bark, juice, fruit, and seed were described as medicine, narcotic, analgesic, anesthetic, delirifacient, aphrodisiac, fertility drug; and its "symbolic parts," originating in its botanical and pharmaceutical properties, were recognized by the whole range of commentators. But it was mandrake's uncanny likeness to the human frame that ushered it into full participation in the human drama. Its upright torso, usually complete with either male or female genitals, caused it to be given the names *anthropomorphos* and *a forma humana;*[13] and some said, though respectable English herbalists did not agree, that mandrake owed its very existence and substance to human "matter":

> . . . it is neuer or very seldome to be found growing naturally but vnder a gallowes, where the matter that hath fallen from the dead body hath giuen it the shape of a man; and the matter of a woman, the substance of a female plant . . .[14]

With the human frame impressed so deeply upon it, we are not surprised to discover that mandrake's primary parts signified its efficacy in arousing sexual desire and stimulating conception. Its erotomaniac effects were noted by botanists and alluded to by poets, who identified it as a plant that participated in Adam's dust and lust. Known from antiquity as *"Circaea, of Circe* the witch, who by art could procure loue: for it hath beene thought that the Root hereof serueth to win love,"[15] mandrake easily found its way into the lascivious vocabulary of Falstaff, who recognized it as a sexual excitant, calling one man "Thou whoreson mandrake" (*II Henry IV,* I. ii. 14) and describing another as "lecherous as a monkey, and the whores call'd him mandrake" (*II Henry IV,* III. ii. 314-315). Donne's "Song," with its outrageous imperative to "Get with child a mandrake root," is thick with the sexual lust and sensuality associated with mandrake. His allusion to the "lustfull woman [who] came this plant to grieve" in "The Progresse of the Soule" (XVII) reflects the traditional portrait of a lewd Venus imploring the mandrake to make her fertile:

> Venus ye goddesse of adultery/which excercisid her lechery wiht [sic] dyuers personis/went to the mandrake & made her prayer mekely & sayde thus/O thowe best and moste frutefull tre. Loke uppon me and despyse not my prayers/but grawnte me of thy goodnes to be partetaker of the that I maye conceyue chyldren of them that be my

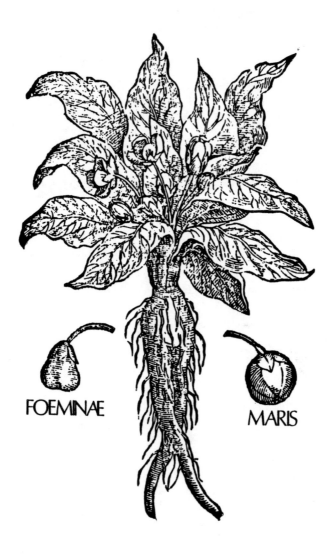

FOEMINÆ   MARIS

Figure 7

Mandrake (from Gerard's Herball, p. 352)

louers . . .[16]

Mandrake in these botanic and poetic settings emerges as an erotic plant in its human physicality. (FIGURE 7)

Mandrake's association with human mortality was observed by botanists, theologians, and poets. Henry Lyte in A *nievve herball* (1578) warned about the lethal properties of an overdose:

> It is most dangerous to receiue into the body, the iuyce of the roote of this herbe, for if one take neuer so little more in quantitie, then the iust proportion which he ought to take, it killeth the body. The leaues and fruit, be also dangerous, for they cause deadly sleepe, and peeuish drowsines like *Opium*.[17]

A Biblical commentator discovered mortal symbols in the botanic habits and habitat of mandrake:

> The roots of the mandrake lie deep under the earth and have the appearance of human bodies. They thus bear upon themselves the image of the dead.[18]

And Donne, in his "Elegie upon the untimely death of the incomparable Prince Henry," placed the mandrake in this same mortuary context:

> Therefore we live; though such a life wee have,
> As but so many mandrakes on his grave.
>   . . . Therefore wee
> May safelyer say, that we are dead, then hee.
> So, if our griefs wee do not well declare,
> We'have double excuse; he'is not dead; and we are.[19]

For Donne the living mourners in the elegy were like mandrakes on Prince Henry's grave because, as creatures who sprang from the dark earth and who will return to it, they wear the image of death. Both mourners and mandrakes would be nourished and sustained by Prince Henry's "putrefaction," as mandrakes were by man's "corruption." By placing mourners and mandrakes in the same mortal category ("This living buried man"), Donne subtly lauded the superior state of the Prince: Risen above mortality, the Prince had joined the heavenly "Quire"; mourners and mandrakes "Still stay, and vexe our great-grand-mother, Dust."[20]

Reminiscent of the voice of an insane human being, mandrake's shrieks and groans were universally heard. So pervasive was the belief that mandrake shrieked or groaned when uprooted that several herbalists strongly denounced the belief and denied a voice to mandrake:

> They ["old wiues, runnagate Surgeons, physicke--mongers"] fable further and affirme, That he who would take vp a plant thereof must tie a dog therunto to pull it vp, which will giue a great shreeke at the digging vp; otherwise if a man should do it, he should surely die in short space after.[21]

Shakespeare's characters, however, along with Ben Jonson's, John Webster's, and Cyril Tourneur's, knew the "sad horror" of the mandrake's voice. For Juliet the mandrake's shrieks epitomized her fear of madness in the tomb should she awake early:

> So early waking — what with loathsome smells,
> And shriekes like mandrakes' torn out of the earth,
> That living mortals, hearing them, run mad — (IV. iii. 46-48)

And for Tourneur's D'Amville, the voice of mandrakes was the voice of insanity and death:

> The cries of mandrakes never touch'd the ear
> With more sad horror than that voice does mine.[22]

It is astonishing to discover that a twentieth-century clinical analysis of the pharmacodynamic properties of mandrake under laborafory conditions corroborates these properties and effects: 1) The chemical fraction of mandrake containing piperidin hydrochloride produced marked aphrodisiac responses (in dogs); 2) the chief constituent of both root and fruit (hyoscine or scopolamine) had a narcotic, sedative, and anesthetic effect and could cause death if overdosed; and 3) the delirifacient action of the belladonna alkaloids on the senses produced maddening effects, acute maniacal manifestations characteristic of atropine poisoning, and hallucinations of sight and hearing.[23]

The poets and earlier botanists were right. Mandrake is "this living buried man" because it shares man's smudge and wears his grief and fears.

II

"the lustiest to look upon"[24]

Human anatomy provided the clues to plant sexuality. As botanists analyzed the genitalia of plants in order to understand plant reproduction, so poets described genitalic plants in order to illumine human conduct. When the founder of the science of plant anatomy, Nehemiah Grew, used the anatomical vocabulary of the human reproductive system to explore botanic anatomy, he gave an excitingly vivid, though not titillating, account of the workings of both:

> And as the young and early *Attire* before it opens, answers to the *Menses* in the *Femal:* so it is probable, that afterward when it opens or cracks, it performs the *Office of the Male.* This is hinted from the Shape of the Parts. For in the *Florid Attire,* the Blade doth not unaptly resemble a small *Penis,* with the Sheath upon it, as its *Praeputium.* And in the *Seed-like Attire,* the several *Thecae,* are like so many little *Testicles.* And the *Globulets* and other small *Particles* upon the *Blade* or *Penis,* and in the *Thecae,* are as the *Vegetable Sperme.* Which, so soon as the *Penis* is exerted, or the *Testicles* come to break, falls down upon the *Seed-Case* or *Womb,* and so Touches it with a *Prolifick Virtue.*[25]

When the poets used phalluses and erotic configurations of plants in their poems, they recognized that the sexual affiliation of humans and plants intensified human experience.

Botanists and poets agreed about the sensuality of orchids. Obtrusively phallic, orchids had whole clusters of scientific and common or popular names which revealed the human (as well as animal and mythical) organs of generation. *Orchid,* a name of Greek origin meaning *testicles,* bore the scientific names *Testiculus hirci, Testiculus Pumilio, Testiculus Serapias,* and the common or popular names of Priest pintell [penis], Ballock grasse, Fooles Balloxe, Serapias stones, sweete Ballocke, Souldiers Cullions, finger Orchis (with a phallic referent), Gelded Satyrion, and Dwarfe

stones.[26] The roots were regarded as testicular, and the shapes of
the flowers as suggestive of shamelessly immoderate copulation.
Gerard, reflecting centuries of opinion, reported that the flowers
resemble

> . . . Flies and such like fruitfull and lasciuious insects, as
> taking their name from *Serapias* the god of the citisens of
> Alexandria in AEgypt, who had a most famous Temple at
> Canopus, where he was worshipped with all kinde of
> lasciuious wantonnesse, songs, and dances, as we may
> reade in *Strabo,* in his seuenteenth Booke.[27]

Through the shape, the aphrodisiac properties were deduced:

> . . . these do so exactly resemble the *Testicles* of Men, and
> Luxurious Animalls, that whosoever sees them, must needs
> confess he knows them.
> . . . it as powerfuly excites Lust as the *Scinus,* being only
> held in the Hand, and more if drunk in Wine, as *Dioscorides,*
> and after him *Lobelius,* testifie.[28]

Appearing for centuries in copulatory contexts, orchids were
regarded as testicular and venerial by both botanists and poets. The
virgin Ophelia in Shakespeare's *Hamlet,* who in mad distraction
sings pitifully of a defiled and abandoned maid, adorns herself with
orchids, whose sexuality is so explicit that in the wearing of them she
seems to bring dishonor upon herself. It is Hamlet's mother who
alludes to Ophelia's testicular funeral garland:

> Queen.   . . . fantastic garlands did she make
>   Of crow-flowers, nettles, daisies, and long
>   purples
>   That liberal shepherds give a grosser name,
>   But our cull-cold maids do dead men's fingers
>   call them.
>   (IV. vii. 168-71)   (FIGURES 8-9)

The botanical literature, with its thorough analysis of the names,
appearance, color, properties, botanico-medical history of orchids,
enables us to identify Ophelia's "long purples" or "dead men's
fingers" as orchids and to see the poignant incongruity of the chaste
Ophelia garlanded in death with flowers so ludicrously obscene.[29]

Mushroom's phallic shape had been observed by the Continental

Figure 8
Male Satyrion (from Gerard's *Herball*, p. 220).

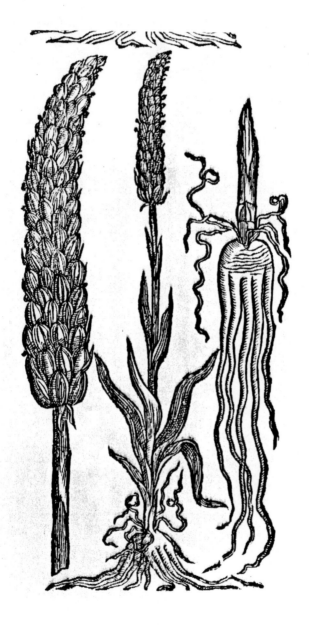

Figure 9
Serapia's Stones (from Gerard's *Herball*, p. 223).

and English herbalists, but the most graphic description (with illustration) was given by Robert Plot, a natural historian, in his *The Natural History of Stafford-shire:*

> . . . *Fungus phalloides,* or *phallus Holandicus* of *Hadr. Iunius,* is frequently found in old dry ditch banks (about the middle of *Iuly* and some-times if a warm *Autumn,* as late as *Michaelmas.* They are ordinarily betwixt 8 or 9 Inches long, and seem to be made up of 3 distinct parts: the *Volua* or round bagg at the bottom representing the *Scrotum;* the *Coles* or body; and the *Capitulum Glandiforme,* or nut of the yard; of which in their order. The *Volua* which is sometimes bigger than a Tennis-Ball . . . is cover'd with a whitish rough *membrane,* which contains a thin *pellucid gelley* of an amber colour; under which there is another very white tunicle, that includes a dirty green *Farinaceous matter,* which *Bauhinus* compares to the *tunica elytroeides* of the testicles; and then a third, smooth on the inside next the *cavity* in the center of the *Volua,* and faviginous like a *hony-comb* or *tripe,* without; and of which last *membrane,* both the *body* and *nut* of the yard, seem to grow . . . the *Cavities* whereof are fill'd with that *dirty green* substance . . .[30] (FIGURE 10)

The herbalist Parkinson describes this mushroom, the *phallus Holandicus,* as "the *Hollanders* working-toole . . . somewhat like a dogges pricke, having a nut or cappe on the toppe an inch thicke."[31] What the low countries contributed to mushroom identification was a working model of an overactive phallus. Whether or not this identification was intended as a lubricious joke, the botanic context helps to clarify Shakespeare's reference to a "holland" in *II Henry IV,* where Prince Hal's allusion to the sexual activites of Poins's "holland" must be recognized as explicit bawdry:

> . . . the rest of the low countries have [made a shift to] eat up thy holland . . . but the midwives say the children are not in the fault, whereupon the world increases, and kinreds are mightily strengthen'd.   (II. ii. 18-27)

Among the fruits that stimulated Eros were oranges and lemons. The "Orange Tree with Horned Fruit" produced an orange that was described by the pomologist Commelyn as "the lustiest to look

Figure 10
Fungus phalloides (from Plot's *The Natural History of Stafford-shire*, p. 221).

upon":

> . . . points sticking out, and dinted Corners, representing
> the Fashion of a Man's Members, others of a Womans . . .
> this Kind is desired here by many Lovers; and is found in
> many Gardens, where it is known by the Name of Cloister
> Apple.[32]

In the citrus orchard hung a lemon whose "Fruit is Oval, or longish
Round, sharp at the End, with a long Point sticking out, almost like
the Nipple of a Womans Brest;" and a lemon "with a little Nipple
pointing out," which was described in the original Dutch as "een
uitstekent mammetje."[33] In a world where nipples, breasts, and
genitals were recognizable forms appearing in orchards, fields, and
in pomological books, Hotspur's playfully serious reference to
"mammets" (I Henry IV) can mean only one thing: nipples. It is
Kate's pleas for physical evidences of Hotspur's love that evoke his
impatient

> This is no world
> To play with mammets and to tilt with lips.   (II. iii. 91-92)

The man who "must have bloody noses and crack'd crowns" is not
one to speak of dolls and puppets (as most of Shakespeare's
commentators would have us believe).[34] The visual human physicality in the mammetje of a lemon (brilliantly engraved in the
pomological treatises and in the memory) shows the currency of the
term in both pomology and poetry. (FIGURES 11-12)

The names of plants in herbals, appearing under the caption
"Lust, Bodily" (both to provoke and to allay), are frequently so
genitalic as to make them particularly susceptible to extravagant
ribaldry — names such as Open-arse, Ladies-buttock, Venus-basin,
Venus lips, Venus-navel. Although the English botanists and
pomologists do not hint at the risibility latent in those names, the
poets do. William Coles, herbalist, was single-mindedly devoted in
Adam in Eden to having his readers recognize the medlar tree as the
one they called "Openarse-Tree, and the fruit Medlars and Open-
arses";[35] but it is Mercutio in Romeo and Juliet who pounces on the
double meanings, coupling open-arse with poperin pear:

> Now will he sit under a medlar tree,
> And wish his mistress were that kind of fruit
> As maids call medlars, when they laugh alone.

Figure 11

Orange Tree with Horned Fruit (from Commelyn, *Nederlantze Hesperides:* Amsterdam, 1676).

Lima met. Zoete vrught.

Figure 12

Lemon (from Commelyn, *Nederlantze Hesperides:* Amsterdam, 1676).

> O, Romeo, that she were, O that she were
> An open [-arse], thou a pop'rin pear!   (II. i. 34-38)

The name *open-arse* came from both the shape and the function of the fruit: the "head of the fruit is seen to be somewhat hollow,"[36] the pharmaceutical properties were regarded as efficacious in reducing the flow of menstrual blood, preventing miscarriage, stanching the bleeding of hemorrhoids, and alleviating the distresses of diarrhoea.[37]

As for the poperin pear, the pomologist Leonard Meager included three poperins in his long list of pears — Russet, Green, and Great — serenely placing them fourteen pears down from "Ladies-buttock" pear.[38] It is Mercutio, however, who, seeing the poperin pear as the male phallus, rampages through Romeo's acutely painful love experience with a pomological pun.

Finally, there was nothing indelicate in the botanists' giving names like *vulvaria, clitoria, labrum veneris, Venus basin, Venus navel* to plants: nor anything inelegant in the poet and priest George Herbert's referring to the vagina of a plant in a formal Latin oration: "modò detis eum in flore, in vaginâ in herbescenti viriditate" *(III Oratio).*[39] The name *Labrum veneris* (Venus lips) did provoke a rare ethical disquisition by the herbalist Parkinson, who resisted seeing an anatomical resemblance to the female labia and urinary bladder in the plant known popularly as *Teasell:*

> . . . I am of a different opinion that it tooke the name of
> *Venus* lips from the effects of a whores lippes, which as the
> leaves the raine, so they are ready to receive all mens offers,
> and as the heads of Teasells, so they are ready to carde and
> teare all mens skins that have to doe with them, untill they
> leave them bare and thin . . .[40]

In addition to the genitalic plants, there were those plants whose carnosity invited identification with the human navel. The fleshy, protruding umbilicus of these plants, which gave them the names *navelwort, umbilicus veneris, Venus-navel,* were by some physicians considered capable of exciting "Amorous Affections," either by the physical appearance of the plants or by their pharmaceutical-aphrodisiac properties, since the human navel, as an extension of the erogenous zone, was the "seat of Luxury."[41] Although Ben Jonson was not alluding to the venerial features of *navelwort* when he called for "*Sweet* Venus *Navill*" in "*Pans Anniversarie* (l. 37), and John Evelyn was not referring to the "seat of luxury" when he spoke of the "navel of every leaf,"[42] the use of *navel* for both the name of the plant and its parts does show the intimate relationship between human anatomy and plants. The "navel" in Milton's *Comus*, which is not a direct reference to a person or plant but to the "navel of this hideous Wood" (l. 520), exudes carnality. Since in the human anatomy the navel was capable of erotic stimulation, and in the botanic was susceptible to sexual suggestibility, the word *navel* in *Comus* alerts us to the imminent betrayal of the young lady by the sly enticer. Donne's "fair Atlantick Navell" in *Elegie XVIII (l. 66)* is clearly a female human navel in the middle of a watery metaphor, tickled into seduction by the prevailing sexuality of all navels, including the botanic.

The persistent appearance of human genitalia in plants and in the plants of poetry was no profanation of either botanic structure or human anatomy. Botanists and poets simply reported that they saw the human reproductive system in plants. For it was the human that environed the vegetable, and the human that made botany and poetry fit hosts for even those plants that are "the lustiest to look upon."

III

"And Bush with frizzl'd hair implicit"[43]

In the sixteenth and seventeenth centuries, the parts of the human body which appeared in a botanical context ranged from head to toe, included external and internal organs, and assisted in plant identification, classification, and prescription. That this did not remain a strictly sixteenth and seventeenth century phenomenon is evident from the vestigial remains found in today's botany: *The Excursion Flora of the British Isles* (1968) identifies a plant by its "Labellum shaped like a man, with long slender lateral lobes (arms) near its base, and a longer narrow central lobe which is forked distally into 2 slender segments (legs)," and another by the "short tooth in the sinus."[44] What made the conversations between botanists and poets so easy was that they were not in bondage to absolute distinctions between metaphor and actuality. For botanists and poets, the eyes of a plant were as actual as the eyes of a human; the hair, joints, ears, blood, even posture of the plant, showed metaphor enlivening actuality, actuality validating metaphor, and the two conjoining to restore an old reality and to create a new one. The "human" parts of plants were not only an inexhaustible source for poets but were the mirror of reality for poets and botanists as well.

For every poet who put plants with heads, cheeks, necks, hair, skin, and blood in his poems, there were botanists who described plants with tongues, hearts, bosoms, faces, teeth, and knees in their botanical writings.[45] It is important to see, however, that neither poets nor botanists forced plants into service merely as allegories for human life: in the "humanizing" process was the elevation of plants, not the obliteration. The daffodil's hanging head, as real as his own mortality, was for Herrick an apt "divination" or even "omen-ation" of his death:

> When a Daffadill I see,
> Hanging down his head t'wards me;
> Guesse I may, what I must be:
> First, I shall decline my head;
> Secondly, I shall be dead;
> Lastly, safely buryed.[46]

Crashaw's struggle with immanence and transcendence in "The Weeper" is resolved on the soil where the "human" parts of plants are replaced by a higher presence:

> We goe not to seek,
> The darlings of Auroras bed,
> The Roses modest cheek
> Nor the violet's humble head . . .
>   We goe to meet
> A worthy object, our lord's *FEET*.[47]

And Milton's "Cowslips wan that hang the pensive head" in *Lycidas* (l. 114) provide the stance required for the emotion appropriate to his grief.

The tangled hairiness of Milton's bush "with frizzl'd hair implicit," created by God to make earth seem like heaven (the "human" having heavenly origins), and the hairy sides of his steep wilderness

of Eden, created "grotesque and wild" to deny Satan access to
Paradise (*PL* IV. 135-137); the hairy groves in which Lord Herbert of
Cherbury walked near Merlow Castle "while the leaves do friss"[48];
the herbalist Gerard's Raspis or Framboise bush identifiable by its
"rough hairiness about the stalkes" and his Furze with hairy leaves;
and the gardener Hanmer's flowers with "bushy haires in tufts"[49]
—all reflect a shared vision by poets and botanists of the unity of
vegetable and human life. Lord Herbert increased his pleasure, and
the pleasure of his readers, by seeing in the "frissing" a "self-
renewing vegetable bliss" (l. 14), a bliss in which he and the vegetable
grove participated.

The mutuality of the terminology of human anatomy and gardening appears at first glance in Shakespeare's *Richard II* to be the rustic
pronouncement of a gardener who naively limited the whole world to
his own small pomological plot:

> [We] at time of year
> Do wound the bark, the skin of our fruit-trees,
> Lest being over-proud in sap and blood,
> With too much riches it confound itself;
> Had he done so to great and growing men,
> They might have liv'd to bear and he to taste
> Their fruits of duty.   (III. iv. 57-63)

In the eyes of the poet's gardener, the skin and blood of humans are
consanguineous with the bark and sap of fruit trees; and, because
the kinship is skin-deep and has blood-ties, the human ought to have
used the governance model provided by the fruit trees. For William
Coles, the anatomical affinity between the human and the vegetable
provided the signs for pharmacy: he defined the *skin* of a plant as
"that wherewith the stalks, boughes, leaves, fruits, and sometimes
the root are covered," and the juice of a plant as "answerable to the
blood in living creatures"[50]; and he used the human signature on
plants to authenticate pharmaceutical efficacy.

The most famous vegetable *eyes* in all of English literature are
Milton's. They have sent more twentieth-century readers to
wandering in a maze of symbols than any other eyes in poems,
including Shakespeare's "winking mary-buds" with their "golden
eyes" *(Cymbeline).*[51] When the readers of Milton's day, however,

read his injunction in *Lycidas* — "Throw hither all your quaint enamell'd eyes/ . . . To strew the Laureate Hearse where *Lycid* lies" (11. 139, 151) — they would have instinctively gone (actually and imaginatively) to the straight paths of gardens and the open fields or sequestered woods to find the flowers with *eyes;* and on that soil they would have found the symbols indigenous to those plants. They knew what has been lost to us: that botanic *eyes* were the *centers* of certain kinds of familiar flowers. Althought the OED cannot help us (this definition does not appear until 1870 [10c]), the botanists can. In 1577 the influential Continental botanist Hieronymus Bock (Tragus) used the phrase "gaelen augen" to describe the centers of *Primula veris;* in 1597 the English herbalist Gerard described the center of *Red Bears eare* as "the middle or eie of the flower," and in 1629 the *Botanicus Regius Primarius* John Parkinson noted that *auricula* has "a white eye or circle in the bottome."[52] With the meticulous joy of a horticulturist, Thomas Hanmer listed the *eye* of each *Beares Eare* in his garden in 1659: "the eye is pale yellow," "a pure white eye," "a large lemmon color eye," "an ill eye," "a reasonable eye," "a durty yellow eye"; and the florist John Rea boasted of his auriculas "with snow-white eyes, that will not wash yellow with rain" (1676).[53]

Floral eyes exist. They could be seen in gardens and fields and woods, in herbals and gardening books. And still can be. Since plant eyes have a botanic existence apart from the poet and the poem, the emotional energy they create in *Lycidas* shatters the private, self-binding grief of the poet. These eyes are not an inert funereal trope. As centers of feeling in botany and poetry, they redouble the grief. The poet, by using plant eyes than can be seen as we walk or as we read, involves us in human grief every time we see an *eye* in a flower. Plants and humans are bonded together by mortality. And yet once more, the lovely paradox: It is the poet, "through the dear might of him that walked the waves," who has made plant eyes immortal. Like Mr. Rea's, Milton's *eyes* "will not wash yellow with" — tears or years.

So, then, as we look back at poems and plants in the sixteenth and seventeenth centuries, we see that humans took their bearings from God, and plants took their bearings from humans. And both bore the marks of the "human face divine."[54]

NOTES

Chapter Four

[1] Milton, *Paradise Lost* III. 44.

[2] Nehemiah Grew, *The anatomy of plants*, 2nd ed. (London, 1682), p. 3.

[3] *Walter Blith was one of the most eloquent spokesmen for re-establishing friendship with the soil through Christ's mediation. See Chapter One.*

[4] Poem of dedication to Oswald Crollius by an un-named friend, in Oswald Crollius, *Philosophy reformed and improved*, trans. H. Pinnell (London, 1657).

[5] Herbert, "Providence," 11. 13-14; Henry Vaughan, "Christs Nativity," *The Complete Poetry of Henry Vaughan*, ed. French Fogle (New York, 1964), 11. 11-12. All subsequent references to Vaughan's poetry are to this text. See also Donne's reference to man's mediatorial obligation to Nature: "our businesse is to rectifie/Nature, to what she was," "To Sr Edward Herbert. at Iulyers.," *The Poems of John Donne*, ed. Herbert J.C. Grierson (Oxford, 1912, 1951), I, 194, 11. 33-34. All subsequent references to Donne's poetry are to this text.

[6] "The Garden," to J. Evelyn Esquire, *Several Discourses by Way of Essays, in verse and Prose*, 8th ed. (London, 1693), p.119.

[7] Petri Laurenberg, *Horticultura* (Francofurti, 1631 [?]), pp. 68-69 (69 misnumbered 66). Laurenberg's lucid statements included the question: "2. Plantarum partes quomodo respondeant partibus corporis humani? . . ." ([The question is] how the parts of the plants correspond to the parts of a human being . . .), and an invitation to further exploration: "Caeterum si quis plantarum anatomian cum humano corpore conferre scrupulosius volet, nae ille inter vtraq; illustrissimam inueniet analogiam & similitudinem proportionis." (Now if anyone desires to compare the anatomy of plants with a human body more precisely, he will indeed find between them a most remarkable resemblance and similarity of symmetry.)

[8] Abraham Cowley, "The Author's Preface to His Two First Books of Plants," *The Complete Works in Verse and Prose*, ed. Alexander B. Grosart (Edinburgh, 1881), II, 237. This was not a simple variation on the theme of man as microcosm of the whole inferior creation. John Donne, for one had polished that orthodoxy into a beautiful paragraph in a brilliant sermon: "The world is a great Volume, and man the Index of that Booke; Even in the body of man, you may turne to the whole world; This body is an Illustration of all Nature; Gods recapitulation of all that he had said before, in his *Fiat lux*, and *Fiat firmamentum*, and in all the rest, said or done, in all the six dayes," "Preached at the funeral of Sir William Cokayne, December 12. 1626, "*The Sermons of John Donne*, ed. Evelyn M. Simpson and George R. Potter (Berkeley, 1954), VII, 272. See also Herbert, "He is in little all the sphere," "Man," 1. 22; Milton, "all summ'd up in Man" (*PL* IX. 113); Andrew Marvell, "I was but an inverted tree," "Upon Appleton House," *The Complete Poems*, ed. Elizabeth Story Donno (Harmondsworth, 1976). 1. 568.

[9] Grew, *The anaomy of plants* (1682), p. 10.

[10] *Stirpium historiae pemptades sex . . . (Antverpiae, 1616): "Flos . . . arborum & herbarbum gaudium dicitur, futuriq;* fructus spes est, vnaquaeq," p. 5.

[11] Donne, "The Progresse of the Soule," 1. 160.

[12] For a definitive study and comprehensive bibliography, see Hugo Rahner, *Greek Myths and Christian Mystery* (London, 1963), pp. 223-277. See also Charles B. Randolph, "The Mandragora of the Ancients in Folk-Lore and Medicine," *Proceedings of the American Academy of Arts and Sciences,* 40 (1905), 487-537; Mircea Eliade, "The Cult of the Mandragora in Romania," *University of Chicago Magazine,* LXV, No. 4 (Jan.-Feb., 1973), 8-16; and David I. Macht, "Mandrakes in the Bible, Literature, and Pharmacology," *American Druggist* (December, 1933), pp. 24-25, 68-76.

[13] Gerard, *Herball,* cites Greek authors, including Dioscorides, p. 352; Parkinson, *Theatrum botanicum,* p. 344.

[14] Gerard, *Herball,* p. 351.

[15] Gerard, *Herball,* p. 352. See also *The Greek Herbal of Dioscorides,* Englished by John Goodyer (1655), ed. Robert T. Gunther (New York, 1959), p. 473; Parkinson, *Theatrum,* p. 344; and Sir Thomas Browne, *Pseudodoxia epidemica:* "Many Mola's and false conceptions there are of Mandrakes, the first from great Antiquity, conceiveth the Root thereof resembleth the shape of Man . . . ," *The Works of Sir Thomas Browne,* ed. Geoffrey Keynes (London, 1928), II, Bk. II, Chap. VI, p. 140.

[16] *Dialogue creaturarum* (Antwerp[?], 1535), M. de Keyser (?), Dialogue 31. See also a Geneva edition of the *Dialogue of Creatures,* Moralized, 1500, which shows Venus imploring a large flowering plant (woodcut, Museum of Fine Arts, Boston, Mass.).

[17] London, p. 438. Cf. Shakespeare's *Othello* where Iago's malicious observation places mandrake in a soporific setting in which Othello's obsessive concern with lust denies him even a mandrake-induced sleep: "Not poppy, nor mandragora/Nor all the drowsy syrups of the world/Shall ever medicine thee to that sweet sleep/Which thou ow'dst yesterday" (III. iii. 330-333).

[18] Philo of Carpasia, *Commentary on the Canticles,* 217, Migne, *Patrologia Graeca,* 40, 136B.

[19] Ll. 53-54, 78-82. See Rahner, p. 264ff., for an exploration of the Christian symbolism emerging from this human-shaped "mortal" root, its subjection to demonic powers, and its conversion into a Christ-image.

[20] See my argument in "Donne's 'Elegie upon the Untimely Death of the Incomparable Prince Henry,' " *Explicator,* 33 (March, 1975), 59. Donne's allusion to putrefaction originates undoubtedly in the long-lived belief that mandrake sprang from the "corruption" of a dying human being.

[21] Gerard, *Herball,* p. 351. See also Sir Thomas Browne, *Pseudodoxia epidemica:* "roots of Mandrakes . . . do give a shriek upon eradication; which is indeed ridiculous," *Works,* II Bk. II, Chap. VI, p. 143.

[22] *The Atheist's Tragedy,* ed. Irving Ribner (London, 1964), V. i. 56-57. See also Ben Jonson, *Masque of Queens:* "I last night lay all alone/O' the ground to hear the mandrake groan," *Ben Jonson: Selected Masques,* ed. Stephen Orgel (New Haven, 1970), 11. 150-151; John Webster, *The Duchess of Malfi:* "I have this night dig'd up a man-drake . . ./And I am growne mad with't," *The Complete Works of John Webster,* ed. F.L. Lucas (London, 1927), II. v. 1-3; and Shakespeare, *II Henry VI:* "Would curses kill, as doth the mandrake's groan," III. ii. 310.

[23] Macht, pp. 74-76.

[24] J. Commelyn, *The Belgic, or Netherlandish Hesperides,* trans. G.V.N. (London, 1683), p. 66.

[25] *The anatomy of plants* (1682), p. 172.

[26] Lyte, *A nievve herball,* p. 222; Gerard, *Herball,* pp. 205-228 *passim.* For other plants with testicles, see Parkinson, *Theatrum,* Goose grasse with "two small round rough seedes joyned together like two testicles," p. 567.

[27] *Herball,* p. 225.

[28] Oswald Crollius, *Signatures of internal things* (London, 1669), p. 5. See also *The grete herball* Satirion "helpeth lechery," CCCxci; the Italian physician Matthioli, "zu boden die Venus begierdt," *Kreutterbuch* (durch Camerarium, Franckfurt, 1600), p. 303; the poet Robert Chester, "There's *Standergras, Hares ballockes,* or great *Orchis,/*Prouoketh *Venus,* and procureth sport," *Loves Martyr* or, *Rosalins Complaint* (London, 1601), p. 94; and William Langham, "The round and full roots of all kindes of Satirion, or *Orchis,* are good in meate and Electuaries to prouoke Venus," *The garden of health,* 2nd ed. (London, 1633), p. 450.

[29] For an enlargement of this argument, see my article "Ophelia's 'Long Purples' or 'Dead Men's Fingers,' " *Shakespeare Quarterly,* 30 (Summer, 1979).

[30] Oxford, 1686, pp. 200-201.

[31] *Theatrum,* p. 1322. Gerard suggested that mushrooms promote lasciviousness: "many haue eaten and doe eat Mushroms more for wantonnesse than for need," *Herball,* p. 345.

[32] Commelyn, *The Belgic . . . Hesperides,* p. 66.

[33] Commelyn, *The Belgic . . . Hesperides,* "The Limon Tree of St. Remo," p. 41; "Lima," p. 46; *Nederlantze Hesperides* (Amsterdam, 1676), p. 11. The Dutch edition has many brilliant illustrations (copper plates).

[34] The gloss in *The Riverside Shakespeare,* ed. G. Blakemore Evans (Boston, 1974), reads: "dolls (like you)," p. 858.

[35] P. 81. See also Hieronymus Bock, *De stirpium* (Argentorati, 1552), for a ribald verse describing the progress of medlar seeds (5 in each fruit) through the body of a chaste young woman: "Kein Jungfraw ward nie so rein/Esse sie drey Mespeln/sie geb von jr fünffzehen stein," p. 1014.

[36] Coles, *Adam in Eden,* p. 82.

[37] Coles, *Adam in Eden,* p. 82; Gerard, *Herball,* p. 1455; Lyte, *A nievve herball,* p. 714; Parkinson, *Theatrum,* p. 1423; Robert Turner, *Botanologia,* p. 197. See also Mats Rydén, *Shakespearean Plant Names* (Stockholm, 1978), p. 61, for a brief discussion of *open-arse.* Rydén is mistaken, however, when he states that the name *open-arse* is not adduced by Gerard. Although Gerard does not use this name in his text, he does list *open-arse* in his Table of English Names.

[38] *The English gardener,* p. 87. See also Parkinson, *Paradisus,* p. 592. For an elaborate sexual treatment of medlar, pear, and other fruits, see Tourneur, *The Atheist's Tragedy* IV. i. 1-42. The poet Robert Chester in *Loves Martyr* speaks of "The Peare-tree and the young mans Medlar," p. 96.

[39] *Works,* p. 445, 1. 20. For an eighteenth-century comment on *Clitoria foliis pinnatus* see John Hill, *Eden: or, a compleat body of gardening* (London, 1757): "It is call'd in *English* the *Clitoris* Flower, from its *Latin* Name *Clitoria;* an indecent one . . . though, in Compliance with *Linnaeus,* it be retain'd in the *Latin,*" p. 53.

[40] *Theatrum*, p. 985. See also Coles, who echoes Parkinson in *Adam in Eden*, Chap. CCLXII.

[41] Crollius, *A treatise of signatures*, p. 4.

[42] *The compleat gard'ner . . . By . . .* Mon. sr de La Quintinye, trans. John Evelyn (London, 1693), II. 63. Geoffrey Grigson, *The Englishman's Flora* (London, 1958), describes a curious Roman use of *Umbilicus Veneris:* the sap of its leaves, when smeared, or combined with wine, relieves constriction in the pudenda, p. 200. See also Coles, *Adam in Eden* on sow-bread "called *Umbilicus terrae*, because as the Navell of a Mans Body strutteth out a little above the Belly, so this sometimes above the Earth," Chap. XL; and Parkinson, *Theatrum*, p. 568.

[43] Milton, *Paradise Lost* VII. 323. Cf. Hanmer, *Garden book:* "Nature seems to sport, imitating in its flowers the shapes of severall creatures, as beasts, birds, flyes, and even Man himself too, and from their resemblances the severall sorts are denominated," p. 48.

[44] A.R. Clapham, T.G. Tutin, and E.F. Warburg (Cambridge, 1968), pp. 486, 484.

[45] Hanmer, *Garden book*, "roots of anemone with many little . . . Tongues," p. 57; Gerard, *Herball*, the fruit of Cloud-berry "like vnto a little heart," p. 1420; the Society of Gardeners, *Catalogus plantarum*, the fruit of the Nettle Tree "growing single in the Bosom of its Leaves," p. 17; Gerard, *Herball*, mushroom with a "face," p. 1582; Gerard, *Herball*, the root of bulbous Fumitorie "resembling teeth," p. 1090; Gerard, *Herball*, Crossewoort as "full of ioints or knees," p. 1123, to mention only a few. R.T. Gunther, *Early British Botanists and Their Gardens (Oxford, 1922)*, observes: "The descriptions [of plants] conform rigidly to the style in vogue at the period . . . 'footstalk' in the sense of petiole, 'knee'-node, 'bosome'-axil (of a leaf), 'pointell'-pistil," p. 44.

[46] "Divination by a Daffadill," *The Complete Poetry of Robert Herrick*, ed. J. Max Patrick (New York, 1968), H-107, 1. 2. All subsequent references are to this text.

[47] "Sainte Mary Magdalene or The Weeper," *The Poems of Richard Crashaw*, ed. L.C. Martin (Oxford, 1927), Stanzas VIII, XXX-XXXI. All subsequent references are to this text.

[48] "Sonnet," *The Poems of Edward, Lord Herbert of Cherbury*, ed. G.C. Moore-Smith (Oxford, 1968), p. 54, l. 10.

[49] *Herball*, pp. 1272, 1320; Hanmer, *Garden book*, p. 35.

[50] *The art of simpling*, p. 22. Cf. My article "Milton's Haemony," *English Literary Renaissance*, V (Winter, 1975), 81-95, where I show that Milton's haemony in *Comus* is *andros-haemon*, a well-known plant so named because of the color of its juice: red, like man's blood (*aner*, gen. *andros*, Greek, *man; haima*, Greek, *blood*).

[51] *Cymbeline* II. iii. 24; for a summary of these interpretations, see *A Variorum Commentary on the Poems of John Milton*, ed. A.S.P. Woodhouse and Douglas Bush (New York, 1972), II, ii, 709-711. See also W.K. Thomas, "Mouths and Eyes in *Lycidas*," *Milton Quarterly*, 9 (May, 1975), 39-42. For a study of Shakespeare's "mary-buds," see David I. Macht, "Calendula or Marigold in Medical History and in Shakespeare," *Bulletin of the History of Medicine*, XXIX (Nov.-Dec., 1955), 491-502.

[52] *Kreütterbuch* (1577), p. 59; *Herball* (1597), p. 641; *Paradisus*, p. 238.

[53] *Garden book*, pp. 172-173; *Flora*, 2nd ed. (London, 1676), p. 151.

[54] The herbalists saw Christ's marks in the dolphin figure in Larkes Heele "by which signe also the heauenly Dolphine is set forth," Gerard, *Herball*, p. 1083, and in the parts of Passion Flower "which resemble a speare and three nayles, the instruments of the passion," Hanmer, *Garden book*, pp. 85-86. See also Herrick, "Thou seest a present God-like Power/Imprinted in each Herbe and Flower," H-662, 11. 31-32; and Stephen Blake, *The compleat gardeners practice*, where the plant commonly known as *Balm of Christ* was so called because Christ's hand appears on it "in the fulness of its perfection," p. 11.

CHAPTER FIVE
THE ONTOLOGY OF
VEGETABLE SMELLS

I
"With grateful Smell"[1]

We cannot assume that because the writers of the sixteenth and seventeenth centuries injected so many smells into their poetry and prose that their olfactory equipment was superior to ours. What we can assume, however, is that their intense concentration on smell shows that it had a greater significance for them than it has for us. Speaking frequently of the intricate process of smell, they analyzed its anatomical, physiological, and sensory functions:

> The Ayre altred with Odours or by an aiery exhalation of odorifferous things is receiued by the Nose . . . the exhalation that is dispersed through the ayre is by inspiration drawne into the nosethrils: and because out of them there are two holes which go into the pallat, the greatest part of

> that ayre so drawn in entreth into lungs but without any
> sense of odours; the rest ascendeth vpward to the instru-
> ments of Smelling . . . Braine is the common instrument by
> which the Sensatiue Soule perceiueth all sensible qualities
> . . .[2]

Moving from process to definition, they described smell as "a more
excellent, and a little more Sublime Faculty, than either Tasting, or
Touching; to wit, because its Object is more subtle, and comes to
the Sensory, with a thinner Consistency."[3] The combination of
"sublimity" of faculty and "subtlety" of object led them to regard the
nose as the instrument of the Sensitive Soul and an avenue of
knowledge. If blindness meant, as Milton so poignantly showed, that
wisdom was "at one entrance quite shut out" (*PL* III. 50), loss of the
sense of smell would in all probability have similar implications and
consequences. Through the olfactory sense, smells had direct
access to the spirit of a human being, where they were converted
into a source of knowledge and wisdom.

Since smell operated in so large an arena, which included the
spiritual as well as the physical, the nature of smell and the effect of
odors on human beings were of interest and concern to poets as well
as to physicians and botanists. Nicholas Culpeper and Abdiah Cole,
who were aggressively involved in mediating medical and pharmaceutical information to the common people, reviewed the ancient
medical and philosophical positions on smell and stated their own
compromise position: smell is both corporeal and spiritual:

> . . . dayly experience teaches, That odoriferous exhalations
> do sundry waies affect the Brain, and very often change the
> temper thereof, and sometimes qualifie and rectifie the
> same, other whiles cause heaviness of head . . . when an
> odoriferous thing is taken away, the smel remains many
> times a long while after in the Air, which cannot be done by
> images alone, which do not remain when the object is
> removed. Al which things teach, that oftentimes there flows
> from odorous bodies a certain corporeal exhalation, which
> hath a power of heating, cooling, and doing other things,
> which cannot be effected by bare species and images. This
> therefore we grant, That from many things a certain
> odoriferous vapor exhales, and that corporeal savory

vapors do flow from things that have smel: but yet we avouch that a spiritual species is required and presupposed to cause the sense of smelling.[4]

Smell, operating on the "holier plane of air,"[5] had a powerful and subtle influence on the human spirit. In Milton's physical and poetic worlds, singed air, buxom air, empyreal air, ambient air, liquid air, inspired air, black air, bleak air, worked through the organ of smell into the spirit of humans (and angels and devils), shaping, influencing, and dispensing knowledge.

Smells, both pleasant and unpleasant, both lethal and life-giving, hovered over the sixteenth and seventeenth centuries. Smells had the power to cure or kill, to woo or to repel. Physicians warned of stinking smells that killed, and recommended strong smells that cured. Stephen Bradwell, in *Helps for svddain accidents* (1633), supplied his readers with case histories of the fatal effects of certain stinking smells:

> One may be choaked also with stinking Scents, such as privies and filthy ditches send forth. As in Saint *Laurence Lane* in *London* a young man fell into a privy vault, about fourteen yeares agoe (as I remember) who with the stinking stuffe was for the time suffocated; but being missed, and by chance, was with much ado gotten to life againe. Neverthelesse, using such onely as wanted skill to encounter such a strange Accident, he died within two or tree dayes after.
>
> Christopherus à Vega . . . tells of two men that being employed among others in cleansing certaine sinkes, and stinking sewers, were so overcome of the evill savours, that by their fellows they were taken up and carried out for dead . . .[6]

In this latter case, strong sweet perfumes were held to the nose to revive these two men. They survived. Also recommended to counteract deadly stinking smells were the plants Sweet Marjoram, Tyme, Penyroyall, Rosemary, and Lavender, which, after being rubbed together betwixt the hands, were held to the nose.[7]

In an age where smells impinged upon sense and soul at every turn, good physical and spiritual health depended, at least partly, upon good smells. Thomas Venner, Doctor of Physicke in Bathe, urged the readers of his *Via Recta* (1622) to live where the air was "not mixt with any grosse moisture, or corrupted with filthy or noisome vapors."[8] He believed that "tenuitie, puritie, and wholsomnesse of the ayre" help to make "cleare, pure, and subtill spirits," spirits that become "witty, nimble, magnanimous and *alta petentes.*"[9] In contrast, the inhabitants of low and marish places by "reason of the evilnesse of the aire, have grosse and earthy spirits . . . dull, sluggish, sordid, sensuall, plainely irreligious . . . deceiptfull, malicious, disdainefull . . ."[10] Thomas Phayre, in *A Treatyse of the Pestilence* (1545), enjoined his readers "to flye from al places that be corrupte, or stynkyng." He pleaded with rulers "to prouide that no filthy donge, nor any deade caryons, be cast into the stretes, for that shulde sore enfecte the ayer, & bryng many men to death."[11] In John Donne's Elegy IV, "The Perfume," although the seducer/narrator does not die because of a bad smell, he is betrayed by his "loud" smell (of sweet vegetable origin), which is quite recognizably different from the "bad smells" (of human origin) arising from the bed of the woman's watchful father "that his own feet, or breath . . . had wrought" (11. 45-46).[12]

For practising gardeners floral fragrance was a valuable commodity which had to be protected from enterprising thieves. The gardener Stephen Blake, a gentle Christian whose floristic commentary is filled with generous thoughts for fellow-humans, found it necessary to devise an olfactory method to prevent the theft of his fragrant investment, his gilliflowers:

> . . . if you shall have any of these Flowers stolen, and if you would be revenged on the party . . . you shall accomplish your desire thus: take an Elecompane root dry and beaten to powder, then sprinkle it upon your Gilliflowers, or put it into the midst, then give your Flowers to the party that you desire to be revenged of, let it be a he or shee they will delight in smelling to it, then they will draw this powder into their nostrils which will make them fall a sneezing, and a great trouble to the eyes, and by your leave will make the tears run down their thighs: other things there are which may be bought at the Apothecaries, which I will not give you the receit of, for fear it should come to a malicious mans hands, then the effect would be evil.[13]

Poets and terraculturalists had the same olfactory concerns that physicians had: they described the stench of dental caries, suppurating sores, and decaying carrion as well as the smells that transformed the air into clouds of fragrances in a world of rot. On the pages of poetry, botany, and medicine the smells of mortality, of piss, blood, assafoetida, musty chaff, rank weeds, of brown bread and garlic, mingled with the smells of immortality, of roses, lilies, gillyflowers, sweet violets, eglantine and woodbine, of amber and perfume. And sometimes intermingled. Shakespeare spoke of decaying roses so foul that women "stopped" their noses when they smelled them, and of festering lilies that smelled "far worse than weeds."[14] The botanist Grew wrote of Dragon plants that stank "like the *pus* of the most *Fetid Ulcer,* of Sena plant that had a "rank *Smell* betwixt that of *Sweat* and *Urine,"* of Scurvygrass Juice that stank like "Humane *Excrements,"* and of Coriander, which "when green and young, stink so basely, that they can hardly be endur'd."[15]

They also wrote of plants whose fragrances exceeded even their visual loveliness. Both poets and terraculturalists were transported by sweet smells. Shakespeare's "the rose looks fair, but fairer we it deem/For that sweet odour which doth in it live,"[16] and Drayton's "odoriferous Pink, that sends forth such a gale/Of sweetnes" and his "sweet Basill rare for smell"[17] were matched by Gerard's roses, the "most glorious floures of the world . . . being esteemed for his . . . fragrant and odoriferous smell"[18] and by Francis Bacon's "the breath of flowers is far sweeter in the air, where it comes and goes, like the warbling of music . . ."[19] Like Dogberry's, their comparisons were *odorous.*[20]

The smells of an age arise from the most basic concerns of an age, and, hence, provide a scientific and social history as well as a literary one. The smells of disease and death; of pollutants; of human breath, blood, and excrement; of copulation; of ethnic groups; of gardens, fields, orchards, plants; of love; of worship; of God, devils, angels, humans —these smells and a hundred more, were discussed with candor and intense plainness. The question of ethnic smells, for example, today a question too inflammatory to be asked, was the occasion for Dr. Thomas Browne's inquiry into whether "Jews stinck naturally, that is, that in their race and nation there is an evil savour," and of his disquisition on human smells, preceded by his comment on vegetable smells:

. . . pleasant smels are not confined unto vegitables . . . We confesse that beside the smell of the species, there may be individuall odours, and every Man may have a proper and peculiar savour . . . We will not deny that particular Men have sent forth a pleasant savour, as Theophrastus and Plutarch report of Alexander the great, and Tzetzes and Cardan doe testifie of themselves. That some may also emit an unsavoury odour, we have no reason to deny; for this may happen from the quality of what they have taken; the Faetor [ill savour] whereof may discover it self by sweat and urine, as being unmasterable by the natural heat of Man, not to be dulcified by concoction beyond an unsavoury condition: the like may come to passe from putrid humours, as is often discoverable in putrid and malignant feavers. And sometime also in gross and humid bodies even in the latitude of sanity . . . But that an unsavoury odour is gentilitious or national unto the Jews, if rightly understood, we cannot well concede; nor will the information of reason or sence induce it.[21]

The power of olfactory words to alter perception, and the power of smell to influence words was a fact of life for poets and terraculturalists. They knew that the nose "is requisite also, to smell out work for th' other senses."[22] Their olfactory descriptions, which constitute an odorous dispensary for twentieth-century readers, still have the power to disgust or delight. Although the England of that day is not our contemporary in smells, the odors linger on in herbals, medical treatises, botanical and floristic books, agricultural and pomological handbooks, natural histories, and poetry — odors that like William Coles' Pasque flower "will bite you by the Nose, if you rub it between your fingers and smell to it."[23] Those smells were born in experiences that the twentieth century may have eliminated, disguised, or deodorized. We practise genocide on a whole race of smells which our forebears endured and described; but the words from those centuries convey smells so tenacious as to be able even now to arouse unpleasant sensations in our noses and perhaps even to offend our stomachs, since smell is wily and dramatically affects taste. We have only to mention *foul, rotten, fishy, stinking, putrid, fetid,* to have our gorge rise, as did Hamlet's when he smelled poor

Yorick's skull. Pah![24] And again when we smell with the herbalist Lyte the plant that "stinketh like rotten corrupt fishe, or lyke stinking fishe broth."[25] On the other hand, there are words that effuse fragrances, words so fragrant as to make our spirits soar while our stomachs remain blissfully tranquil. We have only to think of *ambrosial, perfumed, sweet, fragrant,* to admit with the poet Thomas Traherne that "pleasant Odors do my spirit charm";[26] and smell with the herbalist Parkinson flowers and plants which "comfort, and as it were reuiue the spirits, and perfume a whole house . . ."[27]

Because smells, both pleasant and unpleasant, touched and shaped the spirit of a human being, the smells of the sixteenth and seventeenth centuries must also be studied as part of a larger spirituality. The vegetable world was an active participant in the spiritual community of smells, with botanists defining *odours* as the "Spirits of Plants."[28] Botanists recognized, to be sure, the fact that smell issued from matter through digestion and refinement[29] but that the process of manufacturing odors was essentially an ethereal one: "And for *Odours,* I suppose, That the chief Matter of them, in the *Aerial Ferment* contained in the *Aer-Vessels.*"[30] The human spirit responded so efficiently to the "odorous spirits of plants" because plant spirits and human spirits shared a common ontology. Though earth-bred, plants received their vital spirits from their Creator; plants returned those spirits in the form of an odour into the air, an odour which humans breathed in, converted into a spiritually nutritive substance, and then transpired into a sweet-smelling spiritual sacrifice to God, in and from whose Being all pure smells originated. The spiritual process was carefully outlined by Milton's Raphael to Adam in Paradise:[31]

> O *Adam,* one Almighty is, from whom
> All things proceed, and up to him return,
> If not deprav'd from good, created all
> Such to perfection, one first matter all,
> Indu'd with various forms, various degrees
> But more refin'd, more spiritous, and pure,
> As nearer to him plac't or nearer tending
> Each in their several active Spheres assign'd,
> Till body up to spirit work, in bounds

> Proportion'd to each kind. So from the root
> Springs lighter the green stalk, from thence the leaves
> More aery, last the bright consummate flow'r
> Spirits odorous breathes: flow'rs and thir fruit
> Man's nourishment, by gradual scale sublim'd
> To vital spirits aspire, to animal,
> To intellectual, give both life and sense,
> Fancy and understanding, whence the Soul
> Reason receives, and reason is her being . . .   (V. 469-487)

For the orchardist Ralph Austen, whose ontological view was typical of the age, it was the pleasant smells of fruit trees that constituted their life-giving spiritual gift to mankind:

> But the most *pleasant and wholsome Odors,* are from the *blossomes* of all the *Fruit-trees,* which having in them a condensing and cooling property are therefore, not simply *Healthfull,* but are accompted *Cordiall;* chearing and refreshing the Heart and vitall spirits.
>
> Now the *spirits* . . . are the *Masterworkmen* in the body, and as the *uppermost Wheele* which turneth about the other wheels in the body . . . *Vapours and Affections worke compendiously upon the spirits.*[32]

The unpleasant odors were as spiritual as the pleasant ones. Their origin, too, was spiritual. They originated in Satan, the "Prince of the Air,"[33] and returned to him. Corrupt and corrupting, they invaded the spirits of humans with loathsome noxious vapours. Milton recorded the altered smell of Paradise when, after Adam's fatal choice, Sin entered Earth and "snuff'd the smell/Of mortal change on Earth" (*PL* X.272-73). The vegetable world did not escape the stench: While plants in Paradise had sprung from the "fragrant earth" (*PL* IV. 645), a plant in Milton's England, still under the curse, now "groweth vpon dunghills, and in the most filthy places that may be found, as also about the common pissing places of great princes and Noblemens houses . . . The whole plant is of a most loathsome sauour or smel . . .[34] Dunghills, pissing places, and loathsome stinking plants which sprang from foul nutriments, were associated with Evil and with vile smells. They, like sin, were rank and "smelled to Heaven."[35] Only the Grace of God, which filled Heaven and earth with "ambrosial fragrance" (*PL* III. 135), could purify the foul smells emanating from Sin and Death. In the Son of God, who "breath'd immortal love/To mortal men" (*PL* III. 267-68), the smells of the whole created world would be restored to the pre-lapsarian fragrances of Paradise, where every morning

> . . . all things that breathe,
> From th' Earth's great Altar send up silent praise
> To the Creator, and His Nostrils fill
> With grateful Smell . . .   (*PL* IX. 194-97)

In this environment the smells of plants and poems can now be studied.

II

Lilies that fester smell far worse than weeds.[36]

The sweetest and lushiousest meat turns into the foulest and stinkingst excrement.[37]

From "lilies of all kinds"[38] we expect increase of sweet smells. Lilies ought not to be mentioned in the same breath as rank, noisome, poisonous weeds — hemlock, stinking elder, goats stones, mushrooms, assafoetida.[39] The exquisite smells that lilies breathe out were for poets a benefaction to be turned into an oblation. Poets breathed in the sweet smells of lilies and then breathed out the sweetness of love's breath. The poet of the *Canticles* whispered for all to hear, "My beloved is mine, and I am his: he feedeth among the lilies" (2.16), and the poets of England, following in his "Lilly-Train,"[40] fed on the fragrance and the love. Lilies, celebrated by Spenser, Herbert, Shakespeare, Milton, Traherne, Marvell, and many other poets,[41] were of such surpassing loveliness as to seem impervious to corruption, to decay and stench. But it is an incontrovertible fact of post-lapsarian human life (and of literary history) that the most memorable lilies of the sixteenth and seventeenth centuries are those that stink:

> But if that flow'r with base infection meet,
> The basest weed outbraves his dignity:
>> For sweetest things turn sourest by their deeds;
>> Lilies that fester smell far worse than weeds.[42]

Reeking of his own perversity, Satan befouled the sweetest smells of the poets and terraculturalists.

Although it would be pleasanter to dance with Milton's nymphs and shepherds by "lillied banks"[43]; to lie with Marvell's fawn on "beds of lilies"[44]; to smell with Hercules the lily "of a most delicious Scent" which sprang up from the milk which he spilled as he "Swig'd Immortality" (as the French florist Louis Liger D'Auxerre reported it)[45] than to uncover the smells of base weeds. And pleasanter not to know that the hemlock in the mad Lear's crown [46] was a vile and noisome poison ("the whole plant, and every part, hath a strong headdy illfavoured sent, much offending the senses"[47]) and that this stinking hemlock was commonly used to suppress "venerous dreames"[48] and to discourage the growth of sex organs at the onset of puberty:

> It is therefore a very rash part to lay the leaues of Hemlocke to the stones of yong boyes or virgin brests, and by that meanes to keepe those parts from growing great; for it doth not only easily cause those members to pine away, but also hurteth the heart and liuer, being outwardly applied . . .[49]

And pleasanter to forget the "stinking elder" of *Cymbeline*[50] with its "ranke and stinking smell" and its ugly "excrescence called *Auricula Iudae*, or Iewes eare,which is soft, blackish, couered with a skin,[51] and which, "being dried and put into the cavernous holes of Fistulous ulcers, openeth and dilateth the orifices," and "put up with a little wooll into the mother, bringeth downe women's courses"[52]; and goats stones with a "ranke or stinking smell . . . like the smell of a Goat"[53]; and *Phallus hollandicus* which "stinketh at the best, but withering is turned into a moist blackness, colouring the very ground whereon it falleth: Flies are killed that sit and feede hereon."[54] Yet it is necessary to experience the revolting smells that were so much a part of life, of botany, of poetry of the sixteenth and seventeenth centuries if we are to apprehend the human corruptibility and vegetable corruption of which the botanists and poets were so painfully aware. We must first sniff the weed "of a naughtie strong & unpleasant sauour"[55] and the plant that "stinketh mightily"[56] which assaulted them, if we are to inhale

> . . . the sweet smell
> Of different flowers in odor and in hue.[57]

Shakespeare's "basest weed" smelled of anuses and excrement and grew on dunghills. Base weeds smelled of human and dog piss, of "foule purulentous urines" and grew on pissing places.[58] They smelled of pudenda, of uterine disease, or excoriations of the yard, of "blisters that rise on the yard by inordinate luxury" and of sores in the privities.[59] They smelled of skin cancers that were black and filthy, of "scabbes or running sores or dry sores" on children's heads.[60] They smelled of mucous, of pus,[61] of rotting fish and meat and decaying human flesh; of rammish male goats. All were indescribably loathsome, but familiar. Shakespeare makes a direct appeal to these foul smells when he tells his Beloved to remember that "lilies that fester smell far worse than" these. The poets Donne and Traherne, living in the same olfactory environment as did Shakespeare ("there's not a nose among twenty but can smell him that's stinking"[62]) referred to similar foul smells when they asked the rhetorical questions, "Can dung and garlike be'a perfume?"[63]; "Or can Perfumes from sordid Dunghills breath?"[64] Acknowledging the large number of evil-smelling plants that grew in England in their day, the herbalists devoted whole sections of their herbals to "noysome" plants,[65] many of which plants were efficacious in healing the anatomical parts of which they reeked. For the same botanico-pharmaceutical reason, Jacob Bobart in the seventeenth century raised Stinking Mayweed, Unsavory Mayweed, Great Stinking Hemlock, Broad Stinking Carret or Turbith, Lesser stinking Meadow rue, Stinking Horsehound, in the Oxford Physic Garden (founded in 1621 by Henry Danvers, later Earl of Danby). Beautifully preserved in the Claridge Druce Herbarium in the Department of Botany at Oxford, these plants can still be seen and handled. Three centuries, have, however, removed the stench.[66]

Among the plants of loathsome odors, Stinking Orach was one of the most offensive. It was known by a number of synonyms, all equally repulsive: Stinking Motherworte;[67] Vulvaria;[68] ranke Goate;[69] Garosmus.[70] Gerard's description conveys the stench and explains the use of the stench in the rising of the mother:

> The whole plant is of a most loathsome sauour or smel; vpon which plant if any should chance to rest and sleepe, he might very well report to his friends, that he has reposed himselfe among the chiefe of *Scoggins* heires . . . It groweth vpon dunghills, and in the most filthy places that may be found, as also about the common pissing places of great princes and Noblemens houses. Sometime it is found in places neere bricke kilns and old walls, which doth some-

what alter his smell, which is like tosted cheese: but that which groweth in his naturall place smells like stinking salt-fish, whereof it tooke his name *Garosmus* . . . it smelleth more stinking than the rammish male Goat: whereupon some by a figure haue called it *Vulvaria:* . . . profitable, by reason of his stinking smell, for such as are troubled with the mother: for as *Hyppocrates* saith, when the mother doth stifle or strangle, such things are to be applied vnto the nose as haue a ranke and stinking smell.[71]

Another plant of "ranke and naughty smell . . . The whole plant stinketh," was the plant known in English as Stinking Mayweed, Cotula foetida, Stincking Camomill, Mathers, Dogges Camomil, Dogge Fennel. In Low-Dutch this plant was known as *Pad-debloemen*, that is to say, *Cowdung Flowers*.[72]

Stinking Gladdon, *Spatula foetida* to the Apothecaries, was considered an excremental plant whose leaves when rubbed produced "a stinking smell very lothsome."[73] Associated with anal diseases (hemorrhoides, rifts of the fundament), with urinary disorders and Buboes in the groin, its medicinal uses were dictated by its smell. The country people of Somersetshire reported to Gerard its efficacy as a laxative ("it moueth vnto the stoole")[74]; and women used it to facilitate the birth of a child, to call down the monthly courses, and in a vaginal pessarie to cause abortion.[75]

Assafoetida, whose unsavory odor revealed its devilish origin, was "of so evill a sent, that the *Germanes* call it *Teuffelz drech*, that is *diaboli stercus*, Devils durt . . .[76] Parkinson retells a story originally told by the Portuguese physician Garcias about the King of Bisnager who wanted to buy a horse, except that it was "over subject to breake winde." Garcias put assafoetida in the horse's provender; the horse was cured; and the king said he was cured with "gods meate, yea rather with the devils said the *Portugall*, but softly . . .[77] Ben Jonson notes its efficacy in curing hysterics: "Only a fit o' the Mother!/They burnt old shoes, Goose-feathers, *Assafoetida* . . ."; and Culpeper finds that it "provokes lust exceedingly and expels wind as much."[78]

The abominable plants, which here form a short catalogue of execrable odours, were "dignified" in Shakespeare's comparison of them with festering lilies. The lily that Shakespeare wanted his

Beloved to smell was in all probability the *Day-Lillie*, also called *Lillie for a day* and *Hemorocallis*.[79] It was a lily of exquisite short-lived fragrance and rapid putrescence:

> The Day-Lillie . . . bringeth forth in the morning his bud, which at noone is full blowne, or spred abroad, and the same day in the euening it shuts it selfe, and in a short time after becomes as rotten and stinking as if it had beene trodden in a dunghill a moneth together, in foule and rainie weather . . .[80]

The olfactory element in Shakespeare's sonnet is unpleasantly present and yet, like many smells, is not quite identifiable. The smells of festering lilies and of basest weeds cling to the argument, operating not through metaphoric equivalences but through a banquet of smells, incredibly fragrant today, unbearably putrid tonight. The stench of festering lilies (worse than Stinking Orach, Stinking Mayweed, Stinking Gladdon, Assafoetida) must convince Shakespeare's Beloved that the cultivation of his irresistible power to arouse love in others without reciprocating love is a loathsome, self-gratifying activity; that love so infected by the vanity of self-gratification becomes its own self-contaminating, festering agent; and that the refusal to reciprocate love to those in whom he has aroused love — the poet among others — turns the sweet fragrance of love into the "foulest and stinkingst excrement." Infected love, like infected lilies, decays and sours; festers and stinks. The "Fable of Hemerocale," told by a practising florist in the context of sound horticultural advice on the cultivation of the Day-Lily, breathes into Shakespeare's sonnet the practical gardener's wisdom and the ancient poets' perception about the connection between floral lily fragrance and love's smells:

> *Hemerocale* was a young lady . . . much talk'd of . . . on account of her great Beauty. She had new Lovers every Day . . . all of them labour'd to outvy one another in giving her Proofs of their Passion . . . even the Gods were taken with it.
>
> . . . such a Throng of Admirers, [she] had a mind to enjoy for a long time the Glory of being thus lov'd, believing that when she should think fit to marry, 'twould lie in her Breast to chuse whom she pleas'd for a Husband.

For a certain time indeed this Coyness would not have been amiss: but *Hemerocale* was so fond of her self, that she perceived not her Charms were wasting every Day; nor would she have reflected on it, had she not seen the number of her Lovers fall off on a sudden; but this Alteration made her begin to look about her; insomuch that she resolv'd to bestow her self on him she lik'd best, and who she thought deserved her above all the rest . . .

But she found her self in a Mistake; for her Beauty being quite worn away, all her Admirers forsook her at once; which threw her into so deep Melancholy, as soon brought her to the Grave: and then *Priapus*, who was said to have been in Love with her, chang'd her into the Flower that bears her Name.[81]

The poet's argument operates on the nose through infection and foul odors. The poet's approach to the Beloved is disagreeably bacteriological and botanical. A fetid smell is perceived in the sonnet, a smell which operates on the senses and on the spirit as the smells of fetid plants do: When "the *Oyl* and *Salt* of *Plants*" are "in very great Proportion in any *Plant*, so as to emit violent Steams, offending the Organ of *Smelling*, but chiefly (forcibly) repelling the *Spirits* towards the *Brain*, (which creates an Aversion to it) a *Fetid Smell* is perceived."[82] The poet's "fester" is more virulent than the smells of base weeds. Stench is a powerful persuader: *Teuffelz drech* pollutes the air of the poem.

Today "diesel-fumes cling to wistaria"[83] and assault the senses. In Shakespeare's day foul fragrances cling to devil-spoiled plants: midnight weeds are "thrice blasted" and "thrice infected" with "Hecate's ban."[84] The stench of self-love is devil-inspired, infecting lilies and love:

For sweetest things turn sourest by their deeds;
Lillies that fester smell far worse than weeds.

III

What a new Spirit would these easie [vegetable] Remedies create among the *Inhabitants* of *London?* . . . we, who are compos'd of the *Elements*, should participate of their *qualities:* For as the *Humours* have their source from the

> *Elements;* so have our *Passions* from the *Humors,* and the
> *Soul* which is united to this *Body* of ours, cannot but be
> affected with its Inclinations.[85]

Shakespeare, Milton, Traherne, Evelyn — poets and terraculturalists — knew the power of air to quicken or to kill. Air could be therapeutic or toxic. It could encourage and promote life; it could corrupt and destroy it:

> . . . *Aer* that is corrupt insinuates it self into the vital parts
> immediately; . . . as the Lucid and noble *Aer,* clarifies the
> Blood, subtilizes and excites it, cheering the Spirits and
> promoting digestion; so the dark, and grosse . . . perturbs
> the Body, prohibits necessary Transpiration for the resolu-
> tion and dissipation of ill Vapours, even to disturbance of
> the very Rational faculties, which the purer *Aer* does so far
> illuminate, as to have rendered some Men healthy and wise
> even to Miracle.[86]

Poets and terraculturalists tell of pendulous air that carried plagues and foul contagion;[87] of corrupt and stinking air that defiled the city-walkers with "Pitch."[88] They also tell of air whose "soft delicious" ambience embraced all living things;[89] of air that animated and nourished· vegetable and human life, metamorphosing the physical process into a spiritual "Vehicle of the Soul, as well as that of the Earth."[90]

The "Miracle" of pure air "illuminates" Milton's Paradise: it excites the senses and cheers the spirits of Adam and Eve. Milton gave his "gentle pair" the olfactory appreciation of a pair of seventeenth-century Londoners. Even before the vile vapours of sin smudged the air of Paradise, prohibiting Transpiration and disturbing the rational faculties, Adam and Eve include in their orisons thanks to God for His olfactory gifts (*PL* V. 180-83) — for the fragrant air of Eden so pure as to inspire the heart with "vernal delight and Joy"; so potent as to drive away "All sadness but despair" (*PL* IV. 155-56).

Good air comes from plants giving off fragrances. Evelyn was not the only one who wrote of flowers "whereof are credibly reported to give their sent above thirty Leagues off at Sea."[91] Milton's good air of Paradise comes from flowers exhaling "odoriferous air" and dispensing "native perfumes" so far from Eden that Satan smelled them

on his journey there. The trees, shrubs, and flowers of Paradise, all
unsuspecting, were creating the perfumed air that "entertain'd"
Satan on his depraved mission (*PL* IV. 153-166). The power of air to
"entertain" Satan, and, for that matter, seventeenth-century humans, was larger than the power to please or to delight: it was the
power to *maintain, support, nourish,* even *accommodate.* From the
sweet odors of pure air the miracle of sustenance arose. Sweet,
fragrant air did not stink, pollute, or damage vegetable and human
health. After Satan's successful mission, pure air was corrupted into
impure air. Infected and infecting, it permeated the vegetable
creation, contributing to the foul breath of some plants, which plants
then added their own dense foulness to the air. Lambert Daneau
argued that Satan and his cohorts could transform harmless plants
into harmful ones, could alter the smell of air, could by noxious
smells spread physical and spiritual disease.[92] According to William
Vaughan, foul vegetable air from Nut-trees, Figge-trees, Coleworts,
Hemlockes, competed for olfactory notoriety with the air emanating
from "filthy dunghils, stinkes, stangs, noysome gutters, channels . . .
Carkases, Mine and Forges."[93] The power of vegetable air to
"entertain" was changed to the power to "defile." And those who
were "Inhabitants by reason of the euilnesse of the aire, haue grosse
and earthy spirits . . . dull, sluggish, sordid, sensuall, plainely
irreligious . . . deceiptfull, malicious, disdainefull . . . "[94]

Corrupt and pestilent air infiltrates Milton's Paradise by way of a
simile:

> As one who long in populous City pent,
> Where Houses thick and Sewers annoy the Air,
> Forth issuing on a Summer's Morn to breathe . . .
> The smell of Grain, or tedded Grass . . .
> Such Pleasure took the Serpent to behold
> This Flow'ry Plat . . .   (*PL* IX. 445-56)

Hovering over "This Flow'ry Plat" is the murk of London and of Hell.
Lucifer, disgraced by the singeing air of Hell and the stench of "the
hot Hell that always in him burns" (IX. 467), propels himself toward
the flowery smells of Paradise as one who has lived in the noxious
vapours of industrial and human pollution rushes to the sweet smells
of rural grass and grain. The simile carries the weight of noisome
fact: the city odors which pestered and harassed the seventeenth-

century air were not unlike the acrimonious smells which perpetually re-contaminated the air of Hell with "Sulphur, and strange fire" (*PL* II.69). Around Milton's simile is fuliginously wreathed Evelyn's description of Londoners whose "Spittle and others excrements" were "blackish"[95] and of the London where the burning of seacoal made it resemble the "Suburbs of Hell":

> from . . . *Brewers, Diers, Lime-burners, Salt,* and *Sope-boylers,* and some other private Trades, *One* of whose *Spiracles* alone, does manifestly infect the *Aer,* more, then all the Chimnies of *London* put together besides . . . Whilst these are belching it forth their sooty jaws, the City of *London* resembles the face rather of *Mount AEtna,* the *Court of Vulcan, Stromboli,* or the Suburbs of *Hell,* then an Assembly of Rational Creatures . . . Ecclipsed with such a Cloud of Sulphure . . . the weary *Traveller,* at many Miles distance, sooner smells, then sees the City to which he repairs . . . the very Rain, and refreshing Dews . . . precipitate this impure vapour . . . [It] contaminates whatsoever is expos'd to it.[96]

If poets and terraculturalists lived in or near a city, they breathed the foul, contaminating air which Evelyn described, and, in addition, smelled "those horrid stinks, *niderous* and unwholesome smells which proceed from Tallow, and corrupted Blood."[97] Falstaff's London experience makes him assume that his audience will nose their way through the sweet smells of the herbalists' lane ("Bucklersbury in simple time") to the "hatefull . . . reek of a lime-kill,"[98] smelling the argument in his brief catechism on love.

In the Providence of God, however, the post-lapsarian world boasted more sweet smelling plants than foul, and those sweet vegetable smells made good health possible: "Nothing in the world can so exhilerate and purifie the spirits, as good odours,"[99] observed William Vaughan, knowing full well that plants are most efficient manufacturers of good smells and good air. All that sweet odor in terraculture and poetry, where gillyflowers comfort "the spirites, by the sence of smelling,"[100] and where "the odoriferous Pink . . . sends forth such a gale/Of sweetnes"[101] is not the exotic hyperbole of fanatic environmentalists or ranting poets. Evelyn continued on his aggressive vegetable course of action, pushing his readers along odorous lines, inviting them to transform the pernicious smells of

London into the transporting smells of "Arabia the Happy." "Sir," he said in the epistolary introduction to his *Fumifugium,*

> I prepare in this short Discourse, an expedient how this pernicious *Nuisance* may be reformed; and offer another also, by which the Aer may not only be freed . . . but render not only Your Majesties Palace, but the whole City likewise, one of the sweetest, and most delicious Habitations in the World . . . the culture and production of such things, as upon every gentle emission through the Aer, should so perfume the adjacent places with their breath; as if, by a certain charm, or innocent *Magick,* they were transferred to that part of *Arabia,* which is therefore styl'd the *Happy,* because it is amongst the Gums and precious spices . . . [102]

Milton, who experienced day by day the stinking smells of his and Evelyn's world, knew (as did Evelyn) that what made Arabia *happy* and *blest* was its good vegetable smells. The "native perfumes" of Milton's fragrant Paradise are in sharp contrast to the "fishy fume" penetrating the daily existence of his readers. It is "gentle gales," "odoriferous wings," "balmie spoiles" that will make his readers, like old Ocean, smile:

> now gentle gales
> Fanning their odoriferous wings dispense
> Native perfumes, and whisper whence they stole
> Those balmie spoiles. As when to them who sails
> Beyond the *Cape of Hope,* and now are past
> *Mozambic,* off at Sea North-East windes blow
> *Sabean* Odours from the spicie shoare
> Of *Arabie* the blest, with such delay
> Well pleas'd they slack thir course, and many a League
> Cheard with the grateful smell old Ocean smiles.
>
> (IV. 156-65)

Although plants could create an Arabian Paradise of smells and make a stinking London habitable, they could not take away the stench of moral pollution. The horror in *Macbeth* is that plants which can be smelled "forty miles out to sea" cannot take away the stench of corrupted blood. They cannot cover nor obliterate the smell of murder:

"Here's the smell of the blood still. All the perfumes of
Arabia will not sweeten this little hand."(V. i. 53-55)

Evelyn's fragrant formula for reducing toxins in the air gave hope
to his readers who were "pursu'd and haunted by that infernal
smoake": "And, I am able to enumerate a Catalogue of native *Plants*
. . . whose redolent and agreeable emissions would even ravish our
senses, as well as perfectly improve and meliorate the Aer about
London."[103] His large catalogue of plants that ravish the senses,
meliorate the air, and "emit a *Cardiaque,* and most refreshing
Halitus," is Milton's "flowering odours" and "wilderness of sweets"
(*PL* V. 293-94) and Shakespeare's "thousand fragrant posies."[104] In
Evelyn's catalogue are included the poets' fragrant flowers: sweet-
brier, woodbinds, jessamine, syringas, roses, bays, juniper, lavender, rosemary, sweet smelling sally, lime-tree, pinks, carnations,
clove, stock-gilly-flower, primroses, auriculas, violets, cowslips,
lillies, narcissus, strawberries, musk, lemmon, mastick thyme,
cammomile, balm, mint, marjoram.[105] Of the plants that are indexes
to the odors which exhilarate the spirit and bring repose to wearied
limbs and minds, roses head the list. No one would want to live in a
world without roses, except, of course, those humans whose
contaminated spirits adversely affected their olfactory sense. Since
roses are flowers "wherein airie and spiritual parts are predomin-
ant,"[106] humans who had alliances with the Devil could not tolerate
their scent. The demonic could not host the sweet pure spirits of
roses.[107] On the other hand, those "airie and spiritual" parts of roses
envelope Eve in a "cloud of fragrance" (*PL* IX. 425), spiritualize the
Edenic bower (*PL* IV. 256), aid digestion (*PL* V. 349), and twist
around mirth-inducing windows (*L'Allegro,* 47-48). Herrick's roses
make *Zephirus* emit perfume "when he 'spires/Through *Woodbine*
and *Sweet-bryers [roses]."*[108] And the "rose-breath air" of Titania's
bower was there to purge the air of gross vapours so that her spirit
might sleep undisturbed by nasty dreams or visions.[109]

Evelyn considered shrubs an efficient remedy to air pollution. He
recommended those that "yield the most fragrant and odoriferous
Flowers, and are aptest to tinge the *Aer* upon every gentle emission
at a great distance . . . "[110] Milton's shrubs in Paradise flinging out
"spicy" odors (VIII. 517) are his prescription for heightening the bliss
of his earthly pair. A "land of spices" — the phrase awakened
George Herbert's olfactory sense, reminding him and his readers

that the spicy fragrance of prayer works like a "Cardiaque,"
purifying the corrupt air of sin.[111] When the "aire was all in spice" for
Henry Vaughan, the fragrant air cleansed the polluted soul,
preparing it for spiritual regeneration.[112]

Even grain has a fragrant contribution to make to air. Evelyn's
"blossom bearing Grain as send forth their virtue at farthest distance
and are all of them *marketable* at *London"* are "marketable" also in
Milton's Paradise where "airs, vernal airs,/Breathing the smell of
field and grane, attune/The trembling leaves" (*PL* IV. 264-66);
"marketable" also in Herrick's *Epithalamie* where the sweetest
odors are those that smell "like flowrie Meads",[113] and in Marvell's
expansive northern territory where fields stretch out for miles and
"fragrant as the mead" is an acceptable olfactory tribute to
females.[114]

Arbors were ubiquitous. Even small gardens had them, and no
horticultural manual or poem was complete without them:

> So smell those neat and woven Bowers,
> All over-archt with *Oringe flowers,*
> And *Almond* blossoms, that do mix
> To make rich these *Aromatikes* . . . [115]

Arbors (or bowers) provided beauty and shelter. Lovely to look at
and to be in, they provided shelter from wind, sun, and rain. Beyond
their visual beauty and sheltering structure, they exerted a spiritual
power that sprang from their fragrance. This spiritual scenting
substance protected humans in the arbor from the invasion of
insects, toads, and harmful reptiles. In Lemnius's botanic commentary on the *Canticles* there is reflected an awareness of the
protective powers of scent:

> . . . yeeldeth foorth a most pleasant smell, wherewith the
> hart and braine of man is maruellously recreated, so that it is
> no small solace and delight for a man during the time of the
> flowring thereof, to dine, sup, or otherwise passe away the
> time in conuenient arbor or gallerie vnder this most gallant
> and braue tree.
>
>   It is also saide that the odour and smell of the leaues &
> flowres of this tree be so soueraigne, that no venemous
> beasts wil approch neere thereunto; insomuch as Serpents,
> Snakes, Adders, Toades, and such like, cannot abide to

come neere where it is.[116]

The bower of Paradise was furnished with plants whose scent kept the arbor free of non-human guests, harmless as these animals were in their pre-lapsarian condition:

> Of firm and fragrant leaf; on either side
> *Acanthus,* and each odorous bushy shrub
> Fenced up the verdant wall . . .
> > other creature here
> Beast, bird, insect, or worm durst enter none;
> Such was their awe of man.   (*PL* IV. 695-7; 703-05)

No doubt the fragrance contributed to the awe.

Fruit trees, too, were important in the production of pure and fragrant air. Although the most obvious benefit of raising fruit trees was the production of edible fruit, there were attendant benefits. After forty years of working in an orchard, William Lawson could still smell the sweet odours of fruit trees "decking the ayre and swteening [sic] every breath and spirit."[117] John Beale, among the most active and enthusiastic of the orchardists, maintained that orchards "do not only sweeten, but also purifie the ambient aire."[118] Milton's Eve knew this about fruit trees, too. She had breathed their air and smelled their fragrance. Her most poignant lament after the Fall and just preceding the Expulsion is for fruit trees (understandably, not for their fruit) because of their health-producing odours essential to respiration:

> . . . how shall we breath in other Aire
> Less pure, accustomed to immortal Fruits?
> > > (*PL* XI. 284-85)

What appears to some critics as Eve's irrational babbling after the Fall — what have fruit trees got to do with breathing? — is actually a standard piece of pomological knowledge.[119] Fruit-tree air has everything to do with good air and good breathing, as Ralph Austen patiently explained in his plea for planting fruit trees. Fruit trees create odours that have a salutary effect on the human body and, hence, on the human spirit:

> But chiefly the *Pleasure this sense* meets with is from the
> *sweet smelling blossomes* of all the fruit-trees, which from
> the time of their breaking forth, till their fall, breath out a

most precious and pleasant odor; perfuming the ayre
throughout all the Orchard . . .

And besides the *pleasure* of this perfumed ayre, it is also
very profitable, and healthfull to the body. Here againe,
Profit and pleasure meet and imbrace. An *Odores nutriunt*,
is a question amongst *Philosophers:* some hold sweet
perfumes nourishing, doubtlesse they give a great refreshing to the spirits, and whatsoever delights and cheers
the spirits is without controversie very advantagious to the
health of the body; for the spirits are the chiefe workers in
the body, from which proceed all, or most of the effects
wrought in the body, good or bad, according to the temper
of the spirits.

Sweet perfumes work immediately upon the spirits for their
refreshing . . . sweet and healthfull Ayres are speciall
preservatives to health, and therefore much to be prised.[120]

Finally, it follows both logically and experientially, that if pure
odours purify air, foul odours befoul it; consequently, both pure and
foul odours have an effect on the human mind and spirit, as well as
on the body. The "dead men's fingers" that Ophelia wore in death
not only looked erotic but smelled foul. These genitalic plants gave
off "a ranke or stinking smel or sauour like the smell of a Goat."[121]
Flowers smelling of copulation pollute air, mind, spirit; defile a young
virgin in death. The only antidote is to find a pure plant whose odour
purifies the air and the spirits. When Laertes prays for appropriate
burial plants

> Lay her i' th' earth.
> And from her fair and unpolluted flesh
> May violets spring!
>
> *(Hamlet,* V. i. 238-40)

he recognizes that violets, "stealing and giving odors,"[122] operate
imperceptibly on nose, spirit, mind; as does Milton's "uncouth
swain" when he places violets on the grave of Lycidas (l. 145). Violets
are flowers

which haue a great prerogatiue aboue others, not onely
because the minde conceiueth a certaine pleasure and
recreation by smelling and handling of those most odoriferous flours, but also for that very many by these Violets

receiue ornament and comely grace: for there bee made of them Galands [sic] for the head, Nose-gaies, and poesies, which are delightfull to looke on, and pleasant to smell to, speaking nothing of their appropriate vertues; yea Gardens themselues receiue by these the greatest ornament of all, chiefest beautie and most gallant grace: and the recreation of the minde which is taken hereby, cannot be but very good and honest: for they admonish and stir vp a man to that which is comely and honest: for floures through their beautie, variety of colour, and exquisite forme, do bring to a liberall and gentle manly minde, the remembrance of honestie comelinesse, and all kindes of vertues. For it would be an vnseemely and filthie thing (as a certaine wise man saith) for him that doth looke vpon and handle faire and beautifull things, and who frequenteth and is conuersant in faire and beautifull places, to haue his minde not faire, but filthie and deformed.[123]

Good vegetable smells do not lodge in minds that are "filthie and deformed." But in minds disposed to purity, "odoriferous flours" can awaken the spirit to produce its own matching scent, the scent of virtuous deeds and comely graces. "What a new Spirit would these easie [vegetable] Remedies create . . . the *Soul* which is united to this *Body* of ours, cannot but be affected with its Inclinations."

IV

"A speaking sweet"[124]

The drama of Creation, of the Fall and Restoration, was re-enacted in the world of smells in the sixteenth and seventeenth centuries. The olfactory sense was not exempt from the war between God and Satan. All good smells originated in God, the Creator of the universe, by whose sweet Breath/Spirit the whole world was created; from whose sweet Breath all Nature took its fragrance. All rank, vaporous, putrid smells originated in Satan, by whose foul breath the whole world was contaminated; from whose stink all Nature took its stench. While those who were of Satan's band are "filths [who] savor but themselves"[125] and pollute the air with the "scent of living Carcasses" (*PL* X. 277) and "noxious vapour" (*PL* II. 216), those who were redeemed by Christ sent up sweet odours to God because

> Onely God, who gives perfumes
>   Flesh assumes
> And with it perfumes my heart.[126]

Recognizing the polarity in the world of smell as ontologically significant, poets and terraculturalists worked on a level deeper than analogy when they attributed terrestrial sweet odours to God's Being and traced foul odours to Satan and metaphysical corruption. The nose, as an instrument of both flesh and spirit, engaged in that continuing combat between God and Satan. Timothy Bright, in *A treatise of melancholy,* explored the relationship of sense to soul, arguing that each sense (including the olfactory) has the obligation to prepare a lodging for the Holy Spirit, the soul's perpetual guest. Obviously, sweet and fragrant smells are the most hospitable hosts for a guest whose Breath created sweet smells from the pre-creation Chaos:

> the soule hath a facultie one, single, and essentiall, notwithstanding so many and sundrie parts are performed in the organicall bodies, as wee daily put in practise: neither is it hereof to bee gathered, that the soule affoordeth no more actions, then there bee instruments . . . as the soule, in Organicall actions, vseth one and the selfe-same instrument to changeable Offices, likewise being separated from the bodie, although the facultie bee one, it also exerciseth of herselfe . . . diuers duties . . . Of such Organes, as the soule vseth for instrumentall actions, some are of substance, and nature most quicke, rare and subtile: other some grosse, slow, and Earthie, more or lesse. The subtile instrument, is the Spirit: which is the most vniversall instrument of the soule, and imbraceth at full, so farre as bodily vses require, all the vniversall facultie, where-with the soule is indued, and directeth it, and guideth it, vnto more particular instruments, for more speciall and priuate uses, as to the Eye, to see with, to the Eare to heare, to the Nose to smell . . . whereof this Spirit is made, I take it to bee an effectuall, and pregnant substance, bred in all thinges, at which time the

> Spirit of the Lord did as it were hatch, and breed out all liuing thinges, out of the Chaos mentioned in Genesis. Which Chaos, as it was matter of Corporall, and Palpable Substance to all things, so did it also minister this liuely Spirit vnto them . . . to some more pure, to othersome more grosse, according to the excellencies of the creature, and dignitie of the vses, whereto it is to be employed. From this power of God, sprang the Spirit of man, as I take it, raised from the earth, together with the bodie, whereby it receiued such furniture, and preparation, as it becommeth a lodging for so noble a gest . . . [127]

Since God and Satan are arch-enemies, it follows that all pure, sweet vegetable smells such as Herbe Aloe are "an enemie to all kindes of putrefactions," defending the "body from all manner of corruption";[128] and that the "stench or fog" of weeds is the odour that the unprofitable sinner bequeathes to His Creator.[129] Each putrid smell is ultimately an assault on the purity of God's being and a repudiation of the sweetness of His grace:

> As then we iudge by the nose and sence of smelling which God hath giuen vnto vs, what difference there is betweene a good and stinking smell, and how the one is pleasant and delightsome, and the other vnpleasant and abhominable: so likewise we ought to consider what small pleasure God taketh in the infection and stench of our sinnes, and how hee is delighted with the sweete smell of the iustice and vertues of Christ Iesus, when wee are perfumed therewith, and when he smelleth the sauour thereof in vs . . . For if we turne our faces aside, and stoppe our nose, and euen spit vpon the ground when we meete with some great infection, shall we not thinke that God turneth his face from vs when he findeth vs so stincking & infected?[130]

The "filths [who] savor but themselves" in *King Lear* contaminate the air with the effluvia of sin. The fog and filthy air which is created by the witches in *Macbeth* as the substance necessary to sustain their foul existence; the blasted heath on which they live, which supports no vegetation; the "vap'rous drop profound" in which Hecate raises "artificial sprites"; the "root of hemlock digged i' th' dark" which the witches toss into their stinking brew[131] — give evidence that stinking odours are devil-inspired:

> Anne Bodenham, we read in Henry More, when she raised
> Spirits, made a stinking perfume on Coals, after her Circle
> was drawn, and conjuring Charmes in her Book read; the
> Devil loves, it seems, evil base Odours . . . [132]

Comus and his damned crew in Milton's *Mask* alter the smells of the
sweetest vegetation, turning fragrant woods into the "rank vapors of
this Sin-worn mold," unhallowing the air, spreading their "foul
contagion."[133]

Poets and terraculturalists frequently used vegetable smells to
mark the major events in Redemption history. Associated with
Satan, sin, and death were thankless weeds, stinking breath, foul
plants, filthy savours, sluttish fumes, stinking perfumes, rotten
fruits, rotten blossoms, stinking fens, noisome vapours. All things
pollute and foul owed their stench to Satan, the progenitor of all
impurity. Among the foulest plants in the world was the mushroom
known as "Devil's tool" or "Fungus virilis penis arrecti facie," which
had an egregiously foul smell ("den afgrijffelijcken vuijlen reuch").[134]
The gum assafoetida, whose popular name *"Teuffelzdrech,* that is,
Diaboli stercus"[135] or Devil's Dirt or Dung indicated its diabolical
excremental origin, smelled as foul as its name. Association with
Satan meant adopting his foul smells, being identified with his
stench. The smell of sin in Shakespeare's *King John* hinders
breathing, so stifling is its odour.[136] Lear's imagination has been so
befouled by the stench of sin that he assigns to the Devil the territory
below the waist in women and calls for an ounce of civet to sweeten
his imagination.[137] As Herbert knew, the smell of sin is so noxious
that had not the sweet smells of Christ's body and blood in the
Eucharistic feast "subdue[d] the smell of sin," no vegetable fragrance — flowers, gums, or powders — could have done so:

> To subdue the smell of sinne;
> Flowers, and gummes, and powders giving
>   All their living,
> Lest the Enemy should winne?
>
> Doubtlesse, neither starre nor flower
>   Hath the power
> Such a sweetnesse to impart:

> Onely God, who gives perfumes,
>> Flesh assumes,
> And with it perfumes my heart.[138]

Accompanying the stifling smell of sin is the sick smell of mortality. Sin degrades the whole creation, fatally befouling the sweet air so that Vaughan's Palm-tree "shut from the breath/And air of Eden . . . /thrives no where."[139] Sin's incestuous pairing with Death in *Paradise Lost* produces an odour in Paradise tainted with corruptibility, tinged with "carnage," and with "prey innumerable" (*PL* X. 268). When Sin "snuff'd the smell/Of mortal change on Earth," the air had already turned murky (*PL* X. 267-280); then slow and gradual changes in the air bring "Vapor, and Mist, and Exhalation hot,/Corrupt and Pestilent" (*PL* X. 694-95), "black Air" and "double terror" (*PL* X. 847-50).[140]

There is a quiet terror in the flowers that die in Herbert's hand as he makes a "posie." Touched by Time, which is synonymous with mortality, the flowers wither at noon; their fragrance is altered by the smell of mortality:

> I made a posie, while the day ran by:
> Here will I smell my remnant out, and tie
>> My life within this band.
> But Time did becken to the flowers, and they
> By noon most cunningly did steal away,
>> And wither'd in my hand.
>
> My hand was next to them, and then my heart:
> I took, without more thinking, in good part
>> Times gentle admonition:
> Who did so sweetly deaths sad taste convey,
> Making my minde to smell my fatall day;
>> Yet sugring the suspicion.
>
> Farewell deare flowers, sweetly your time ye spent,
> Fit, while ye liv'd, for smell or ornament,
>> And after death for cures.
> I follow straight without complaints or grief,
> Since if my sent be good, I care not if
>> It be as short as yours.[141]

The smell of his "fatall day" in the poet's hand penetrates into his heart. Yet in the death of flowers lies the consolation for the Christian poet: those sweet deaths, "sugring the suspicion" of his own death, tell him that if the "sent" of his life "be good," his death can be as fragrantly curative and salvific as theirs.

But the smell of mortality menaces all human and vegetable life. Drawing on his olfactory memory of his olfactory sensations in graveyards, Herbert puts into his poems the deadly smells of decaying flesh

> And after death the fumes that spring
> From private bodies make as big a thunder,
>   As those which rise from a huge King[142]

and of bodies that

> in noisome vapours grow
> To a plague and publick wo.[143]

In Herbert's day, the trees in graveyards, in combination with human flesh, united to threaten public health. The "double fatal yew," for instance, was well known for its unhealthful qualities in burial grounds. Robert Turner's botanical analysis of the poisons exuded by human carcasses and sucked in by yews serves to identify the source of foul fragrances and deadly fumes and to explain Vaughan's references in "Buriall" to the "blasts" or "exhalations" of putrifying bodies:

> Yew is hot and dry in the third degree, and hath such an attractive quality, that if it be set in a place subject to poysonous vapours, the very branches will draw and imbibe them: Hence it is conceived, that the judicious in former times planted it in Church-yards on the West side, because those places being fuller of putrefaction and gross oleaginous Vapours exhaled out of the Graves by the setting Sun, and sometimes drawn into those Meteors called Ignes fatui, divers have been frightened, supposing some dead bodies to walk; others have been blasted, &c. not that it is able to drive away Devils, as some superstitious Monks have imagined; nor yet, that it was ever used to sprinkle Holy-Water, as some quarrelsome Presbyters . . . have fondly conceived. Wheresoever it grows, it is danger-ous and deadly both to man and beast, according to most Authours, how much more then if it be encompassed with

Graves, into which the lesser Roots will run and suck
nourishment, (poisonous mans flesh being the rankest
poison that can be) yet a certain Vicar unwilling to own the
effects thereof upon his Cows would fain deny it to be so:
Other Creatures as Rabbits have been poisoned with it, and
the very lying under the shadow hath been found hurtful:
Yet the growing of it in a Church-yard is useful, and
therefore it ought not to be cut down upon what pittiful
pretence soever.[144]

The yew tree attracted mortality: it was a squalid reminder of the
power of sin over the vegetable world. For centuries the terraculturalists associated the yew tree with stinking gums and with fatality:

I like the land that of it selfe doth yeeld,
The mighty Elme that branches broad doth beare,
And round about with Trees bedecks the field,
With Trees, that wild beares Apple, Plumme, and Peare,
But will no Bearefoot breed, nor stincking Gumme,
Nor Yewe nor Plantes, whence deadly poisons come.[145]

Amelioration of smells — escape from infection, toxicity, and
fatality — relief and restoration, a new nose and a new olfactory
environment: for these Heaven was the source, and the Person of
Christ the new fragrance and fragrancer. The odours of Grace for
which St. Augustine cried, "You shed your fragrance about me; I
drew breath and now I gasp for your sweet odour,"[146] were sprinkled
on the events of Christ's Humiliation and Exaltation. It is the birth of
Christ that radically transformed the winter season and the season's
smells. When Herrick carols the birth of Christ, he smells the
Christly fragrances of Restoration, of December turned to May, of
frozen fields to new-mown meadows:

That sees *December* turn'd to *May*.
If we may ask the reason, say;
The why, and wherefore all things here
Seem like the Spring-time of the yeere?
Why do's the chilling Winters morne
Smile, like a field beset with corne?
Or smell, like to a Meade new-shorne,
Thus, on the sudden? Come and see
The cause, why things thus fragrant be . . . [147]

For Vaughan, the day of Christ's birth is the day when the sun

"Breathing Perfumes, doth spice the day."[148]

The Name of Jesus — Saviour — has a significance beyond its sound. Its influence extends to all the senses, not excluding the olfactory. The fragrance of the Name of Jesus transforms smells and changes olfactory perceptions: Crashaw shows how a poet's vocabulary, a poet's catalogue of metaphors, is altered by the Name of Jesus, whose Name disinherits all mistaken comparisons and gives "New Similes to Nature."[149] No created thing can be compared with the loveliness of Christ. The sweetest fragrance in the world —the fragrance of the vegetable creation — has no fragrance apart from Christ. All earthly fragrances are derivative: they are fragrant only insofar as they admit their olfactory dependence on Jesus. In his Being is their fragrance:

> All force of so Prophane a Fallacy
> To think ought sweet but that which smells of Thee.
> Fair, flowry Name; in none but Thee
> And Thy Nectareall Fragrancy,
>   Hourly there meetes
> An vniuersall Synod of All sweets;
>   That no Perfume
>   For euer shall presume
> To passe for Odoriferous,
> But such alone whose sacred Pedigree
> Can proue if Self: some kin (sweet name) to Thee,
> Sweet Name, in Thy each Syllable
> A Thousand Blest Arabias dwell;
> A Thousand Hills of Frankincense;
> Mountains of myrrh, & Beds of spices,
> And ten Thousand Paradises . . . [150]

The Body of Christ, broken for the sake of mankind, is the perfume that substitutes its own fragrance for the vile smells of man's corrupt and carnal heart. Herbert celebrates in the Eucharist the sweetness of Christ's flesh, the Pomander whose fragrance is made and enhanced by bruising:

> But as Pomanders and wood
>   Still are good,
> Yet being bruis'd are better sented:
> God, to show how farre his love

> Could improve,
> Here, as broken, is presented.[151]

Pomanders were prepared in the following way:

> Take two ounces of Labdanum, of Beniamin and Storax
> one ounce, muske sixe graines, ciuit sixe graines, Amber
> griece sixe graines, of Calamus Aromaticus and Lignum
> Aloes, of each the waight of a groate: beate all these in a hot
> mortar, and with an hote pestell till they come to paste, then
> wet your hand with Rosewater, and roll vp the paste
> sodainly.[152]

The broken-ness creates the sweetness.

Since evil appeared to be ubiquitous and evil smells permeated all
aspects of life, pomanders had to be worn "against foule stinkyng
aire" by both old and young to "purifie the spirits":

> . . . it is most certaine that good smels doe make the heart
> ioyfull and merrie, and purifie the spirits. I am of opinion
> therefore, that it were good for olde men to carrie about
> them some good odours, as chaines and belles of Muske,
> that they haue alwaies in their chamber some good
> parfumes, that they wash their beards, hands and faces with
> sweete waters.[153]

The Pomander of Christ's flesh is eternally present in the Eucharist,
making the heart pure, perfuming all that it touches.

The final victory over Satan, and the restoration of fragrance to its
heavenly qualities, occurred in Christ's Resurrection. His Resurrection challenged the whole creation and altered the response of
the senses to the natural creation. The sun, as many poets had
observed, could not on Easter Day compete with the brilliance of the
resurrected body of the Light of the World; nor could the perfumes
emanating from the sun presume to contest with the perfumes
arising in the resurrected flesh of the risen Lord. Herbert's Easter
poem establishes the New Order and the new Odour:

> The Sunne arising in the East,
> Though he give light, & th' East perfume;
> If they should offer to contest
> With thy arising, they presume.[154]

The sweetest flowers and the most fragrant boughs could not

sweeten the Way of the Christ, who, arising from the tomb, out-
fragranced even the fragrant remnants of His creation. His
resurrected fragrance of incarnate sweets is the Victorious Way in
which He censes His creation. Herbert's "Easter" charts the radical
shift in the sinner's floral experience at Christ's resurrection:

> I Got me flowers to straw thy way;
> I got me boughs off many a tree:
> But thou wast up by break of day,
> And brought'st thy sweets along with thee.[155]

The poet's *vade-mecum*, like the florists', compels all men to take
the new Way that "gives us breath"[156] — the breath that we know
gives life to all the world and sweetens humans and flowers.

The concern with fragrance and sweet breath can best be
understood if we recall that theirs was a world of "fuliginous Reeks of
Mens Bodies,"[157] and of a stinking breath so foul that it was "capable
to perfume a whole Room."[158] Arm-holes, mouth, and body were
notorious offenders in Herbert's day. For stinking arm-holes the
herbalists prescribed not a deodorant to cover the stench but a
vegetable concoction of artichoke steeped in wine to be drunk so
that the cause of the odour could be attacked; after drinking this
vegetable potion, the owner of the stinking arm-holes would send
"forth plenty of stinking vrine, whereby the ranke and rammish
sauour of the whole body is much amended."[159] Even worse smells,
the kind to which Herrick has such an aversion, also originated in
internal pollution:

> Fie, (quoth my Lady) what a stink is here?
> When 'twas her breath that was the *Carrionere*.[160]

> *Skoles* stinks so deadly, that his Breeches loath
> His dampish Buttocks furthermore to cloath.[161]

With what tremendous relief the poets and terraculturalists must
have received the news that in Christ's death the "Original Curse is
Reversed."[162]

The culminating event in Christ's salvation mission is His
Ascension. A sharer in Christ's victory, the poet Vaughan partici-
pates in the fragrances of Ascension Day. It is a bright and glorious
morning redolent with floral perfumes. The scents are created by
Christ as He ascends; the poet smells Christ's fragrance as he
celebrates the event at "one remove":

> I smell her spices, and her ointment yields,
> As rich a scent as the now Primros'd fields . . . [163]

These are the kinds of fragrances that the orchardist William Lawson cherished — the scents that he smelled in his orchard and garden:

> The Rose . . . the faire and sweet senting Woodbind . . .
> Primrose double and single. The Violet nothing behinde the
> best, for smelling sweetly. And 1000. more . . . [164]

The rich sequence of redemptive events that were breathing out Christ's fragrance was to be recapitulated in the life of the believer. Only ingratitude could cause a believer to stink like a weed:

> Thus thou all day a thankless weed doest dress,
> And when th' hast done, a stench, or fog is all
>   The odour I bequeath.[165]

The life of gratitude — of repentance, self-sacrifice, good deeds, prayer — has its fragrant odours, odours borrowed and derived from the Saviour. The Christian life is rooted in the Being of its Saviour and is guided by the testimony of the Scriptural Revelation:

> Now thanks be unto God, which always causeth us to
> triumph in Christ, and maketh manifest the savour of his
> knowledge by us in every place. For we are unto God a
> sweet savour of Christ, in them that are saved, and in them
> that perish: To the one we are the savour of death unto
> death; and to the other the savour of life unto life.[166]

The gifts of the Philippians to the Apostle Paul are "an odour of a sweet smell, a sacrifice acceptable, well pleasing to God."[167] The restoration was constantly being completed by the offerings of sweet-smelling sacrifices to God. In the consciousness of the Puritan preacher Thomas Adams, for example, the relationship between floral fragrance and the life of sanctification is indicated by the title of his sermon "A Contemplation of the Herbes" and by his reference to the repulsive stench of assafoetida:

> Man is naturally delighted with pleasant sauours, and
> abhorres noysome and stinking smels. But our God hath
> purer nostrils, and cannot abide the polluted heapes of
> iniquities . . . no carryon is so odious to man, as mans

impieties are to God. Yea the very oblations of defiled hands
stinke in his presence . . . As if *Assafoetida* was the onely
plant of their gardens . . . The sweete smoke of a holy,
sacrifice, like a subtill ayre, riseth vp to heauen; and is with
God before man sees or smels it.[168]

The sanctified perception of the poet operates in "The Odour,"
Herbert's fragrant poetic meditation on II Corinthians 2:15. Herbert
smells the Christian life as a sweet "traffick" between man and God,
between man's call to God and God's response:

For when *My Master,* which alone is sweet,
    And ev'n in my unworthinesse pleasing,
        Shall call and meet,
    My servant, as thee not displeasing,
That call is but the breathing of the sweet.[169]

All the smells in the poem (spices, pomanders, cordials, amber
greece, orientall fragrancie, broth of smells) perfume the poem as
Christ perfumes the Christian's life, making the poem, and the
"minde" and breath of the poet, "a speaking sweet."[170]

NOTES

Chapter Five

1 Milton, *Paradise Lost* IX. 197. For *grateful* as an olfactory adjective to describe musk and civet, see John Floyer, *Touch-stones of medicines* (London, 1687): "while fresh, they stink; afterwards, in a small quantity, they are more grateful," I, 36.

2 Helkiah Crooke, *Microcosmographia,* 2nd ed. (London, 1631), p. 620. Crooke, a "Dr. of Physicke," based his writing on the medical treatises of "the best authors of Anatomy, esp. Gaspar Bauhinus & Andreas Laurentius."

3 Thomas Willis, *Two discourses concerning the soul of brutes,* trans. S. Pordage (London, 1683), p. 88. Willis, an English physician and Professor of Natural Philosophy at Oxford, wrote authoritatively in Latin on anatomy and physiology, relating them to the soul and its functions.

4 *The rationall physitian's library* (London, 1661), p. 376. Cole and Culpeper drew on Greek, Arabic, and Latin sources and applied their medical skills with "reason and experience" to olfactory issues.

5 Donald Davie, in "Observances," an unpublished poem read at Calvin College, Grand Rapids, Michigan, March 1979; the poem concludes, "The smoke fuliginously wreathing,/But air, sweet air,/We folk of God are simply breathing."

6 London, 1633, pp. 111-112.

7 Bradwell, p. 113.

8 2nd ed. (London, 1622), p. 1. See also André Du Laurens, *A discourse of the preservation of sight . . . ,* trans. Richard Svrphlet (London, 1599): "It is good daily to carrie some good smell . . . The ayre then . . . will serue to repaire our first substance, which the Phisitions call spirituall," p. 181.

9 Venner, p. 7.

10 Venner, p. 7.

11 London, 1545, sig. Avii.

12 Donne, I, 85. See also Shakespeare's *The Tempest,* "the foul lake/O'erstunk their feet," IV. i. 183-84, and "I do smell all horse-piss, at which my nose is in great indignation," IV. i. 199-200.

13 *The compleat gardeners practice,* p. 27.

14 *Antony and Cleopatra* III. xiii. 39; Sonnet 94, 1. 14.

15 *The anatomy of plants* (1682), pp. 292-93.

16 Sonnet 54, 11. 3-4.

17 *Poly-Olbion, Song XV,* 180-81,187, *The Works of Michael Drayton,* ed. J. William Hebel (Oxford, 1961), IV, 307-308.

18 *Herball,* p. 1259.

[19] "Of Gardens," in *Bacon's Essays*, ed. Richard Whately (Boston, 1871), pp. 443-44.

[20] *Much Ado About Nothing* III. v. 16.

[21] *Works*, II, 297-98.

[22] Shakespeare, *The Winter's Tale* IV. iv. 672-73. See also *Twelfth Night*, "To hear by the nose, it is dulcet in contagion," II. iii. 56-57.

[23] *The art of simpling*, p. 43.

[24] *Hamlet* V. i. 200.

[25] *A nievve herball*, pp. 548-49.

[26] "Goodnesse," *Centuries, Poems, and Thanksgivings*, ed. H.M. Margoliouth (Oxford, 1958), II, 184, 1. 60. All subsequent references are to this text.

[27] *Paradisus, The epistle to the reader.*

[28] Grew, *The anatomy of plants* (1682), p. 82.

[29] Francis Bacon, *Sylva sylvarum, The Works of Francis Bacon*, ed. James Spedding, *et al.* (New York, 1869): "But where there is less heat, there the spirit of the plant is digested and refined, and severed from the grosser juice," pp. 347-48.

[30] Grew, p. 94.

[31] See also Henry Vaughan, *"Isaacs* Marriage," "The thankful Earth unlocks her self, and blends/A thousand odours, which (all mixt,) she sends/Up in one cloud, and so returns the skies/That dew they lent, a breathing sacrifice," 11. 59-62.

[32] *A treatise of fruit-trees* (1657), p. 23.

[33] Milton, *Paradise Lost* X. 184-85, XII. 454, and Ephesians 2:2, where Satan is called the "prince of the power of the air."

[34] Gerard, p. 327.

[35] *Hamlet* III. iii. 36.

[36] Shakespeare, Sonnet 94, 1. 14.

[37] Blake, *The compleat gardeners practice*, p. 23. See also Milton's quotation from Ariosto: "Then past hee to a Flowry Mountaine greene,/Which once smelt sweet, now stinks as odiously," *Of Reformation*, I, 560.

[38] *The Winter's Tale* IV. iv. 126.

[39] Herbert's poem "Assurance" has bitter "rank poyson" in it, 11. 1, 3, 6, 14; and Lyte's herbal devotes the third part to medicinal and purging plants and "noysome weedes" and "dangerous plantes."

[40] Traherne, "Admiration," II, 123, 1. 23.

[41] Spenser, *The Shepheardes Calendar* "Aprill," l. 141; Herbert, "Poems from Walton's *Lives*," (Sonnet 2, l. 6); Shakespeare, Sonnets 98, 99, *The Winter's Tale* IV. iv. 126; Milton, *Arcades*, l. 97, *Mask*, l. 862, Sonnet XX; Traherne, "Admiration," l. 23; Marvell, "The Nymph Complaining for the Death of Her Fawn," ll. 73, 77, 81-82, 90.

[42] Shakespeare, Sonnet 94.

[43] *Arcades*, ll. 96-97.

[44] "Nymph Complaining," l. 77.

[45] *The compleat florist* (London, 1706), pp. 285-86.

[46] *King Lear* IV. iv. 4.

[47] Parkinson, *Theatrum*, p. 932.

[48] Parkinson, *Theatrum*, p. 934.

[49] Gerard, p. 1063. See also Parkinson, *Theatrum*, p. 932, and Culpeper, *The English physitian enlarged* (London, 1653): "the whole Plant and every part has a strong, heady, and ilsavor'd scent, much offending the Senses . . . applied to the privities, it stops lustful thoughts," pp. 122-23.

[50] *Cymbeline* IV. ii. 59.

[51] Gerard, p. 1421.

[52] Parkinson, *Theatrum*, p. 211.

[53] Gerard, p. 209.

[54] Parkinson, *Theatrum*, p. 1322. The names of mushrooms are clues to their foul smells: "because it groweth among dung is called *Fimetarius*"; and *Columna* calleth *Lupi crepitus* . . . hath a very stinking savour, whereof commeth the name, and is much devoured by flyes that eate it," pp. 1321-23.

[55] Lyte, p. 176.

[56] Blake, *The compleat gardeners practice*, p. 17.

[57] Shakespeare Sonnet 98, ll. 5-6.

[58] Parkinson, *Theatrum*, p. 1627; see also Gideon Harvey, *Morbus Anglicus* (London, 1672), where the "corrosive steams" exhaled by "Houses of Office, Pissing places, and other nasty stinks and fumes," p. 146.

[59] Parkinson, *Theatrum*, p. 1028.

[60] Parkinson, *Theatrum*, p. 1028.

[61] Culpeper, *English physitian*, describes the herb Pilewort and its uses: "the very Herb born about ones Body next the skin, helps in such Diseases . . . I cured my own Daughter of the Kings Evil, broke the sore, drew out a quarter of a pint of Corruption, and Cured it without any Scar at al, and in one Weeks time," p. 60.

[62] *King Lear* II. iv. 70-71.

[63] Donne, "To Sr *Henry Wotton*," l. 17.

[64] Traherne, "The Enquiry," l. 9.

[65] Lyte and Parkinson, to mention only two herbalists.

[66] I am indebted to Mr. F. White, Curator of the Herbaria, for permitting me to examine the plants preserved by Jacob Bobart.

[67] Gerard, p. 328; Lyte, p. 548.

[68] Gerard, p. 328; Lyte, p. 549; Culpeper, *English physitian*, p. 15.

[69] Lyte, p. 548.

[70] Gerard, p. 327.

[71] Gerard, pp. 327-28. Cf. Lear's description of his hysteria as "this mother swells up toward my heart!" II. iv. 56. See also Lyte, pp. 548-49 and Parkinson, *Theatrum*, p. 749.

[72] Gerard, p. 756. See also Lyte, pp. 185-87.

[73] Gerard, pp. 59-60. See also Parkinson, *Theatrum*, p. 257.

[74] Gerard, p. 60.

[75] Gerard, p. 60.

[76] Lyte, pp. 303-4. See also William Coles, *Adam in Eden*, Chap. CCCX.

[77] *Theatrum*, pp. 1569-70.

[78] *The complete herbal* (1850), p. 272. See also Ben Jonson, *The Magnetic Lady, Ben Jonson*, ed. C.H. Herford and Percy Simpson (Oxford, 1927, 1954), "Only a fit o' the Mother!/They burnt old shoes, Goosefeathers, *Assafoetida*," III, V. i. 11-12.

[79] Gerard, p. 99.

[80] Gerard, p. 98. See also Parkinson, *Paradisus*, p. 148.

[81] D'Auxerre, *The compleat florist*, pp. 290-91.

[82] Floyer, *Touch-stones of medicines*, I, 34.

[83] Donald Davie, "For Doreen. A Voice from the Garden," *Collected Poems* 1950-70 (Oxford, 1972), p. 128.

[84] *Hamlet* III. ii. 258.

[85] John Evelyn, *Fumifugium* (London, 1661), p. 22.

[86] *Fumifugium*, pp. 1, 3.

[87] *King Lear* III. iv. 67; *King John* V.iv.33; *Henry V* III. iii. 31; Lambert Daneau, *A dialogue of witches . . .*, trans. Thomas Twyne (London, 1575): "some pestilent smell or vapour doth in such wise infect an whole region through which it breatheth, ye most greeuous and infectious diseases are thereby engendred," sig. Euir.

[88] Traherne, "The City," ll. 34-35; Evelyn, *Fumifugium*: "the very Rain, and refreshing Dews . . . precipitate this impure vapour . . . contaminates whatsoever is expos'd to it," p. 6; Thomas Phayre, *A treatyse of the pestilence* (London, 1545), Air; Robert Burton, *The anatomy of melancholy*, ed. A.R. Shilleto (London, 1903), II, *"Air rectified. With a digression of the Air,"* 40-80∤

[89] *Paradise Lost* II. 400; VII 89-90: " . . . the ambient Air wide interfus'd/Imbracing round this florid Earth . . . " See also *Macbeth*: "The temple-haunting [marlet], does approve,/By his lov'd [mansionry], that the heaven's breath/Smells wooingly here," I. vi. 4-6.

[90] Evelyn, *Fumifugium*, p. 1. Evelyn observes that the ancient Philosophers believed this.

[91] Evelyn, *Fumifugium*, p. 24.

[92] *A dialogue of witches:* "And as for Herbes, Trees, with their berries and fruites, and all such like thinges, truely they may be by them intoxicated," sig. Eviv.

[93] *Directions for health*, 6th ed. (London, 1626), p. 3. See also Du Laurens, *A discourse:* "There are certaine plants which a man must hardly come neere vnto . . . because they haue a contrary qualitie vnto the animall spirit," p. 180.

[94] *Via recta*, p. 7. See also Surflet, *Maison rustique:* "it [Indian Gilliflower] ingendreth an infectious aire . . . the flower thereof is venemous," p. 304.

[95] *Fumifugium*, p. 12.

[96] *Fumifugium*, p. 6.

[97] *Fumifugium*, p. 21.

[98] *The Merry Wives of Windsor* III. iii. 72-79.

[99] *Directions for health*, p. 158.

[100] Lawson, *A new orchard*, p. 1.

[101] Drayton, *Poly-Olbion, Song XV*, ll. 180-81.

[102] Evelyn's description of air pollution that "kills our *Bees* and *Flowers* . . . suffering nothing in our Gardens to bud" shows the close inter-relationship between plant and human health, pp. 7-14.

[103] *Fumifugium, epistolary introduction.*

[104] *The Merry Wives of Windsor* II. i. 20.

[105] *Fumifugium*, pp. 24-25.

[106] Gerard, p. 1268.

[107] See George Abraham Mercklin's summary of this accepted olfactory dogma of the day, *Sylloge physico-medicinalium casuum incantationi adscribi solitorum* (Nürnberg, 1698): "Caussam ego referrem in odium Diaboli, quo genus humanum prosequitur, . . . at noluit id admittere, ne odium Dei omnipotentis, vanè hoc modo laborando, contra odium Diaboli . . . ," p. 44.

[108] *H-149A*, ll. 67-68.

[109] *A Midsummer Night's Dream* II. i. 250-54.

[110] *Fumifugium*, p. 24.

[111] "Prayer," l. 14.

[112] "Regeneration," l. 45.

[113] *H-149A*, ll. 63-64.

[114] "Upon Appleton House," l. 429.

[115] Herrick, *H-375*, ll. 11-14.

[116] *An herball for the Bible*, pp. 17-18.

[117] Lawson, *A new orchard*, p. 57.

[118] *Herefordshire orchards*, p. 7.

[119] See William Empson, *Some Versions of Pastoral* (London, 1950), p. 162.

[120] Austen, *A treatise of fruit-trees* (1657), pp. 37-58.

[121] Gerard, p. 209. For a study of the foul odours associated with sexual intercourse, see Helen Lemay, "The Stars and Human Sexuality: Some Medieval Scientific Views," *Isis* 71 (1980): "In the *Centiloquium* Ahmad ibn Yusuf states that if Mars is in the ascendent at a person's conception, he will take delight in terrible odors, and if Saturn should also be in his nativity, he will want to smell feces during coitus," 133.

[122] *Twelfth Night* I. i. 6-7.

[123] Gerard, pp. 849-50.

[124] Herbert, "The Odour," l. 17.

[125] *King Lear* IV. ii. 39.

[126] Herbert, "The Banquet," ll. 22-24.

[127] Pp. 53-55.

[128] Gerard includes in corruption "stinking breath proceeding from the imperfection

of the stomacke," p. 508.

129 Vaughan, "Unprofitableness," ll. 17-18.

130 Peter de la Primavdaye, *The French academie* (London, 1618), p. 397.

131 *Macbeth* IV. i. 25.

132 William Drage, *Daimonomageia* (London, 1665), p. 20.

133 Ll. 17, 757, 467, *Lycidas*, l. 127.

134 Rembert Dodoens, *Cruydt-Boeck*, enlarged with commentary from other writers and Carolus Clusius (Antwerp, 1664), p. 786.

135 Coles, *Adam in Eden*, Chap. CCCX; Lyte, p. 304.

136 *King John* IV. iii. 111-13.

137 *King Lear* IV. vi. 125-31.

138 "The Banquet," ll. 15-24.

139 "The Palm-tree," ll. 5-7.

140 Cf. Blith, *The English improover*: ". . . Sinne, the Root that brings forth all: First brought forth the Curse, and ever since the Fruit thereof," p. 94; see Chapter One. Cf. also *Hamlet*: The whiff of death at first excites Hamlet and the thought of death lures him to escape from the rottenness in Denmark where murder is "most foul," offenses are so "rank" they "smell to heaven," air is a "foul and pestilent congregation of vapors," and love creates a "rank sweat" on an "enseamed bed."

141 Herbert, "Life."

142 Herbert, "Content," ll. 22-24.

143 Herbert, "Dooms-day," ll. 23-24.

144 Vaughan, "Buriall," ll. 25-27. Turner, *Botanologia*, p. 362.

145 Heresbachius, *Foure bookes of husbandrie* (1601), refers to Columella, pp. 49-50. See also Lyte: "Ewe is not profitable for mans body, for it is so hurtful and venemous, that suche as do but onely sleepe under the shadowe thereof become sicke, and sometimes they die, especially when it bloweth," p. 768.

146 *Confessions*, trans. R.S. Pine-Coffin (Baltimore, 1961), X. 27, p. 232.

147 "A Christmas Caroll," *N-96*, ll. 10-18.

148 "Christs Nativity," l. 6.

149 "To the Name Above Every Name, the Name of Iesvs," l. 96.

150 "To the Name," ll. 171-87.

151 Herbert, "The Banquet," ll. 25-30.

152 H. Plat, *Delights for ladies* (London, 1617), Sig. G8v-G9r. See also Bacon, *Sylva*: "Most odours smell best broken or crushed . . . but flowers pressed or beaten do leese the freshness and sweetness of their odour [Arist. Prob. xxxiii. 3], p. 348.

153 Du Laurens, *A discourse*, p. 192. See also Vaughan, *Directions*: "You must vse, after the example of *Galen*, to carry about you a sweet Pomander, and to have alwaies in your chamber some good perfumes," p. 158.

154 Herbert, "Easter," ll. 23-26.

155 Herbert, "Easter," ll. 19-22.

[156] Herbert, "The Call": "Come, my Way, my Truth, my Life:/Such a Way, as gives us breath," ll. 1-2.

[157] Boyle, *A free enquiry into the vulgarly receiv'd notions of nature* (London, 1658), p. 320.

[158] Gideon Harvey, *The vanities of philosophy & physick* (London, 1699), *Introduction*.

[159] Gerard, p. 1154.

[160] Herrick, *H-598*.

[161] Herrick, *H-650*, ll. 1-2.

[162] Letter from Beale to Hartlib, 9 April 1657, *Hartlib Papers LII*, in Webster, *The Great Instauration*, pp. 481-82.

[163] Vaughan, "Ascension-day," ll. 21-22.

[164] *A new orchard*, p. 57.

[165] Vaughan, "Unprofitableness," ll. 16-18.

[166] II Corinthians 2:14-16.

[167] Philippians 4:18.

[168] *The Workes of Tho: Adams* (London, 1630), p. 1037.

[169] Herbert, "The Odour," ll. 21-25.

[170] Herbert, "The Odour," l. 17. See also Traherne, "The Odour," "My Members all do yield a sweet Perfume," ll, l. 5; and "Admiration,' "Can Bodies fill the hev'nly Rooms/With welcom odours and Perfumes!," ll, ll. 8-9.

CHAPTER SIX
THE PARADISAL ESCHATOLOGY OF PLANTS IN POEMS

I

"Fill thy brest with home"[1]

Throughout this study the interdependence of plants and poems has become apparent: Vegetable philosophy, terracultural values, the hortulan saints, had a profound impact on poetry, providing it with Nature's treasures and with an exciting view of the place they occupied in the Grand Design of God; lyric, epic, and dramatic poetry captured the vegetable experience and vision, thrived on it, encouraged and enlarged it. Together plants and poems shared a Christian view of origin and destiny; combined they recalled and recreated Paradise, articulating and proclaiming a Paradisal eschatology. In the loveliness and energy of plants, the Paradise of

Adam and Eve and of the Paradise-to-come were reborn in the earth, in the books about the earth, and in the poetry. Poetic references to Paradise and all subsequent Paradises, and descriptions of all the vast creation of vegetable strength and beauty (by both terracultur-alists and poets), supported the growth of the kind of natural spiritual knowledge which originally had given Adam's life such dignity and joy:

> Only what Adam in his first Estate
>> Did I behold;
> Hard Silver and dry Gold
> As yet lay under ground: My happy Fate
>> Was more acquainted with the old
> And innocent Delights which he did see
> In his Original Simplicity.[2]

The power of plants and poems together to revitalize life, to freshen religious experience, to put eternity within reach, to reveal "th' Eternall root/Of true Love,"[3] was realized over and over again. In this chapter we shall look at 1) the hidden strength of plants, conferred upon them by God through the divine force of natural magic, to repel demons and to prevent demonic intervention in the vegetable creation for the distortion or destruction of human life; 2) at the crucial role plants played in counteracting death, lightening death's stain on human life, and foreshadowing Heaven; and 3) at the final integration of plants and poems, where "inserted into Him,"[4] vegetable actuality participated in metaphor, where vegetable metaphor glowed with actuality, and where both helped to fill the "brest with home."

II

"pleasing poison"[5]

Demonic intervention in nature to manipulate, distort, and deface human life is nowhere more obvious than in Milton's *A Mask at Ludlow Castle*. Comus, as imitative as is Satan in *Paradise Lost*, promises Paradise to his followers and to the young lady. Purporting to exalt God's vegetable creation by affirming its potency, Comus uses plants, as his mother taught him, to establish a false Paradisal bliss:

> I have oft heard
> My Mother *Circe* with the Sirens three,
> Amidst the flow'ry-kirl'd *Naiades*,
> Culling their Potent herbs and baleful drugs,
> Who as they sung, would take the prison'd soul,
> And lap it in *Elysium* . . .[6]   (252-257)

Comus and his rout spoil everything: They defile the beauties of the rural scene, they abort the natural wholesome uses of plants, they degrade human love, they distort the uses to which the Creator's beneficence should be put. They use nature unnaturally.

Milton's masque is interpenetrated by two kinds of magic: the unnatural magic practiced by Comus and the elves, and the natural magic practiced by the Attendant Spirit and Sabrina. These two kinds of magic, well known in Milton's day, were dealt with in many "Books of Secrets." Probably the most popular and representative statement concerning the distinction between the two kinds of magic was made by Giambattista della Porta in his *Natural Magick*. Della Porta defines magic as "Wisdom, and the perfect knowledge of natural things," and clearly outlines the differences:

> There are two sorts of Magick: the one is infamous, and unhappie, because it hath to do with foul spirits, and consists of Inchantments and wicked Curiosity: and this is called Sorcery; an art which all learned and good men detest . . .The other Magick is natural: which all excellent wise men do admit and embrace, and worship with great applause . . . The Platonicks, as Plotinus imitating Mercurius, writes in his book of Sacrifice and Magick, makes it to be a Science whereby inferiour things are made subject to superiours, earthly are subdued to heavenly; and by certain pretty allurements, it fetcheth forth the properties of the whole frame of the world . . .
>
> . . . Moreover, it is required of him, [the natural magician] that he be an Herbalist, not onely able to discern common Simples, but very skilful and sharp-sighted in the nature of all plants: for the uncertain names of plants, and their neer likeness of one to another, so that they can hardly be discerned, hath put us to much trouble in some of our

works and experiments . . . so the knowledge of plants is so
necessary to this profession, that indeed it is all in all.[7]

The herbalists, whose major concern was with the discovery of
the natural virtues of plants, warn of the unnatural uses of plants.
Gerard, for example, after describing the multiple uses of mullein,
refers to a tale in Apuleius where mullein was used by Ulysses,
Mercury, and Circe in "their incantations and witchcrafts."[8]
One of the less dynamic forms of unnatural magic mentioned in
the masque is that practiced by the elves. It is counteracted by the
natural magic of Sabrina's "precious vial'd liquors." The Attendant
Spirit praises Sabrina's natural uses of nature, referring to the fact
that the shepherds garland her herbal interventions in unnatural
magic:

>   . . . and oft at Eve
> Visits the herds along the twilight meadows,
> Helping all urchin blasts, and ill-luck signs
> That the shrewd meddling Elf delights to make,
> Which she with precious vial'd liquors heals.
> For which the Shepherds at their festivals
> Carol her goodness loud in rustic lays,
> And throw sweet garland wreaths into her stream
> Of pansies, pinks, and gaudy Daffodils.   (843-851)

Included in the occupational hazards of farming in Milton's day were
vegetable blight (diagnosed as "blasting") and the malady of
domestic animals described as "elf-shot." Reginald Scot, who in the
Discoverie of Witchcraft places urchins, elves, hags, fairies in the
same category, attributes blasts and diseases of cattle to these
malignant creatures.[9] William Perkins, also a writer on witchcraft,
considers the causes of blasting as unnatural: " . . . The wonders
done by Inchantment are, 1. The raising of stormes and tempests;
windes and weather, by sea and by land: 2. The poysoning of the
ayre: 3. Blasting of corne . . ."[10] Scot suggests a course of action to
counteract these malignant forces:

> But if you desire to learne true and lawfull charmes, to cure
> diseased cattell, even such as seeme to have Extra-
> ordinarie sicknesse, or to be bewitched, or (as they saie)
> strangelie taken: looke in *B. Googe* his third booke, treating
> cattell, and happilie you shall find some good medicine or

> cure for them: or if you list to see more ancient stuffe, read
> *Vegetius* his foure bookes thereupon: or, if you be un-
> learned, seeke some cunning bullocke leech. If all this will
> not serve then sett *Jobs* patience before your eies.[11]

Sabrina's precious liquors were a natural product, obtained from
herbs and prepared naturally:

> For the operations of Simples, do not so much consist in
> themselves, as in the preparing of them; without which
> preparation, they work little or nothing at all. There be
> many wayes to prepare Simples, to make them fitter for
> certain uses. The most usual wayes are, Steeping, Boiling,
> Burning, Powning, Resolving into ashes, Distilling, Drying,
> and such like.[12]

The minor demonic powers, though lower on the diabolic scale
than Satan, his angels, and Comus, nevertheless had a naggingly
disturbing effect on nature, on animals, and on humans. Milton
shows that it took no major angelic power to combat the "ill-luck
signs" of meddling elves and that the natural creation provided
plants for cures. Here again, Satan, interfering in Nature even at
petty levels to make Nature unnatural, is thwarted by the natural
remedies administered by one who has resisted demonic attractions.

The young lady in the masque is a long way from home when, deep
in the woods, she approaches the sensual snares of the demon-lover
Comus, and is misled by him to his "sensual sty." He comes from
illustrious demon stock: Bacchus and Circe are his nefarious
parents; his dazzling spells, magic chains, hellish charms, baleful
drugs and potent herbs, pleasing poison, orient liquor, gums of
glutinous heat, and limed-twig snares, show him as a skilled
naturalist in putting the vegetable creation to demonic unnatural
uses. He turns the salubrious virtues of plants into the salacious
faculties of plants cultivated by a long line of sorcerers — Medea,
Circe, and assorted "cacochymists." According to Pliny,

> . . . tales everywhere are widely current about Medea of
> Colchis and other sorceresses, especially Circe of Italy,
> who has even been enrolled as a divinity . . . Strong
> confirmatory evidence exists even today in the fact that the
> Marsi, a tribe descended from Circe's son, are well-known
> snake-charmers. Homer indeed, the first ancestor of

ancient learning . . . express[es] in several passages great
admiration for Circe . . . [13]

Comus himself is skilled in unnatural pharmacy. Having observed
his mother culling potent herbs and baleful drugs for evil purposes,
he excels even his mother in pharmaceutical skills:

> Excels his Mother at her mighty Art,
> Off'ring to every weary Traveller
> His orient liquor in a Crystal Glass,
> To quench the drought of *Phoebus,* which as they taste,
> (for most do taste through fond intemperate thirst)
> Soon as the Potion works, their human count'nance,
> Th' express resemblance of the gods, is chang'd
> Into some brutish form of Wolf, or Bear,
> Or Ounce, or Tiger, Hog, or bearded Goat,
> All other parts remaining as they were
> And they, so perfect is their misery,
> Not once perceive their foul disfigurement,
> But boast themselves more comely than before,
> And all their friends and native home forget,
> To roll with pleasure in a sensual sty.   (63-77)

The Attendant Spirit warns the young brothers of Comus's herbal
skills, especially in concocting potions to procure "venerial
delicacies":

> Deep skill'd in all his mother's witcheries,
> And here to every thirsty wanderer,
> By sly enticement gives his baneful cup . . .   (522-524)

In trying to entice the lady to amorous activities, Comus has
prepared an aphrodisiac potion made of vegetable spirits and
syrups:

>   . . . this cordial Julep here,
> That flames and dances in his crystal bounds
> With spirits of balm and fragrant Syrups mixt.
> Not that *Nepenthes* which the wife of *Thone*
> In *Egypt* gave to *Jove*-born *Helena*
> Is of such power to stir up joy as this,
> To life so friendly, or so cool to thirst.   (672-678)

Both natural and unnatural aphrodisiacs were available for

centuries. Natural aphrodisiacs, used to remedy impotence ("Venus imperfect") as well as to arouse sexual appetites, were known to have had varying degrees of success. The aphrodisiacs known to Chaucer's Merchant, for example, were found in *De Coitu* by Constantinus Africanus, and were vouched for by Constantinus's claims to successful clinical tests. Largely herbal, his recipes include such plants as asparagus, rag-wort, colewort, crocus, poppy, anise, hellebore, scammony.[14]

Theophile Bonet's *Mercurius compitalitius,* a practical medical guide to physicians (gathered from ancient as well as contemporary sources), includes a section on aphrodisiacs and prescriptions against salacity. In his description of Cantharides as an aphrodisiac, Bonet gives the case history of "two Noble-men, who used *Cantharides,* the one to gratifie his Whore, the other his new married Wife, but wholly with ill success: . . . first fell into a most dangerous pissing of Blood, of which he was Cured with great difficulty: And the other the second day after he was married, died of an Apoplexy."[15]

Herbalists and physicians listed herbs that provoked venery. William Coles devotes twenty-six chapters to those herbs that inflame the venereal instincts, and he singles out the Tree of Cacao and Chocolate as one that "vehemently incites to Venus," especially if "relented in Milke."[16] Gerard's entries on aphrodisiacs are numerous; he mentions that corne-flag, "the vpper root proueketh bodily lust,"[17] that Rocketseeds, Garden Cresses, Annise, Cheruill, Spignell, Herbe Ferula, ash, and many more, whether in distilled, roasted, powdered, or boiled form, all work for Venus. Herbalists also listed those herbs that are effective in abating lust: Coles recommends Agnus or chaste-tree, Hempe, Water Lilly, Hemlock, Camphire; and Gerard says that *"Agnus Castus* is a singular medicine and remedy for such as would willingly liue chaste, for it withstandeth all vncleannes, or desire to the flesh, consuming and drying vp the seed of generation, in what soeuer it bee taken, whether in pouder onely, or the decoction drunke, or whether the leaues be carried about the body . . . "[18]

Since the effects of aphrodisiacs were common knowledge, Milton had no difficulty in establishing their credibility in the masque. Within easy memory was the case of Sir John Colquhoun of Luss in

Dumbartonshire, who had married Lady Lilian Graham, a daughter
of the earl of Montrose, in 1633. "Her younger sister, the Lady
Katherine, came to reside with the married pair, and the faithless
baronet conceived an unlawful affection for his sister-in-law. At first
she remained cold to his advances, so he applied to a necromancer
for a love potion . . . which so worked upon the senses of the Lady
Katherine that she became infatuated with Sir John and finally
eloped with him to London . . . "[19] Another case which can be cited
is that of Lord Balmerino, a Scottish peer, who "died in 1612 from the
effects of a love philtre administered to him by a serving-maid in his
house . . . "[20] And then there were the unmentionable crimes of the
brother-in-law of the Earl of Bridgewater. He was beheaded on
Tower Hill May 14, 1631, for the crimes of rape and sodomy
perpetrated upon his wife, her daughter, his male servants. And,
although the Earl's trial records do not accuse him of using
aphrodisiacs, his pornographic methods of stimulating lust in his
victims were designed to create sensuality of the grossest sort, as
were Comus's lust-provoking potions.[21]

   Comus's demonic powers in the potions created diabolic side-
effects: his unnatural aphrodisiacs transformed humans into brutes.
The spiritual transformation of those who chose to drink was
accompanied by a change in physical appearance. While it was an
ancient commonplace that a brutish man begins to look like a beast,
the subject of physical metamorphosis was vigorously debated in the
Renaissance. William Perkins believed transformation to be a
delusion and the intervention of the devil in the visual processes:

> Delusion is then performed, when a man is made to thinke
> he sees that which indeede he sees not. And this is done by
> operation of the devill diuersly, but especially three waies.
> First, by corrupting the humor of the eye, which is the next
> instrument of sight. Secondly, by altering the ayre, which is
> the meane by which the object or *species* is carried to the
> eye. Thirdly, by altering and changing the object, that is, the
> thing seene, or whereon a man looketh.[22]

Della Porta, attributing transformation to natural magic, describes the phenomenon of altered perceptions as the direct result of using hallucinogenic herbs in potion form:

> For by drinking a certain Potion, the man would seem sometimes to be changed into a Fish; and flinging out his arms, would swim on the Ground: sometimes he would seem to skip up, and then to dive down again. Another would believe himself turned into a Goose: now and then sing, and endeavour to clap his Wings. And this he did with the aforenamed Plants [Stramonium, Solanum Manicum, Bella Donna]: neither did he exclude Henbane from among his Ingredients: extracting the essences by their Menstruum, and mix'd some of their Brain, Hart, Limbs, and other parts with them. I remember when I was a young man, I tried these things on my Chamber-Fellows: and their madness still fixed upon something they had eaten, and their fancy worked according to the quality of their meat. One, who had fed lustily upon Beef, saw nothing but the formes of Bulls in his imagination, and them running at him with their horns: and such-like things. Another man also by drinking a Potion, flung himself upon the earth, and like one ready to be drowned, struck forth his legs and arms, endeavouring as it were to swim for life: but when the strength of the Medicament began to decay, like a Shipwrack'd person, who had escaped out of the Sea, he wrung his Hair and his Clothes to strain the Water out of them; and drew his breath, as though he took such pains to escape the danger.[23]

And the physician John Cotta supported "local translation" by attributing to "the Divel, and his associates, Enchaunters, Witches, and Sorcerers" the power to enter into and possess human and animal bodies, and to work magic and mischievous effects "as is evident by the generally knoune power of the Magicke cups of the inchaunted Filtra or loue draughts."[24]

Whether or not there was metaphysical alteration in Milton's masque, the visual evidence of Comus's deceptions is everywhere apparent. While his potions promised heavenly ecstasies, they actually transformed humans into sub-rational and sub-moral creatures; and while Comus described his life and loves as spiritual, they were actually the reduction of life and loves to an imbruting physicality. The brothers in the masque, too inexperienced to know about demonic power over vegetables and still impervious to lust's charms, are persuaded by the mature experience of the Attendant Spirit of the power of Comus's herbal potions to incite to lust, to disfigure the human countenance, and to create depraved tastes by shackling the soul to the body.

After the young lady has successfully resisted Comus's entice-ments, Comus is still determined to trap the young "Nightingale" in his "deadly snare." Having glued the young lady to a "marble venom'd seat/Smear'd with gums of glutinous heat" (915-916), Comus presses her to reconsider swallowing his licentious baits. The gums that he has smeared on the seat operate through his "hellish charms." Their viscosity has been used unnaturally to immobilize the lady, though her virtuous will remains free. Physi-cians, herbalists, apothecaries, on the other hand, used gums "full of glutinous moisture"[25] for natural wholesome purposes — the gum sarcocola "sodereth and gleweth together woundes and cuttes of the flesh, euen as glewe doth ioyne togyther timber."[26]

Gums participated in a long natural and unnatural history. For legitimate practical purposes fowlers in Milton's day used a gummy glue to make lime-twig snares for birds. Even fifty years after Milton's masque, Worlidge devoted several pages of his *Systema Agricul-turae* to the making of lime from English holly berries to attract birds into lime-twig snares:

> Besides the Art of taking Fowl with Nets, there is a very ingenious way of taking them with Bird-lime, which seems very ancient; for *Pliny,* who lived about 1600 years since, not only mentions the use of it, in liming of Twigs to catch Birds withal, but the manner how the *Italians* prepared the same, of the *Berries* of *Misseltoe* . . . we have here in *England* a more easie and effectual way of preparing it with the Bark of that common and so well known Tree the *Holly;* which Preparation is thus . . . When you intend to use your Bird-lime for great Fowl, take of Rods long, small, and streight, being light, and yielding every way; Lime the upper parts of them before the Fire, that it may the better besmear them.

Then go where these Fowl usually haunt, whether it be
their Morning or Evening haunt, an hour to two before they
come, and plant your Twigs or Rods about a foot distance
one from the other, that they cannot pass them without
being intangled . . . [27]

Long before Milton wrote his masque, however, and before
Shakespeare wrote of "lay [ing] lime to tangle her desires," and his
Malvolio thanked Jove for having "lim'd her,"[28] the physical actuality
of lime-twigs and the spiritual reality of liming had coincided,
merged, blended, and eventually had totally united. Antedating
Worlidge's *Systema* were the treatises describing the use of the
Misseltoe tree glue *(Ixia)* for lime-twigs to catch birds and to ensnare
humans in sensual traps. The use of lime-twigs for actual bird snaring
is described for his countrymen by the native English herbalist
William Turner, whose early Greek source was Dioscorides:

The best missel byrde lyme/is freshe resemblinge a leke in
color within/but somthynge yelow wythoute . . . It is made
of a certayn round fruyte that groweth in an oke the leafe of
the bushe/that beareth it/is lyke unto boxe . . . This Missel
doth grow no other wayes/but by ye sede in such places
where as byrdes haue shitten out theyr excrementes in the
tre.
   Virgil also declareth the same in these two verses
folowynge.
      Quale solet syluis brumalis frigore viscum
      Fronde virere noua, quod non sua seminat arbos.
   By these places rehearsed/a man maye learne to vnder-
stande this prouerbe:
      Turdus ipse sibi malum cacat.
The thurse [*sic* thrush] shyteth mischefe to her self: She
shiteth out the miscel berries well prepared in her
bodye/and layeth them upon the tre/the berries grow into
abushe/and the bushe bringeth furth berries/ and of the
berries the fouler maketh byrde lyme/where wyth afterward
he taketh the thrushe/and so the thrushe hath shitten oute
her owne destruction. I neuer sawe more plentye of righte
oke miscel/then Hugh Morgan shewed me in London. It
was sente to hym oute of Essex . . . [29]

The spiritual reality, in which lime or glue had as venerable a use as the actual smearing of twigs for bird snares, draws on the actuality of lime-twigs to make the extended metaphor possible: "Turdus ipse sibi malum cacat." Pierre Courcelle, in his fundamental research on the word *glue* in the neo-platonic and Christian traditions, unravelled the intricate history of liming and discovered that birdlime was used to describe the descent of the soul into the body; the peril of pursuing sensible, secondary objects; carnal covetousness; and the devil as fowler, as well as other sensual activities.[30] St. Augustine used bird-lime in both spiritual and psychological contexts. In a rhapsodic passage in the *Confessions*, he praises God for beautiful objects apprehended by the senses, but he expresses the fear that the soul may be trapped by the lime or glue of these sensible objects and be unable to ascend to the Creator of this beauty:

> Let my soul praise you for these things, O God, Creator of them all; but the love of them, which we feel, through the senses of the body, must not be like glue to bind my soul to them. For they continue on the course that is set for them and leads to their end, and if the soul loves them and wishes to be with them and find its rest in them, it is torn by desires that can destroy it.[31]

In addition, Courcelle points out that several writers use *lime* or *glue* to describe the psychology of fornication:

> Of course, it is the sexual which is the stickiest of all these passions. The philosophy expressed in the *Phaedo* is here congruent with the teaching of Christianity. Indeed, St. Paul, in commenting on the verse in Genesis about a man and a woman being joined in a single flesh, writes that the man who cleaves to a prostitute forms a single body with her. According to Ambrosiaster, Augustine provides in a sermon an acute psychological analysis of fornication: even if other sins are engendered by the body, that sin which enslaves the soul to the highest degree, he states, is the sexual act, because at such a moment the soul is at this point glued to the body with which it becomes one, and no longer does there remain any possibility of its thinking of other subjects . . .
>
> This idea of the "sticking together" of a man and a woman

> through this illicit relation is found as a matter of course very
> often in patristic treatises . . . responsibility for this attach-
> ment is charged sometimes to the man, more often to the
> woman, viewed as the limed snare held by the devil-fowler.[32]

Comus is a clever, diabolical fowler: he knows the ancient tricks
for snaring "birds" in his "lime-twig" traps. As devil-fowler, he reveals
his lascivious ancestry by showing his skill in sorcery. His is the art of
transposing the natural uses of vegetables into their unnatural uses
where nature is so abused that those who are ensnared by this
attractive glue "roll with pleasure in a sensual sty" (78), all unaware
that they are hopelessly glued to and by their own lusts. Only natural
spiritual intervention by the Attendant Spirit and Sabrina can free
the young lady from the poisonous fetters of his glue. Sabrina, with
chaste palms and drops of water from her pure fountain, unglues the
lady. The Attendant Spirit uses the plant haemony (what has come
to be the most famous plant in seventeenth-century poetry) to
escape entrapment ("Enter'd the very lime-twigs of his spells,/And
yet came off" [646-647]) and to enable the young brothers to "assault
the necromancer's hall" (649) without peril.

Since many literary critics who have written on haemony are
unfamiliar with the natural powers of the vegetable world to
counteract demonic influence,[33] it will be necessary to establish its
identity as a natural substance with spiritual powers. The Attendant
Spirit gives a complete botanico-spiritual description of the plant:

> How to secure the Lady from surprisal,
> Brought to my mind a certain Shepherd Lad
> Of small regard to see to, yet well skill'd
> In every virtuous plant and healing herb
> That spreads her verdant leaf to th' morning ray.
> He lov'd me well, and oft would beg me sing,
> Which when I did, he on the tender grass
> Would sit, and hearken even to ecstasy,
> And in requital ope his leathern scrip,
> And show me simples of a thousand names,
> Telling their strange and vigorous faculties;
> Amongst the rest a small unsightly root,
> But of divine effect, he cull'd me out;
> The leaf was darkish, and had prickles on it,

But in another Country, as he said,
Bore a bright golden flow'r, but not in this soil:
Unknown, and like esteem'd, and the dull swain
Treads on it daily with his clouted shoon,
And yet more med'cinal is it than that *Moly*
That *Hermes* once to wise *Ulysses* gave;
He call'd it *Haemony,* and gave it me,
And bade me keep it as of sovran use
'Gainst all enchantments, mildew blast, or damp,
Or ghastly furies' apparition . . .   (618-641)

Milton's haemony is difficult to identify because it is described in the botanic vocabulary of the pre-Linnean world. It appears to belong to a genus of plants called *Hypericum L.,* which genus includes a number of species with an array of vernacular and scientific names such as St. John's Wort, Fuga Daemonum, Perforata (Porosa), and Androsaemon. Adding to the confusion is the fact that these various species were often mistaken for one another. John Hill, in *The British Herbal* (1756), more than a century after the masque, comments on the persistence of this problem in the *hypericum* genus and observes that these are all "frivolous and idle distinctions, and all tending to create confusion in the science; because the plants are all truly and properly allied."[34] William Salmon in *Botanologia* (1710) makes similar observations on *hypericum:* "There are two generick Kinds of *Hypericon,* or *Johnswort,* viz. I. *Hypericon vulgare,* which some have called *Fuga Daemonum* i.e. Drive Devil, and some *Androsaemum,* because the Flowers yield a bloody color . . ."[35] Other earlier botanists attempted to identify their contemporary plant with the androsaemon of Dioscorides, and called it "Hypericon. Androsaemon, Fuga Demonum. Perforata," and many other names.[36] It is obvious from the herbal accounts that the terms were interchangeable and that the distinctions made were flexible. Although John Parkinson lists fifteen varieties under *hypericon,* including St. John's Wort and Androsaemum,[37] and the Bobart Herbarium preserved at least five different types of Androsaemum (Androsaemum alterum hirsutum; Androsaemum foetidum, sive Tragodes; Androsaemum perfoliatum et perforatum; Androsaemum maximum bacciferum; Androsaemum flore maxime),[38] the characteristics and qualities of the plants overlap. The names under which haemony may be found are the following:

a. *Hypericum* (Latin), *Hypericon* (Greek). The name springs from the function. Etymology: *hyper* (Gr. *above, superior*); *eikon* (Gr. *image, specter*). Function: counteracts hallucinations, visions, phantasms, and apparitions caused by demons.

b. *St. John's Wort* (English). The name is commemorative for St. John the Baptist, on the eve of whose day (Midsummer Night's Eve) this plant was gathered as an efficacious demonifuge.

c. *Fuga Daemonum* (Latin). The name springs from the function. From antiquity it was reputed to be a potent demonifuge.

d. *Perforata; Porosa* (Latin). The name springs from its appearance, its leaves being pellucido-punctate.

e. *Androsaemum* (Latin), *Androsaemon* (Greek). The name springs from the appearance and function. Etymology: *aner*, gen., *andros* (Gr. *man*); *haima* (Gr. *blood*). The herbalists (whether English or continental) are unanimous in their explanation of this name: " . . . from the colour of the juyce which is in the Flowers [or leaves], resembling Mans blood, for so the Greek word signifies."[39]

Milton uses this name, *androsaemon*, for his haemony. Haemony, the *haemon* of *andros-haemon*, with the addition of y to anglicize it, fits the Attendant Spirit's herbal description of his demonifuge.[40]

The root of haemony is "small" and "unsightly." The herbalists describe the root of hypericon-androsaemon as "small and long,"[41] and as "hard and woody, with divers strings and Fibers at it."[42] The "darkish" leaf is the "deep green" of hypericon-androsaemon; the "prickles on it" are not thorns or spines but minute points or dots. One of the most prominent features of hypericon-androsaemon is its pellucido-punctate leaves, and Lyte's *Herball* leaves no doubt that the prickles on the leaves refer to these translucent dots — "as though they were pricked thorough with the poyntes of needels."[43] The "bright golden flowre," the "Goldfarben blümen" of the German herbalist Tragus,[44] is the color of the flower on the continent; in England it is yellow. Haemony is "Unknown, and like esteem'd"; *unknown* is a technical term used by herbalists to indicate that apothecaries did not recognize the pharmaceutical uses of a plant.[45] As for the "dull swain" treading on it daily "with his clouted shoon," the reference to the treading down of herbs by herbal clods is virtually a commonplace. George Herbert in his poem "Man" alludes to the fact that man "treads down that which doth befriend him,/When sicknesse makes him pale and wan"; and Donne, following Clement of Alexandria, says, "We tread upon many herbs negligently in the field, but when we see them in an Apothecaries shop, we begin to think that there is some vertue in them."[46]

It is its anti-enchantment properties that make it so potent a force against the demonic influence of Comus. The natural spiritual name *fuga daemonum* testified to God's beneficence in the creation of hypericon-androsaemon: "Since then because of the ready power of God and the light touch of his finger adverse powers are put to flight, and since God shows such marvelous pity on mankind through his creatures that *perforta herba* and *hipericon* through this heavenly power put demons to flight; and since for that reason it is regularly called by many people *fuga daemonum* . . . "[47] Paracelsus strongly recommends the use of hypericon-androsaemon to rout demons: ". . . you may carry it in your cap, or in your bosom: in the night you may lay it under your pillow: hang it about the chamber; and you may hang some of it in every room of your house."[48]

An account in Aubrey's *Miscellanies* helps to validate Milton's use of haemony in the masque. Aubrey relates an incident in which Henry Lawes, Milton's musical collaborator in the masque, had a direct experience with haemony's qualities as a demonifuge: "A House (or Chamber) somewhere in *London* was Haunted; the Curtains would be rashed at Night, and awake the Gentleman that lay there, who was Musical, and a familiar acquaintance of *Henry Laws, Henry Laws* to be satisfied did lie with him; and the Curtains were rashed so then: The Gentleman grew lean and pale with the frights, One Dr. _____ Cured the House of this disturbance, and Mr. *Laws* said, that the principal Ingredient was *Hypericon* put under his Pillow."[49]

The testimony is universal to the effectiveness of hypericon-androsaemon in combating enchantment. Not only does it cure a person who is "bewitched or inchanted, or forespoken," reports William Langham in *The Garden of Health*, but "kept in the house it suffereth no wicked spirit to come there."[50]

Its anti-"mildew blast, or damp" properties combat the "vaporous blastes and pestilent windes" produced by demons.[51] Wier recommends both moly and hypericon (an interesting juxtaposition since Milton compares moly and haemony in the masque) to combat the noxious harmful vapors of demons: "noxios malorum daemonum uapores."[52]

Hypericon-androsaemon was eminently successful in dispelling "ghastly furies' apparition," a magico-medical disease, with either external or internal causes. Milton vividly describes this kind of assault in *Paradise Regained:*

> . . . nor yet stay'd the terror there.
> Infernal Ghosts, and Hellish Furies, round
> Environ'd thee, some howl'd, some yell'd, some shriek'd,
> Some bent at thee thir fiery darts . . .
> And grisly Specters, which the Fiend had rais'd
> To tempt the Son of God with terrors dire.
>
> (IV. 421-24; 430-31)

Hypericon-androsaemon occupied a prominent place among the suggested remedies:

(1) William Coles prescribes hypericon-androsaemon: "It is called super imagines et Spectra dominum habeat . . . "[53]

(2) Burton cites and interprets Argentine: "*Rich. Argentine, de praestigiis daemonum cap.* 20 adds *hypericon* or S. John's wort, *perforata herba,* which by a divine virtue drives away Devils, and is therefore called *fuga daemonum:* all which rightly used by their suffitus, *Daemonum vexationibus obsistunt, afflictas mentes a daemonibus relevant, et venenatis fumis,* expels Devils themselves, and all divilish illusions . . . "[54]

(3) Oswaldus Crollius explains why hypericon-androsaemon is so effective: "The Strings upon the Leaves of *St. Johns-Wort* have the Signature, which being porous . . . expel all *Phantasmes* and *Phantastick Spirits* from and without man . . . it is also called *Fuga Daemonum* . . . *Portus Neapolitanus* affirms, that Malignant Spirits, that rejoyce in Darkness: So *St. Johns-wort* (among Solar Herbs accounted the chief) by *Paracelsus* dignified with the name of *Terrestrial Sol,* is found to be of like efficacy."[55]

(4) Paracelsus regards hypericon-androsaemon as a plant associated with light and as therefore possessing potent ingredients for dispelling the forces of darkness: "The straikes in the leaves like veines, shew us, that this herb drives away from a man Ghosts and night spirits, and spirits begot by imagina-

> tion, whether they be within a man or without; and these phantastick Spirits, which are begot by Phansie, do beget Ghosts, so that a man shall see spirits, visions, and hear such phansies . . . And for this disease there are no more remedies known that are created by God, but only Coral and St. Johns wort . . . As the sun-beam pierceth through glasses; so this vertue pierceth through the Spirits of men and beasts . . ."[56]

As a sorcerer-detection device hypericon-androsaemon was also well known. Milton's age did not underestimate the wiles of the devil, since he could go about disguised as an angel of light. The problem lay in the detection of such a sorcerer. Addressing himself to this problem, Lambert Daneau discusses the issue with dispassionate awareness of the devil's charms. Using etymology as well as myth, he defines the term *sorcerer* and describes the activities of the sorcerer to include enchantment, witchcraft, necromancy, magic. The realm of sorcery is as large as the world: sorcery can be performed on the air, herbs, trees, water, and can extend to metamorphosis. The point of Daneau's dialogue is to bring to the attention of the reader the sources available for detection and expulsion of sorcerers. Ultimately, he urges his readers to look to God, who had placed in the air a whole army of angels to protect believers from the sorcerer's assaults.[57] Milton, standing in that tradition, stresses this same source of strength: "A thousand liveried Angels lackey her,/Driving far off each thing of sin and guilt" (455-456). But, in addition, there were herbal amulets that were efficacious in sorcerer-detection. Hypericon-androsaemon was used to defend a young virgin's chastity by helping her to identify her lover as a sorcerer. According to the *Magna Vita S. Hugonis Episcopi Lincolniensi*, for example, a young girl was able to identify her young lovers as demons by their response to the St. John's Wort which she wore as an amulet in her bosom and which herb she had also scattered about her house. The demon-lovers could not consummate their love for her because they could not tolerate the smell of this herb: a devil finds the smell of hypericon-androsaemon putrid.[58] Thomas Jackson's *A Treatise Containing the Originall of Vnbeliefe, Misbeliefe, or Misperswasions* tells of a "maide that liked well of the devill making love to her in the habit of a gallant young man, but could not enjoy his company, nor he hers, so long as shee had

Vervine and *S. Iohns* grasse about her . . .[59]

Finally, the Attendant Spirit arms the young brothers with this anti-enchantment herb which also functions as a demonifuge. Natural means are employed to drive away the necromancer. Sinistrari's treatise on *Demoniality* gives the philosophical basis for the use of hypericon-androsaemon to rout demons:

It is indeed a trite philosophical axiom, that agent and patient must have a common subject: pure matter cannot act on any purely spiritual thing. Now, there are natural agents which act on those Incubi Demons: these are therefore material or corporeal. Our minor is proved by the testimony of Dioscorides, Pliny, Aristoteles and Apuleius, quoted by Guaccius, *Comp. Malef.* b. 3, ch. 13, fol. 316; it is confirmed by our knowledge of numerous herbs, stones and animal substances which have the virtue of driving away Demons, such as rue, St.-John's wort . . . and a hundred others: wherefore it is written: *For such as are assaulted by the Demon it is lawful to have stones or herbs, but without recourse to incantations.* It follows that, by their own native virtue, stones or herbs can bridle the Demon: else the above mentioned Canon would not permit their use, but would on the contrary forbid it as superstitious.[60]

The brothers, carrying the root of haemony, *"rush in with Swords drawn, wrest his Glass out of his hand, and break it against the ground; his rout make signe of resistance, but are all driven in"*; but they have not "snatcht his wand" (815). Haemony does not fail in the functions established by the Attendant Spirit; it is human error, not herbal failure, that causes the sister to remain in her "stonie fetters."

The foul-minded, the Comus-inspired, found poisons pleasing and depravities attractive, while Christians prayed that they might "from poyson be exempt."[61] Comus's offer of poison-induced bliss has the eschatology of a false Paradise: It is a substitute for the pre-lapsarian Paradise and for the Paradise-to-come. With the help of his "cordial julep" and "lime-twig" snares, Comus has filled his Paradise with humans and demons whose wills fetter them, whose appetites control them, whose natural powers betray them, whose lusts disfigure and transform them, and whose sorceries banish them eternally from human, angelic, and divine society. To virtuous humans, however, lackeyed by a "thousand liveried Angels," Heaven stoops to help. It provides divine antidotes in which Nature and Grace collaborate in attacking the devil's charms and false claims. The herbalists constantly pointed to the Providence of God in providing antidotes to poisons: "And yet let vs consider the fatherly care and prouidence of God, who hath prouided a conqueror and triumpher ouer this plant so venomous, namely his Antigonist . . ."[62]

In Milton's masque, andros-haemony emerges as the potent demonifuge whose natural qualities work a mighty spiritual effect. Haemony forces evil to recoil and dwell no more with Goodness. Milton's poetry shows that haemony, the living, perfect vegetable antidote to "pleasing poison," is indeed the "root of divine effect" whose effective demonifuge action in field and poem declares "thEternall root/Of true love."

III

"A Garland, where comes neither rain, nor wind"[63]

The most eschatological of garlands was the epicedial garland. Sixteenth and seventeenth century poets and terraculturalists understood that if the process of mourning was to be more than a series of stages to overcome grief, or to keep alive the quickly fading image of the dead, it was imperative to evoke the memory of "Eden so divine and fair"[64] in order to raise the hope of living in Paradise, forever "past changing," "where no flower can wither."[65] Not to reflect on Paradise at a death was to squander valuable God-given opportunities for comfort. Plants and poems were used regularly to evoke Paradise. Plants — "some Flowers and some Bays/For thy Hearse to strew the ways"[66] — served to "sticke and decke forth" the bodies and hearses of the dead:

Laurus, the Bay Tree.
   The Bay leaues . . . serue both for pleasure and profit, both for ornament and for vse, both for honest Ciuill vses, and for Physicke, yea both for the sicke and for the sound, both for the liuing and for the dead: And so much might be said of the Reader, as the Relater: but to explaine my selfe; It

serueth to adorne the house of God as well as of man . . . to
crowne or encircle as with a garland, the heads of the liuing,
and to sticke and decke forth the bodies of the dead: so that
from the cradle to the graue we have still vse of it, we have
still neede of it.[67]

And poems offered a "melodious tear" for a "destin'd Urn."[68] Since
death is an "uncouth hideous thing,"[69] plants and poems served to
beautify its ugly visage with solemn garlanded assurances of an
unspoiled life in a new Paradise. Epicedial poetry was itself garlanded
with funebrial plants — "with Funerall Wreath's ingarlanding His
Browes";[70] plants wove themselves dexterously into the sense of
poems. There was scarcely a funeral elegy to be found that did not
use plants to alleviate the suffering of the mourners; to lighten
death's dark stain on human life by providing some intimations of
immortality; to attest to the certainty of a Paradise after death (in
Hebrew and Christian burials) where garlands never fade and
humans never die. In garlands, as in death, "beginnings touch their
END[71] and "ends crowne our workes, but thou crown'st our
ends"[72]; from the end of life the crown of life is fashioned, and, in the
beginning of the new life, a never-fading garland is formed.

The ancients saw the aptness of garlands for the dead. As Dr.
Thomas Browne observed, "flowry Crowns and Garlands is not of
slender Antiquity, and higher than I conceive you apprehend it. For,
besides the old Greeks and Romans, the AEgyptians made use
hereof . . . in Gestatory, Portatory, Suspensory, Depository
form."[73] Plants crowd the pages of funebrial history and poetry,
displaying themselves in representational form on sarcophagi and
monuments, in catacombs and forums, and later in both actual and
representational form in churches.

In ancient drama the funerary garland was essential to proper
burial. In Euripides' The Women of Troy Talthybios tells Hecabe
how Andromache has pleaded with the Greek Neoptolemos for
Astyanax to be given a proper burial; that is, laid on Hector's shield
rather than in a cedar or stone coffin and put in Hecabe's arms "so
that she would wrap the corpse with funeral robes and garlands."[74]
In the elegiac tradition, the shade of Cynthia, Propertius's mistress,
reproaches him for not giving her a proper funeral; it is her old
servant, Petale, who has correctly observed her death by bringing
garlands to the sepulchre:

> nostraque quod Petale tulit ad minumenta coronas,
> codicis immundi unicula sentit anus.[75]

In earliest times, it seems that the garland was placed on the head of the dead person by his close relative or by his dearest friend: Pericles himself placed a funerary garland on the head of his dead son.[76] And sometimes, perhaps to add to the poignancy, the funerary garland was placed awry on the head:

> et stygio sum sparsa lacu, nec recta capillis
> uitta data est.[77]

Even the bark which conveyed the shades across the Styx was wreathed: "ecce coronato pars altera rapta phaselo"[78]; in that same spirit Herrick, sailing to the haven of eternal life, asks that his bark be garlanded:

> MY wearied Barke, O Let it now be Crown'd!
> The Haven reacht to which I first was bound.[79]

As archaeological evidence has shown, the garlanding of the dead played a major part in Judaic burial rites. In his study *Martyrer-kranz*, Antonius J. Brekelmans calls special attention to a votive picture in a mosque-column which is immured in a wall at Djamiel-Kebir in Gaza where a Hebrew inscription is flanked by a palm and the garland consists of laurel leaves and a band of ivy leaves.[80] The significance of the garland lay in its ability "to intensify the symbolic value for immortality."[81]

In paleo-Christianity, the eschatological garland was often found in the context of martyrdom and death: "Auf einer jetzt verlorenen Grabplatte an der Via Salaria wurde von Liberalis, einem ehemaligen Konsul, gesagt: 'gratia cui trabeas dederat, dedit ira coronam.' "[82] It is to this type of garland that Milton refers in *Epitaphium Damonis:*

> Ipse, caput nitidum cinctus rutilante corona,
> Laetaque frondentis gestans umbracula palmae,
> Aeternum perages immortales hymenaeos . . .   (215-217)

That sixteenth and seventeenth century England continued the practice of garlanding the dead is evident from a letter which was published in *The Gentleman's Magazine* of 1747:

> In this nation . . . by the abundant zeal of our ancestors,

virginity was held in great estimation; insomuch that those which died in that state were rewarded, at their deaths, with a garland or crown on their heads, denoting their triumphant victory over the lusts of the flesh . . . And, in the year 1733, the present clerk of the parish church of *Bromley* in *Kent,* by his digging a grave in that church-yard, close to the east end of the chancel wall, dug up one of these crowns, in filagree work with gold and silver wire, in resemblance of myrtle (with which plant the funebrial garlands of the ancients were compos'd.) . . .

Besides these crowns, the ancients had also their depository garlands, the use of which were continued even till of late years (and perhaps are still retain'd in many parts of this nation, for my own knowledge of these matters extends not above 20 or 30 miles round *London*) which garlands, at the funerals of the deceas'd, were carried solemnly before the corps by two maids, and afterward hung up in some conspicuous place within the church, in memorial of the departed person . . .

About 40 years ago these garlands grew much out of repute, and were thought, by many, as very unbecoming decorations for so sacred a place as the church; and at the reparation, or new beautifying several churches, where I have been concern'd, I was oblig'd, by order of the minister and church-wardens, to take the garlands down, and the inhabitants strictly forbid to hang up any more for the future. Yet notwithstanding, several people, unwilling to forsake their ancient and delightful custom, continued still the making of them, and they were carried at the funerals, as before, to the grave, and put therein, upon the coffin, over the face of the dead; this I have seen done in many places.[83]

A garland was a "guerdon" — a reward, a recompense. Poets and gardeners, among others, asked for this guerdon at their deaths. The young poet Milton in *Lycidas,* for example, brings a garland and a poem (or a poetic garland, or a garlanded poem) for his young friend drowned at sea:

Yet once more, O ye Laurels, and once more
Ye Myrtles brown with Ivy never sere,
I come to pluck your Berries harsh and crude,
And with forc'd fingers rude,
Shatter your leaves before the mellowing year . . .

> He must not float upon his wat'ry bier
> Unwept, and welter to the parching wind,
> Without the meed of some melodius tear.   (1-5, 12-14)

And the gardener Rea, in a poem at the end of his gardening book, craves flowers for his grave and "one sprig of Bays" for his hearse:

> And for my guerdon this is all I crave,
> Some gentle hand with Flowers may strew my Grave,
> And with one sprig of Bays my Herse befriend,
> When as my Life, as now my Book, doth End.[84]

Both Milton and Rea knew how important this guerdon was, since plants and poems spoke eloquently in death of the new life in Paradise:

> So *Lycidas*, sunk low, but mounted high,
> Through the dear might of him that walk'd the waves,
> Where other groves, and other streams along,
> With *Nectar* pure his oozy Locks he laves,
> And hears the unexpressive nuptial Song,
> In the blest Kingdoms meek of joy and love.   (172-177)

Not to bring a garland was to create a harsh silence about the hope of Heaven, for "what is so shrill as silent tears?"[85]

Even empty tombs, according to John Weever, the Renaissance historian of ancient and contemporary burial practices, were erected and garlands made for those whose bodies had perished and who left no physical remains for burial:

> A Cenotaph is an emptie Funerall Monument or Tombe, erected for the honour of the dead, wherein neither the corps, nor reliques of any defunct, are deposited, in imitation of which our Hearses here in England are set vp in Churches, during the continuance of a yeare, or for the space of certaine moneths ... The second kinde of Cenotaphs were made *Religionis causa*, to the memory of such whose carcases, or dispersed reliques, were in no wise to be found, for example, of such as perished by shipwracke ... To these *inania busta*, or *vacua Sepulchra*, the friends of the defunct would yearely repaire ...[86]

For Edward King, the young Cambridge scholar who drowned in the Irish Sea on August 10, 1637, death came too soon. His was an

empty hearse, a *vacua Sepulchra,* to which his young friend John
Milton brought a garland woven of immortal poetry and immortal
plants. This garland was not the kind of garland that was banned
from churches, though it was made of funebrial plants used in both
pagan and Christian garlands. In choosing laurels, myrtles, and ivy
for Lycidas's garland, the poet calls to mind the values and vision of
burial garlanding. Laurel, which is evergreen, has "a dark greene
barke," and "berries that are a little long as well as round, whose
shell or outermost peele is greene at the first."[87] Used for centuries in
magic, folklore, medicine, pharmacy;[88] as a symbol of victory,
salvation, rescue;[89] and especially in funeral garlands, as Parkinson
observed, "to sticke and decke forth the bodies of the dead," it
shaded the tomb of King Bebryx at the Harbour of Amycus,[90] the
grave of Milton's Samson (" . . . and plant it round with shade/Of
Laurel ever green," 1734-1735), appeared on the stone of Susannah
Jayne in Marblehead, Massachusetts, 1776, where it crowns an
elaborately carved skeleton,[91] was placed as a wreath on the tomb of
the Unknown Soldier in Rome by Emperor Haile Selassi of
Ethiopia,[92] and is the tree that Herrick chose to assure him of
personal immortality:

> A Funerall stone,
> Or Verse I covet none;
> But onely crave
> Of you, that I may have
> A sacred Laurel springing from my grave:
> Which being seen,
> Blest with perpetuall greene,
> May grow to be
> Not so much call'd a tree,
> As the eternall monument of me.[93]

Laurel's eschatological context is most apparent in the Post-
Apostolic age, where it appears on the Passion Sarcophagi. The
most famous of these sarcophagi can be seen in the Lateran
Museum: On the left "Simon of Cyrene carrying the Cross and the
'crowning' of Our Lord with the wreath of victory; the crown of
thorns is replaced by one of laurel. In the central niche the focal point
is the cross-monogram of Christ; the wreath hangs from the beak of
an eagle . . . The sarcophagus dates from about 350. The motif of the

'Trophy of the Cross' was adopted into the liturgy and also into the preaching . . . It is still heard during Holy Week in the hymns of Venantius Fortunatus on the Cross . . ."[94] The laurel of military victory was transformed by Christ's death and resurrection into the laurel of eternal victory over sin and death. In the garland of the laureled Christ was the embodiment of the promise of life everlasting for believers — "Today shalt thou be with me in Paradise."

Myrtle, which as we have seen in the letter in *The Gentleman's Magazine* was "most artificially wrought in filgaree work with gold and silver wire, in resemblance of myrtle (with which plant the funebrial garlands of the ancients were compos'd.)," is evergreen, is "couered with a browne bark," and in "England they neuer beare any fruit."[95] Used in wedding garlands,[96] in cultic religions,[97] in purifications[98]; as a wreath of ovation,[99] as a festive garland at circuses,[100] myrtle was regarded from antiquity as an appropriate funebrial plant. The Euripidean Electra weeps for desolation:

> And Agamemnon's tomb is set at naught:
> Drink-offerings never yet nor myrtle-spray
> Had it, a grave all bare of ornament.[101]

In the context of Elysium, the poet Suckling asks for bays "or myrtle bough" for the "noble martyrs here . . ."[102]

Ivy, the leaves "abiding fresh and greene Winter and Summer," did not flower in England until July, and the "berries are not ripe usually untill about Christmas."[103] As early as the Mycenean epoch, ivy leaves were painted on vases and continued to appear in ancient art on vases, drinking cups, columns, statues, sarcophagi.[104] Archaeologists discovered ivy as a funerary plant on an ivy-decorated mask in an Etruscan grave, and in still another grave a metal ivy wreath with leaves and berries.[105] In the elegiac tradition, the shade of Cynthia pleads with her survivor Propertius to plant ivy on her tomb:

> pone hederam tumulo, mihi quae praegnant corymbo
> mollis contortis alliget ossa comis.[106]

An illustrious garland plant, ivy was woven into the wreath that Alexander wore when he returned from India with his victorious army.[107]

Ivy's eschatological uses were so widespread in the Greco-Roman world that ivy leaves became a part of the symbolic vocabulary of artisans. A glance at sarcophagi reveals the ubiquity of ivy as a symbol of immortality:

> Toutes les essences à feuillage persistant, qui restent verdoyantes quand la nature se meurt, comme le pin, le cyprès, le laurier sont pour ce motif devenus des plantes funéraires. . . A Vence . . ., un cyprès se dresse de chaque côte du croissant. Pareillement le lierre, dont le feuillage n'est point caduc, et qui appartient à Bacchus, dieu d'une religion de salut, semblait doué d'un pouvoir de renouveau, qui faisait triompher du trépas . . .[108]

The Jewish symbols of the Greco-Roman period abound in affirmations of the after-life. Goodenough's statement that "Pagan motifs in Jewish synagogues and the graves have already led us to suspect that Jews used them to express faith in heaven, in the love of God, in coming victory,"[109] is supported by his studies of the paintings of the Dura Europas synagogue. What art historians had at first regarded as decorative borrowings from the pagan world emerged, upon investigation, as a full set of symbols to express confidence in the existence of the life after death. Bacchus, dolphins, and ivy on Christian sarcophagi, Goodenough concludes, "refer to hope of life after death . . . refer that is, to heaven."[110]

There is in Lycidas's laurel-myrtle-ivy garland a special pain and sadness. The berries are unripe for garlanding: laurel berries are still green, myrtle berries never ripen in England, and ivy's season for fruiting has been disturbed. These berries are no more ripe for plucking than Lycidas is for death. The poet's fingers — "forc'd fingers rude" — are the fingers of one too young to participate in preparing a funerary garland. It is for the old to die, for the old to garland the old; and, although the young are occasionally called upon to weave a funerary garland for one of their peers, there is something inexperienced, clumsy, poignant, about the young burying the young. Because of the death of his young friend, there is in Milton's life a dislocation; and there is a consequent dislocation in Nature where laurel, myrtle, and ivy leaves must be "shattered before the mellowing year." *To shatter* is not to "do damage ruinously or to damage or destroy by fracture of the parts," but it is, according to the agriculturalists, "to cause (seed, leaves, etc.) to fall or be shed."[111] Rising from the opening lines of *Lycidas* is the image of a premature death and burial, of an immature funebrial poet-garland-weaver, and of three immature funerary plants with unripe berries. All belong at the funeral of one too young to die.

Milton begins *Lycidas* by calling on laurels, myrtles, and ivy to function "Yet once more" as funebrial plants. Twice before, at two untimely deaths, Milton had to weave a funerary garland: for the Fair Infant Dying of a Cough and for the Marchioness of Winchester. For the Marchioness he chose bays (laurels) — the laurels that through the "laurelled Christ" lead the mourners to see the transformation of the marchioness into "bright saint" now sitting high in glory. For Lycidas Milton chose laurels, myrtles, and ivy — in whose leaves, bark, and berries eschatology had been woven and interwoven for centuries of Christian burials. This garland leads the mourners from the sad sight of the body of Lycidas hurled to "the bottom of the monstrous world" to the vision of Lycidas "mounted high . . ./In the blest Kingdoms meek of joy and love." Victimized by that "perfidious bark," Lycidas is a victor "Through the dear might of him that walk'd the waves." The strains of the opening dirge are replaced by the resonances of the solemn and victorious song: "Yet once more" is counterpointed by "Weep no more." In the funerary garland for Lycidas is the preparation for celebration. The process of mourning has been turned into the litany of singing:

> There entertain him all the Saints above,
> In solemn troops, and sweet Societies
> That sing, and singing in their glory move,
> And wipe the tears for ever from his eyes.   (178-181)

Garlands, then, by their form and substance were a continuing witness to victory over death. Christians who looked forward to singing in those sweet societies of Heaven, to joining Lycidas in the "blest Kingdoms meek of joy and love," saw that in the crown of life was the shape of the crown of thorns. Not all garlands, to be sure, functioned eschatologically. But for those that did, their "bright shoots of everlastingness" were rooted in the death and resurrection of the One "Which cannot die, yet cannot chuse but die."[112] It was the cross that spawned immortal crowns. At the dawning of the day of Christ's return to earth, Vaughan has a vision of culmination and fruition: he sees Christ's "locks crown'd with eternitie"[113] and knows that he will share in that crowning.

For those poets and terraculturalists who practiced the craft of garlanding, both actual and symbolic, there was the spontaneous confession that all mortal fingers were rude and unfit. They relied on the God of Nature, who was also the God of Grace, to transform mortal fingers into graceful and fit instruments for eternal garlanding. In garlands Nature and Grace met, intertwined, and never parted. Stephen Blake, gardener, when surrounded by hortulan saints whose faithfulness to terraculture had earned them an earthly crown, prayed for translation to the realm where, surrounded by saints and angels, faithful gardeners would receive "an immortal crown."[114] Marvell, although he dismantled "all the fragrant towers" to prepare a garland for the Savior's head, failed; his own mortal craftlessness disqualified him for garlanding the Saviour. Marvell prays, therefore, that Christ will prepare His own garland.[115] Donne, too, in the exquisite poetic garland woven for Christ in the poet's "devout melancholy," knows how frail poetic bays are; he asks that the thorny garland of Christ will replace the frail bays with "A crowne of Glory, which doth flower always."[116] Crashaw's garland for the "Dread Lambe" at His Nativity is transfigured into the garland of God's death with the promise of life that shall never die."[117] For Herbert, life itself is a garland, a wreath, woven out of the "simplicitie" that directs the Christian's life to Christ's "wayes." As the poet Herbert reaches the end of His life-garland, the Lord of Life shows the poet the startling truth that the wreath of life has become a "crown of praise" to be given by the human recipient back to the Divine Giver.[118] It is Vaughan's "ensuing story" that tells the full tale of eschatology. A garland gives coherence to life and to death. The garland on earth, made of plants and poetry, will "quite vanish and decay." It must vanish and decay before the heavenly garland can be worn — "A Garland, where comes neither rain, nor wind."

IV

All things here shew him heaven . . .
trees, herbs, flowres, all
Strive upwards stil, and point him the way home.[119]

Since the terraculturalists of the sixteenth and seventeenth centuries were so influential in restoring Nature to its rightful place in the universe of God's love, and in reinstating all forms of terraculture to their proper place in the vocational order of God's love, poets could not help enjoying the effects of that effort and sharing in the adventure by giving terraculture a sacred place in the created world of their own poetry. God was for terraculturalists and for poets (as He was for centuries of Christendom before them) the "pre-eternal husbandman" of all creation[120] — the husbandman, also, of the plants, gardens, gardeners, terraculturalists that lived in their contemporary world and in their poetry. The plants, then, that appeared in the poetry were not private poetic, metaphorical creations whose reality was established, defined, and limited by a poem. Because the plants that existed in a poem had a reality outside the poem as well as inside the poem, plant and poem participated in a kind of hypostatical union: the flesh of the plant was united to the spirit of the poem, the spirit of the plant was united to the flesh of the word. In this hypostatic union it was inconceivable to speak of a "merely literal" meaning of a plant in poem, just as it was not possible to think of a plant existing in the natural world apart from its spiritual source and identity. As God's creation of plants was more than an aesthetic act, so the presence of terraculture in poetry and the recognition of the value of plants was more than an aesthetic act on the part of the poet. As Traherne knew, and as he urged his readers to suppose with him:

> Suppose . . . an Herb: GOD knoweth infinit Excellencies in it more than we: He seeth how it relateth to Angels and Men; How it proceedeth from the most perfect Lover to the most Perfectly Beloved; how it representeth all His Attributs; How it conduceth in its Place, by the best of Means to the Best of Ends: And for this Caus it cannot be Beloved too much. GOD the Author and GOD the End is to be Beloved in it: Angels and Men are to be Beloved in it: And it is highly to be Esteemed for all their Sakes . . . Who can lov any Thing that God made too much? . . . What a World would this be, were evry thing Beloved as it ought to be![121]

One of our contemporary poets, Norman Nicholson, expressing frustration with the twentieth-century mental and imaginative process that is so bent on determining what is "literal" and what is "metaphoric" in Nature and Grace, attempts to understand the relationship of symbol to what-is-symbolized by exploring the relationship of God to the burning bush in which He actually appeared to Moses. Nicholson discovers that to cut the actual fire and bush from the spiritual reality of God-in-the-burning-bush is to make a fatal incision — fatal for the reality of both Nature and God:

> When Moses, musing in the desert, found
> The thorn bush spiking up from the hot ground,
> And saw the branches on a sudden bear
> The crackling yellow barberries of fire,
>
> He searched his learning and imagination
> For any logical, neat explanation,
> And burned to go, but turned again and stayed
> And faced the fire and knew it for his God.
>
> I too have seen the briar alight like coal,
> The love that burns, the flesh that's ever whole,
> And many times have turned and left it there,
> Saying: "It's prophecy — but metaphor."
>
> But stinging tongues like John the Baptist shout:
> "That this is metaphor is no way out
> It's dogma too, or you make God a liar;
> The bush is still a bush, and fire is fire."[122]

The plants that appeared in an eschatological setting in the poems of the sixteenth and seventeenth centuries retained their existence in the natural world as they witnessed in the world and in the poem to the Paradise-to-come. As Biblical types retain their actuality as they simultaneously reveal their antitypes, so the natural world retained its actuality as it revealed its eschatological reality. Buds, flowers, herbs, roots, weeds, trees, gardens, gardeners, which were actual outside the poem, existed in the poem in a kind of "hypostatical union" with the "flesh" and "spirit" of the poem, becoming one "person" with the "nature and Godhead" of the poem. This is to say, there was no separating of the actual natural world outside the poem from the actual and symbolic world within the poem; just as there was no separating the actual plants in the world of nature from the spiritual world of the Creator whose presence filled the natural world and whose Grace rehabilitated it.

It was a habit of mind, a mode of apprehension, a vision of reality, a religious faith, that enabled poets and terraculturalists to see eternity in the temporal, the supernatural in the natural, the Creator in the creature, the symbol in the actual, and to retain the identity of each. In his address to his "Critical Peruser," Traherne regards the hypostatic union between God's created world and world of poetry as significant because, only when plants in poems are united to "God's diviner Works," can the eyes of human beings be open to "Great *Felicity*," to a view of eternity — not through "Poëtick Strains and Shadows" but through God's real works, not the poet's "verbal Ones."[123] Recalling human Edenic innocence at birth, Traherne catches in the natural world the resemblance of eternity.[124] As Traherne travels through the "World of Delight," he remembers Paradise as he sees

> That Prospect was the Gate of Heav'n, that Day
> The ancient Light of Eden did convey
> Into my Soul: I was an Adam there,
>   A little Adam in a Sphere
> Of Joys! O there my Ravisht Sence
> Was entertaind in Paradice . . .[125]

Walking on through life, Traherne admires "the pretty Flow'rs/With their sweet Smell" and knows that by them the final glory of eternity is conveyed:

> While in those pleasant Paths we talk
> 'Tis *that* tow'rds which at last we walk;
>   But we may by degrees
>   Wisely proceed
> Pleasures of Lov and Prais to heed,
>   From viewing Herbs and Trees.[126]

If we are to catch Vaughan's vision in "The Constellation," where he observes that "The herb he treads knows much, much more,"[127] we must see the hypostatical union of herb and poem as Vaughan saw them. Vaughan's herb knows its Father, the "pre-eternal husbandman"; knows its Redeemer, Christ the "All Heal"; knows its divinely ordained function in the actual world: to heal human diseases and wounds; knows its place in the poem and in the symbolic order: to reveal the One who heals all human diseases and wounds, both physical and spiritual. When Vaughan speaks of the leaf that "hath his *Morning*-hymn" and sees that "Each *Bush*/and *Oak* doth know I AM,"[128] he is not wandering in a labyrinth of cosmic symbols nor is he trapped by the metaphors of his poem; he is remembering, however, that all created reality has also a spiritual reality and that the Creator who described Himself as I Am when he spoke to Moses from the burning bush (Exodus 3:14) is the same I Am of the New Testament (John 8:58) who redeems mankind and leaves, bushes, and oaks and continues to reveal His redemptive presence in them. Leaves, bushes, oaks, take their significance in Vaughan's poem from their natural-supernatural presence in the created and redeemed worlds outside the poem.

For Vaughan "Mornings are Mysteries." Each morning is an occasion for an unveiling of the human body and soul, with nature providing the model for such radiant worship:

> True hearts spread, and heave
> Unto their God, as flow'rs do to the Sun.[129]

In Vaughan's Christian world, *mystery* takes its meaning from the Latin *mysterium*, where, as part of the long Christian tradition, *mysterium* means *sacrament, symbol, revelation*.[130] This *mystery* reveals rather than conceals, illumines rather than obscures. Vaughan's "morning mystery" declares itself and then points to a reality greater than itself: it shows that all mornings are awakenings because they receive their light from the Light of the World, whose created and resurrection light is mysteriously infused into all mornings. At the Resurrection point, all mornings are mysteries — witnesses to Christ's rising from the dead, to our risings from the deathbed of sin, and to "The Dawning" of our eternal rising with Him. The eschatology emerges in Vaughan's poetry as a result of his primary experience in the plant world:

> *Mornings* are *Mysteries;* the first worlds *Youth,*
> Mans *Resurrection,* and the futures *Bud* . . .[131]

As natural mornings receive their light from the Eternal Morning, so the plant All-Heal in the natural world and in Herbert's poem receives its healing graces from Christ, the All-Heal. By drawing the two natures of Christ into his poem "An Offering," Herbert also reveals the two natures of the Plant All-Heal — the actual and the symbolic. Offering to the believer a kind of hypostatic union with the Saviour through His All-Heal powers, the poet tenderly observes that "In Christ two natures met to be thy cure." The open wounds of the heart are healed by All-Heal:

> There is a balsome, or indeed a bloud,
> Dropping from heav'n, which doth both cleanse and close
> All sorts of wounds; of such strange force it is.
> Seek out this All-heal, and seek no repose,
> Untill thou finde and use it to thy good:
> Then bring thy gift, and let thy hymne be this . . .[132]

Citing the spiritual case-history of All-Heal — Christ has healed hearts of "many holes" — Herbert also reminds the reader of the vivid case-histories recorded by the herbalists of the miraculous power of the plant All-heal to cure flesh wounds, almost mortal wounds:

> The leaues hereof stamped with *Axungia* or hogs grease, and applied vnto greene wounds in manner of a pultesse, healeth them in short time, and in such absolute manner, that it is hard for any that haue not had the experience thereof to beleeue: for being in Kent about a Patient, it chanced that a poore man in mowing of Peason did cut his leg with a sithe, wherein he made a wound to the bones, and withall very large and wide, and also with great effusion of bloud; the poore man crept vnto this herbe, which he bruised with his hands, and tied a great quantity of it vnto the wound with a piece of his shirt, which presently stanched the bleeding, and ceased the paine, insomuch that the poore man presently went to his dayes worke againe, and so did from day to day, without resting one day vntill he was perfectly whole . . . my selfe haue cured many grieuous wounds, and some mortall, with the same herbe; one for example done vpon a Gentleman of Grayes Inne in Holborne, Mr. *Edmund Cartwright*, who was thrust into the lungs, the wound entring in at the lower part of the *Thorax*, or the brest-blade, euen through that cartilaginous substance called *Mucronata Cartilago*, insomuch that from day to day the frothing and pussing of the lungs did spew

forth of the wound such excrements as it was possessed of, besides the Gentleman was most dangerously vexed with a double quotidian feuer; whom by Gods permission I perfectly cured in very short time . . .

In like manner I cured a Shoo-makers seruant in Holburne, who intended to destroy himselfe for causes knowne vnto many now liuing: but I deemed it better to couer the fault, than to put the same in print, which might moue such a gracelesse fellow to attempt the like: his attempt was thus; First, he gaue himselfe a most mortall wound in the throat, in such sort, that when I gaue him drinke it came forth at the wound, which likewise did blow out the candle: another deep and grieuous wound in the brest with the said dagger, and also two others in *Abdomine* or the nether belly, so that the *Zirbus* or fat, commonly called the caule, issued forth, with the guts likewise: the which mortall wounds, by Gods permission, and the vertues of this herbe, I perfectly cured within twenty dayes: for the which the name of God be praised.[133]

In Herbert's poem, *All-Heal* reveals His Father, the "pre-eternal husbandman." The whole world is God's garden: the herbs in it are His and are placed there by Him for healing man's wounds.[134] The poem shows *All-Heal* as Redeemer; as the source of virtue of the actual plant All-Heal; and as the Living Plant from whom all actual created plants receive their life and power.

Man was not always miserable and in need of healing. Originally he lived in Eden where "He was a garden in a Paradise"; but "sinne hath fool'd him," cutting him off from a "glimpse of blisse,"[135] blighting his garden: his bud, flowers, leaves, shrivelled and died, his ground grew barren. Ultimately, he was reduced to such a fearful state that, although the cross and the "cordials and cathartics" of Christ's blood[136] promised him restoration, judicious pruning by Christ the Gardener was necessary to prepare him for life in the eternal Paradisal Garden. Following the terraculturalists like Blith, Gerard, Parkinson, Coles, Grew, Worlidge, Gilbert, Blake, Beale, Austen, who believed that England could be restored to a Paradisal state through the grace of the Redeemer's blood and through subsequent intelligent terracultural practices, Herbert proved to be a poetic terraculturalist in his poem "Paradise" by demonstrating that through careful pruning his poem could make a Paradise of words properly pruned and showing that the actual pruning practices of the terraculturalists of his day were a reflection of the work of Christ the Gardener, who Himself pruned the lives of his disciples to make them fruitful here on earth and to prepare them for a garden life in the Paradise-to-come:

> When thou dost greater judgements SPARE,
>   And with thy knife but prune and   PARE,
>   Ev'n fruitfull trees more fruitfull   ARE.
>
> Such sharpnes shows the sweetest FREND:
>   Such cuttings rather heal then   REND:
>   And such beginnings touch their   END. [137]

If ever there was to be a true Paradise again, the ground which was cursed at the Fall had to be healed and reclaimed. The transformation of barren ground into fertile soil was made by Christ at His resurrection. Through and by His resurrection, He, the Resurrection Gardener, made the ground so fruitful that this restored ground now bears healing herbs for sinners' wounds:

> Christ hath took in this piece of ground,
> And made a garden there for those
>   Who want herbs for their wound.[138]

Healed by the herbs of His flesh and blood, sinners now find that their eyes are opened to this Paradisal Garden who is Christ Himself; that this ground is sacred; that these herbs will bring into the eternal Paradise all who have grace to use Christ's herbs for their mortal wounds.

Finally, there is an unfolding of beauty: Paradise's flower is exempt from poison.[139] The ground, Christ, bears the flower, Christ:

> What hallow'd solitary ground did bear
>   So rare a flower,
> Within whose sacred leafs did lie
> The fulness of the Deity.[140]

From the ground of Christ's flesh springs the "unfading flower" of His life. He is Himself the flower:

> Then was there truly a *Rose* amongst *Thorns,* when through his Crown of *Thorns,* you might see his title, *Jesus Nazarenus:* for, in that very name *Nazarenus,* is involved the signification of a *flower;* the very word signifies a *flower*

> . . . *Behold him* therefore *Crowned with the Crown that his Mother gives him: His Mother, The Earth.*[141]

Because Christ the Creator and Redeemer of the earth is Himself the ground, the flower, the herb, the gardener, the terraculturalist, all ground, flowers, herbs, gardeners, terraculturalists are eternized. This is the "mystery of things": that human beings who are "inserted into Him" in a kind of hypostatic union will again be a "garden in a Paradise."[142] Their home is with God, the "Gard'ner of Universe," where "trees, herbs, flowrs" are "Environ'd with Eternity."[143]

NOTES

Chapter Six

[1] Vaughan, "The Proffer," l. 45.

[2] Traherne, "Innocence," ll. 29-35.

[3] Donne, "A Hymne to Christ, at the Authors last going into Germany," ll. 15-16. See also Vaughan, "Rules and Lessons": "Each *tree, herb,* flowre/Are shadows of his *wisedome,* and his Pow'r," ll. 95-96.

[4] Traherne, "On Christmas-Day," l. 35.

[5] Milton, "A Maske," l. 526.

[6] Cf. James Hart, *The diet of the diseased* (London, 1633), where Satan is regarded as the "chiefe actor in the action" of magical spells, p. 351.

[7] Derek J. Price, ed., Giambattista della Porta, *Natural Magick* (New York, 1957), pp. 2-3. First published in full and expanded form in 1558, it went through at least twelve editions in Latin, four in Italian, seven in French, two in German, and two in English.

[8] *Herball,* p. 776.

[9] London, 1584; reference to the edition by Hugh Ross Williamson (London, 1964), p. 139.

[10] *A discourse of witchcraft* (Cambridge, 1609), p. 629. Cf. Shakespeare, *A Midsummer Night's Dream,* where Titania claims that the quarreling fairies are the "parents and original" of "contagious fogs," rotting corn, and the "progeny of evils," II. i. 81-117.

[11] *The discoverie of witchcraft,* p. 240.

[12] *Natural Magick,* p. 24.

[13] Pliny, *Naturalis historia* XXV. 11-12; trans. from the Loeb Classical Library (London, 1956); see also the contemporary warnings of Robert Turner, *Botanologia, To the reader.*

[14] Editions of his work continued to appear; for example, one was published in Basel, 1536. For the first English translation of this work, see Paul Delany, "Constantinus Africanus' *De Coitu:* A Translation," *The Chaucer Review,* IV (1970). Constantinus treats in detail those aphrodisiacs which "we ourselves have tried and which our authors have used" (Delany, p. 63.).

[15] London, 1684, p. 545. One prescription for males who "would render a Woman very delectable, and so as to love you much in Coition," is to "take of *Euphorbium, Pyrethrum,* Cubebs and Pepper each a like quantity, powder them and incorporate them, when you would lye with a Woman anoint the Yard, and do the work," p. 547.

[16] *Adam in Eden,* chap. 277.

[17] *Herball,* p. 106.

[18] *Herball*, p. 1388. See also Jacques Ferrand, *Erotomania*, trans. Edmund Chilmead (Oxford, 1640): "there may be Medicines . . . of a power provoking to Lust: of which kinde you shall meet with diverse Catalogues," p. 306ff.

[19] Lewis Spence, *The Magic Arts in Celtic Britain* (London, 1945), p. 71.

[20] Spence, p. 71.

[21] Barbara Breasted, "Comus and the Castlehaven Scandal," *Milton Studies*, III (Pittsburgh, 1971), 201-224.

[22] *A discourse of witchcraft*, p. 635. See also Ferrand, *Erotomania*, on love potions which "deprave the judgement, and corrupt the bloud," p. 12.

[23] *Natural Magick*, pp. 219-220; for an illustration of the transformation of men into horses, see Gioseffe Petrucci, *Prodomo apologetico* (Amsterdam, 1677).

[24] *The triall of witch-craft . . .* (London, 1616), pp. 39-43, 91.

[25] Parkinson, *Theatrum*, p. 1392 ff.

[26] Lyte, *A nieuve herball*, p. 311.

[27] 3rd edn., 1681, pp. 243-244.

[28] *The Two Gentlemen of Verona* III. ii. 68; *Twelfth Night* III. iv. 74.

[29] *The seconde parte of Vuilliam Turners Herball* (Collen, 1568), fol. 165. See also Gerard, whose diction is somewhat more elegant: "Some of the Learned haue set downe that it comes of the dung of the bird called a Thrush, who hauing fed of the seeds thereof, as eating his owne bane, hath voided and left his dung vpon the tree, whereof was ingendred this berry, a most fit matter to make lime of to intrap and catch birds withall," p. 1350; and ". . . glutinous and clammy a substance . . . *Ixia* is the glue that is made of the berries of Misseltoe . . . and with his slimie and clammy substance doth so draw together, shute and glue vp the guts," p. 1351.

[30] "La colle et le clou de l'âme dans la tradition néo-platonicienne et chrétienne," *Revue belge de philologie et d'histoire*, XXXVI (1958), 72-95.

[31] *Confessions* IV, 10, 15, 19, ed. Labriolle (Paris, 1950), p. 78; Courcelle, p. 82; for additional references to Augustine, see Courcelle, pp. 81-84. Although George Herbert does not use *lime* or *glue* in his poem "Home," he uses the image of the limed bird to describe the soul "Which now is pinion'd with mortalitie,/As an intangled, hamper'd thing" (ll. 62-64).

[32] Courcelle, pp. 82-84. See also a 1533 reference in Jacob und Wilhelm Grimm, *Deutches Wörterbuch* (Leipzig, 1897), 700-701, to the "lijmrode des duvels."

[33] For a comprehensive survey of interpretations see *A Variorum Commentary on The Poems of John Milton*, ed. A.S.P. Woodhouse and Douglas Bush, II, 932-949.

[34] P. 174. Hill observes that Tutsan is called *Androsaemum maximum frutescens* by C. Bauhine and *Hypericum maximum androsaemum vulgare dictum* by Ray (p. 175); that Perfoliate Saint John's Wort is called *Androsaemum perforatum & perfoliatum* by C. Bauhine (p. 176).

[35] P. 572.

[36] Hieronymus Bock (Tragus), *Kreütterbuch* (Strassburg, 1577), pp. 27-29. This nomenclatural difficulty is apparent in the herbal of Dioscorides (which was the inspiration for centuries of botanists). Dioscorides (in John Goodyer's translation, *The Greek Herbal of Dioscorides*, 1655, ed. Robert Gunther, Oxford, 1934), uses androsaemon as an alternate name for hypericon: "*Hypericum crispum* or *H. barbatum* . . . but some call it Androsemon"; *Askuron. Hypericum perforatum*

. . . but some call it . . . Androsemon"; *Androsaimon. Hypericum perfoliatum* or *H. ciliatum Sibth. Tutsan. Androsemon"* (pp. 395-396). Further evidence for the predominance of androsaemon as a synonym for hypericon (or as an even earlier botanical term than hypericon) can be found in Sir James Smith's botanic history, *The English Flora* (London, 1828), III, 322-30.

[37] *Theatrum*, pp. 572-77.

[38] Section VA in the Claridge Druce Herbarium, Department of Botany, Oxford University.

[39] Coles, *Adam in Eden*, ch. CCLXXXV. Coles in the *Art of Simpling* describes the juices of plants: " . . . the colour of most of them be green, or of a watrish colour . . . There is hardly a Plant that yeildeth a red juice . . . ," pp. 46-47. See also Turner's *Herball* (1568), p. 18: "Androsemon . . . som have called it mans blode." Gerard's *Herball* adds that the color of the juice is "not like blacke bloud, but Claret or Gascoigne wine (pp. 530, 543). See also Bock (Tragus), *Kreütterbuch*, p. 29.

[40] The *h* in andros-haemon is, of course, the rough breathing in Greek. The addition of *y* to anglicize haemon has a parallel in Paeony, "from its Inventor Paeon . . . ," *The Magick of Kirani* (English trans., 1685), p. 11; see also Parkinson on Paeony, *Theatrum*, p. 1381.

[41] *Theatrum*, pp. 572-573.

[42] Coles, *Adam in Eden*, chap. 332.

[43] P. 63.

[44] Bock (Tragus), *Kreütterbuch*, p. 27.

[45] Lyte, *A nievve herball*, p. 66; Dodoens, *Cruyde-Boeck* (Tantwerpen, 1554) on androsaemon: "In die Apoteke eest onbekent," cap. XLII.

[46] "Man," ll. 45-46; Donne, XXVI Sermons, 8, p. 11. See also John Aubrey, *The natural history of Wiltshire*, ed. John Britton (London, 1847), p. 48: "God Almighty hath furnished us with plants to cure us, that grow perhaps within five or ten miles of our abodes, and we know it not."

[47] Richard Argentinus, *De praestigiis daemonum* (Basel, 1568), p. 208 (my translation).

[48] *His dispensatory and chirurgery*, trans. W.D. (London, 1656), p. 60.

[49] London, 1696, p. 111.

[50] 2nd ed., pp. 581-583; see also Andrew Boorde, *The breviarie of health* (London, 1575), chap. 119: " . . . there is an herbe named Fuga Demonum, or as the Grecians do name it Ipericon. In English it is named saint Johns wort, the which herbe is of that vertue that it doth repell maliciousnes or spirites."

[51] Gulielmus Gratarolus, *A direction for the health of magistrates and students*, trans. N. Newton (London, 1574), n. pag.

[52] J. Wier, *De praestigiis daemonum* (London, 1568), V, 18, 508.

[53] *Adam in Eden*, chap. CCCXXXII.

[54] *The anatomy of melancholy*, III, 490-491.

[55] *Signatures of internal things*, p. 14.

[56] *His dispensatory and chirurgery*, pp. 55-57; see also Ioannis Danielis Mylius, *Antidotarium* (Francofvrti, 1620), p. 69.

[57] *A dialogue of witches*, chaps. III, VII.

[58] Ed. James F. Dimock (London, 1684), V, viii, 269-273; cf. Sir James George Frazer, *The Golden Bough* (3rd ed., London, 1955), II, 55: "In Saintonge and Aunis the flowers served to detect the presence of sorcerers, for if one of these pestilent fellows entered a house, the bunches of St. John's wort . . . immediately dropped their yellow heads as if they had suddenly faded." And Sarah Hewett reports a variation on this in the folkore of Devon, *Nummits and Crummits* (London, 1900), p. 80: "Anoint your eyes for three days with the combined juices of the herbs, dill, vervain, and St. John's wort, and the spirits in the air will become visible to you."

[59] 1625, p. 177.

[60] Luigi Maria Sinistrari, English trans. (Paris, 1879) pp. 133-135.

[61] Donne, "A Litanie," l. 238.

[62] Gerard, p. 967.

[63] Vaughan, "The Garland," ll. 33-36.

[64] Traherne, "The Salutation," l. 35.

[65] Herbert, "The Flower," ll. 22-23.

[66] "An Epitaph on the Marchioness of Winchester," ll. 57-58.

[67] Parkinson, *Paradisus*, pp. 598-599.

[68] Milton, *Lycidas*, ll. 14, 20.

[69] Herbert, "Death," l. 1.

[70] Drayton, II, 431.

[71] Herbert, "Paradise," l. 15.

[72] Donne, *La Corona*, I, l. 9.

[73] "Of Garlands and Coronary or Garland-Plants," *Works*, III, 49-50. For a discussion rich with archaeological documentation, see J.M.C. Toynbee, *Death and Burial in the Roman World* (London, 1971); see also J.M. Gesnerus, *De coronis mortuorum* (Göttingen, 1748), and Laum, *Der Totenkranz* (Köln, 1910).

[74] *The Women of Troy*, ll. 1143-1144; Schol. Eurip. Phoen. 1632; Aristophane, *Lys.* 602. See also August F. von Pauly and Georg. Wissowa, *Pauly's Real-Encyclopädie der Classischen Altertumswissenschaft* (Stuttgart, 1893-1956), XI. 2.1594, 1603; hereafter designated as *PW*.

[75] IV. vii. 43-44; ed. W.A. Camps (Cambridge, 1965).

[76] Plutarch, *Pericles*, 36, 25; *PW*, XI. 2.1596.

[77] Propertius, IV. iii. 15-16.

[78] Propertius, IV. vii. 59.

[79] *H-1127*.

[80] Rome, 1965, pp. 10-11.

[81] Edwin R. Goodenough, *Jewish Symbols in the Greco-Roman Period* (New York, 1964), IX. 53.

[82] Brekelmans, p. 116, n. 35.

[83] XVII (June, 1747), 264-265.

[84] *Flora*, p. 239.

[85] Herbert, "The Familie," l. 20. The garland in *Lycidas* has been widely

misunderstood and interpreted only as a poetic garland by critics unfamiliar with funeral garlanding.

[86] *Ancient Funerall Monuments* (London, 1631), p. 41. Weever gives a long list of empty tombs in the ancient world and an elaborate and detailed description of monuments in various dioceses in England (Canterbury, London, Norwich).

[87] Parkinson, *Paradisus,* pp. 598-599.

[88] *PW,* XIII. 2. 1432-1442 passim; see also M.B. Ogle, "Laurel in Ancient Religion and Folklore," *AJP,* XXXI, 287ff.

[89] Josef Murr, *Die Pflanzenwelt in der Griechischen Mythologie* (Innsbruck, 1890; Groningen, 1969), p. 93; see Plutarch qu. *graec.* 12; Pausanias, VIII. 48, 2.

[90] Pliny, XVI. 239.

[91] Allan I. Ludwig, *Graven Images* (Middletown, Conn., 1966), plate 6, p. 78. See also Frederick Burgess, *English Churchyard Memorials* (London, 1963), p. 188.

[92] For the continuity of tomb-garlanding, see James Henry, *Aeneidea* (Dublin, 1878), II, 376-377: "Throughout continental Europe at the present day, the making of wreaths and garlands for tombs gives employment to a vast number of persons, these wreaths and garlands being periodically renewed during a long series of years by the affection of relatives or friends, or even of strangers. The fresh wreath still hangs on the ancient monument of Abelard and Heloise in the cemetery of Père la Chaise at Paris."

[93] *H-89,* "To Laurels."

[94] F. van der Meer and Christine Mohrmann, *Atlas of the Early Christian World* (London and Edinburgh, 1958), p. 143. For further studies on the "Trophy of the Cross" cliche, see H. von Campenhausen, "Die Passionssarkophage," *Marb. Jahrb. f. Kinstwiss.,* 5 (1929), 29f.; F.W. Deichmann and T. Klauser, *Frühchrist-liche Sarchophage* (Basel, 1966), cf. Tafel 16. See also Drayton's "sixth Eglog": "Upon thy toombe shall spring a Lawrell tree,/Whose sacred shade shall serve thee for a hearse," ll. 145-146, I, 76.

[95] Gerard, pp. 1411-1413; Parkinson, *Paradisus,* pp. 427-428.

[96] *PW,* XVI. l. 1180-1182.

[97] *PW,* XVI. l. 1179.

[98] Pliny, XV. 119-120.

[99] Pliny, XV. 125-126.

[100] Pliny, XV. 126.

[101] Euripides, *Electra,* ll. 323-325; trans. from the Loeb Classical Library (New York, 1924). Later the Old Man pays reverence to Agamemnon's tomb by crowning it with myrtle-sprays, ll. 510-512.

[102] Sonnet III, ll. 29-32.

[103] Parkinson, *Theatrum,* pp. 678-681.

[104] *PW,* V. 2. 2839-2846.

[105] *PW,* V. 2.2845-2846.

[106] Propertius, IV. vii. 79-80.

[107] Pliny, XXIV. 75-80, XVI. 144-152.

[108] Franz Cumont, *Recherches sur le symbolisme funéraire des Romains* (Paris, 1966), pp. 11, 219-220.

[109] Goodenough, IX, 7.

[110] Goodenough, IX, 54. See also *Reallexikon für Antike und Christentum* (Stuttgart, 1945), II. 29: "H.U. v. Schoenebeck . . . sieht in den Bäumen u. Hirtsenszenen gewisser Sarkophage von der Ark des. Sark. von La Gayolle Hinweise auf den Grabgarten; in diesem Sinn spricht er von der Gruppe der Paradeisossarkophage . . ."

[111] *A New English Dictionary* (Oxford, 1888). See also M. Conrad Heresbachius, *The whole art and trade of husbandry,* trans. Barnaby Googe, I (London, 1586), 32: "Least the whot weather shatter the seedes." For a contemporary note, see Graham Greene, *The Human Factor* (New York, 1979), where in Suffolk there is "the long weedy path lined with laurels that never flowered," p. 189.

[112] Donne, *La Corona,* "Annunciation," l. 4.

[113] Vaughan, "The Dawning," l. 12.

[114] See Chapter III, p. 102, and p. 107, n. 44.

[115] Marvell, "The Coronet."

[116] Donne, *La Corona,* Sonnet 1, ll. 2-8.

[117] Crashaw, "The Holy Nativity," ll. 99-102.

[118] Herbert, "A Wreath." See also "To All Angels and Saints," "Where ev'ry one is king, and hath his crown,/If not upon his head, yet in his hands," ll. 4-5.

[119] Vaughan, "The Tempest," ll. 25, 27-28.

[120] See Chaps. I and II. See also the Orthodox Liturgy, Triodion 12a, Tone One, Vespers in Saturday Evening, Sunday of the Prodigal Son, where God is describd as "the pre-eternal husbandman."

[121] *Centuries,* II. 67.

[122] "The Burning Bush" in *The New British Poets,* ed. Kenneth Rexroth (New York, 1949), pp. 160-161.

[123] Traherne, "The Author to the Critical Peruser," ll. 8, 11-14, 32-36.

[124] Traherne, "Wonder," l. 5.

[125] Traherne, "Innocence," ll. 49-54.

[126] Traherne, "Walking," ll. 39-54.

[127] Vaughan, "The Constellation," l. 28.

[128] Vaughan, "Rules and Lessons, ll. 15-16.

[129] Vaughan, "Rules and Lessons," ll. 3-4.

[130] C. Mohrmann, "Sacramentium dans les plus anciens textes chétiens," *Études sur le latin des chrétiens* (Rome, 1958), pp. 233-244.

[131] Vaughan, "Rules and Lessons," ll. 25-26.

[132] Herbert, "An Offering," ll. 19-24.

[133] Gerard, pp. 1004-1006. See also Parkinson, *Theatrum:* "to heale burstings or ruptures," "to dry up the moysture and fluxe of humors in old fretting ulcers, and cancres," "it hath his name *Heraclee,* by priviledge of excellency, as an *Hercules* or mastertamer of the strong," pp. 588-589.

[134] As Thomas Dekker observes in a plague pamphlet, physicians are "in Gods garden, gathering herbes: and soueraine rootes to cure thee," "London looke backe," *The Plague Pamphlets of Thomas Dekker,* ed. F.P. Wilson (Oxford,

1925), p. 188. In *King Lear* Cordelia, recognizing that plants contain "blest secrets" for healing the mind, prays that they will be "aidant and remediate/In the good man's distress!" (IV. v. 15-18).

[135] Herbert, "Miserie," ll. 70-75.

[136] Vaughan, "The Agreement," l. 58.

[137] Herbert, "Paradise," ll. 10-15.

[138] Herbert, "Sunday," ll. 40-42.

[139] Donne, "A Litanie," ll. 237-238.

[140] Vaughan, "The Night," ll. 15-18.

[141] Donne, *Fifty Sermons* (London, 1649), p. 303. See also *The Golden Legend of Jacobus de Voragine*, trans. Granger Ryan and Helmut Ripperger (New York, 1969), "Nazareth means flower. Whence Bernard says that the Flower willed to be born of a flower, in flower, and in the season of flowers," p. 204.

[142] Cf. Donne, *Fifty Sermons:* "I shall see him in my flesh, which shall be mine as inseparably . . . as the hypostatical union of God and man in Christ makes our nature and Godhead one person in him." p. 106.

[143] Traherne, "The City," l. 20. Although Traherne is describing a city, it is not a confined space but a place of bowers and everlasting hills, from which the Christian can "view His wide Eternity" (l. 65).

BIBLIOGRAPHY

Adams, Thomas. *The Workes of Tho: Adams.* London, 1630.

Agricola, G.A. *A philosophical treatise of husbandry and gardening.* Trans. and revised by Richard Bradley. London, 1721.

Argentinus, Richard. *De praestigiis daemonum.* Basel, 1568.

Aubrey, John, *Brief Lives.* Ed. A Clark. Oxford, 1898.

_____ . *Miscellanies.* London, 1696.

Austen, Ralph. *A treatise of fruit-trees.* Oxford, 1653, 1657, 1665.

_____ . *The spiritual use of an orchard or garden of fruit trees,* Oxford, 1657; rpt. London, 1847.

Bacon, Francis. *Bacon's Essays.* Ed. Richard Whately. Boston, 1871.

_____ . *The Works of Francis Bacon.* Ed. James Spedding, *et al.* New York, 1869.

Barrough, Philip. *The method of phisicke.* London, 1583.

Beale, John. *Herefordshire orchards.* London, 1657.

Blake, Stephen. *The compleat gardeners practice.* London, 1664.

Blith, Walter. *The English improover*. London, 1649.

_____ . *The English improover improved*. 3rd impression. London, 1652.

Blount, Sir Thomas Pope. *A natural history*. London, 1693.

Bock, Hieronymus (Tragus). *Kreütterbuch*. Strassburg, 1577.

_____ . *De stirpium*. Argentorati, 1552.

Bonet, Theophile. *Mercurius compitalitius*. London, 1684.

Boorde, Andrew. *The breviarie of health*. London, 1575.

Boyle, Robert. *The Works of the Honourable Robert Boyle*. London, 1772.

Bradwell, Stephen. *Helps for suddain accidents*. London, 1633.

Breasted, Barbara. "Comus and the Castlehaven Scandal." *Milton Studies*, III (1971), 201-224.

Brekelmans, Antonius J. *Martyrerkranz*. Rome, 1965.

Browne, Sir Thomas. *The Works of Sir Thomas Browne*. Ed. Geoffrey Keynes. London, 1928.

Burgess, Frederick. *English Churchyard Memorials*. London, 1963.

Burton, Robert. *The anatomy of melancholy*. Ed. A.R. Shilleto. London, 1903.

Campenhausen, H. von. "Die Passionssarkophage." *Marb. Jahrb. f. Kinstweiss., 5 (1929)*.

Chester, Robert. Loves Martyr or, Rosalins Complaint. London, 1601.

Clapham, A.R. et al. *The Excursion Flora of the British Isles*. Cambridge, 1968.

Coles, William. *Adam in Eden*. London, 1657.

_____ . *The art of simpling*. London, 1656.

Commelyn, J. *The Belgic, or Netherlandish Hesperides*. Trans. G.V.N. London, 1683.

_____ . *Nederlantze Hesperides*. Amsterdam, 1676.

Cook, Moses. *The manner of raising, ordering, and improving* forrest-trees. London, 1676.

Cotta, John. *The triall of witch-craft* . . . London, 1616.

Courcelle, Pierre. "La colle et le clou de l'âme dans la tradition néo-platonicienne et chrétiénne." *Revue belge de philologie et d'histoire*, XXXVI (1958), 72-95.

Cowley, Abraham. *The Complete Works in Verse and Prose.* Ed. Alexander B. Grosart. Edinburgh, 1881.

Crashaw, Richard. *The Poems of Richard Crashaw.* Ed. L.C. Martin. Oxford, 1927.

Crollius, Oswald. *Philosophy reformed and improved.* Trans. H. Pinnell. London, 1657.

——————. *Signatures of internal things.* London, 1669.

Culpeper, Nicholas. *The complete herbal.* London, 1850.

——————. *The English physitian.* London, 1652.

——————. *The English physitian enlarged.* London, 1653.

Culpeper, Nicholas and Abdiah Cole. *The rationall physitian's library.* London, 1661.

Cumont, Franz. *Recherches sur le symbolisme funéraire des Romains.* Paris, 1966.

Curtis, William. *A catalogue of the British, medicinal, culinary, and agricultural plants cultivated in the London botanic garden.* London, 1783.

Daneau, Lambert. *A dialogue of witches.* Trans. Thomas Twyne. London, 1575.

——————. *The wonderful workmanship of the world.* Trans. Thomas Twyne. London, 1578.

Davie, Donald. *In the Stopping Train.* Manchester, 1977.

——————. "Observances," an unpublished poem read at Calvin College, Grand Rapids, Michigan, March, 1979.

D'Auxerre, Louis Liger. *The compleat florist.* London, 1706.

Deichmann, F.W., and Klauser, T. *Frühchristliche Sarcophage.* Basel, 1966.

de la Primavdaye, Peter. *The French academie.* London, 1618.

Della Porta, Giambattista. *Natural Magick*. Edited by Derek J. Price. New York, 1957.

Dialogue creaturarum. M. de Keyser(?). Antwerp(?), 1535.

Dioscorides. *The Greek Herbal of Dioscorides*. Englished by John Goodyer. Ed. Robert T. Gunther. New York, 1959.

Dodoens, Rembert. *Cruyde-Boeck*. Antwerp, 1554.

_____ . *Cruydt-Boeck*. Enlarged with commentary from other writers and Carolus Clusius. Antwerp, 1664.

_____ . *Stirpium historiae pemptades sex . . .* Antverpiae, 1616.

Donne, John. *The Poems of John Donne*. Ed. Herbert J.C. Grierson. Oxford, 1912, 1951.

_____ . *The Sermons of John Donne*. Ed. Evelyn M. Simpson and George R. Potter. Berkeley, 1954.

_____ . *Fifty Sermons*. London, 1649.

_____ . *XXVI Sermons*. London, 1661.

Drage, William. *Daimonomageia*. London, 1665.

Drayton, Michael. *The Works of Michael Drayton*. Ed. J. William Hebel. 5 vols. Oxford, 1961.

Drope, Francis. *A short and sure guid*. Oxford, 1672.

Du Laurens, André. *A discourse of the preservation of sight . . .* Trans. Richard Svrphlet. London, 1599.

Dymock, Cressy. *An essay for advancement of husbandry learning*. London, 1651.

Evelyn, John. *Fumifugium*. London, 1661.

_____ . *Sylva*. London, 1664.

_____ . *The compleat gard'ner*. By Mon.sr de La Quintinye. London, 1693.

_____ . *The Diary of John Evelyn*. Ed. E.S. de Beer. Oxford, 1955.

Floyer, John. *Touch-stone of medicines*. London, 1687.

Fussell, G.E. *The Old English Farming Books from Fitzherbert to*

Tull 1523-1730. London, 1947.

Gerard, John. *The herball or generall historie of plantes.* London, 1597; enlarged and amended by Thomas Johnson, London, 1633, 1636.

Goodenough, Edwin R. *Jewish Symbols in the Greco-Roman Period.* 3 vols. New York, 1964.

Gratarolus, Gulielmus. *A direction for the health of magistrates and students.* London, 1574.

Grew, Nehemiah. *An idea of a phytological history propounded.* London, 1673.

Gunther, R.T. *Early British Botanists and Their Gardens.* Oxford, 1922.

Hanmer, Thomas. *The garden book of Sir Thomas Hanmer Bart. With an introduction by E.S. Rohde.* London, 1933.

Harrison, William. *First Two Editions of Holinshed's Chronicle, A.D. 1577, 1587.* Ed. Frederick J. Furnivall. London, 1877.

Hart, James. *The diet of the diseased.* London, 1633.

Hartlib, Samuel. *Legacie of husbandry.* Unsigned petition in Sheffield University Library, Hartlib Papers LXVI 22.

——————. *The reformed husband-man.* London, 1651.

Harvey, Gideon. *Morbus Anglicus.* London, 1672.

——————. *The vanities of philosophy & physick.* London, 1699.

Henrey, Blanche. *British Botanical and Horticultural Literature Before 1800.* 3 vols. London, 1975.

Herbert, George. *The Works of George Herbert.* Ed. F.E. Hutchinson. Oxford, 1967.

Herbert, Sir Edward, Lord H. of Cherbury. *Autobiography.* Ed. S. L. Lee. London, 1886.

——————. *The Poems of Edward, Lord Herbert of Cherbury.* Ed. G.C. Moore-Smith. Oxford, 1968.

Heresbachius, M. Conradus. *Four bookes of husbandry.* Trans.

Barnabe Googe. Increased and enlarged by Gervase Markham. London, 1577.

_____. *The whole art and trade of husbandry.* Trans. Barnaby Googe. London, 1586.

Herrick, Robert. *The Complete Poetry of Robert Herrick.* Ed. J. Max Patrick. New York, 1968.

Hewett, Sarah. *Nummits and Crummits.* London, 1900.

Hill, John. *The British herbal.* London, 1756.

_____. *Eden:* or, *a compleat body of gardening.* London, 1757.

Jonson, Ben. *Ben Jonson.* Ed. C.H. Herford and Percy Simpson. Oxford, 1927, 1954.

_____. *Selected Masques.* Ed. Stephen Orgel. New Haven, 1970.

Kessler, Herbert L. *The Illustrated Bibles from Tours.* Princeton, 1977.

Kirschbaum, Englebert. *Lexicon der Christlichen Ikonographie.* Rom, Freiburg, Basel, Wien, 1970.

Langham, William. *The garden of health.* 2nd ed. London, 1633.

Laurenberg, Petri. *Horticultura.* Francofurti, 1631(?).

Lawrence, Anthony and John Beale. *Nurseries, orchards, profitable gardens, and vineyards encouraged.* London, 1677.

LeGendre, Curate of Henonville. *The manner of ordering fruit-trees.* Trans. John Evelyn(?). London, 1660.

Lemay, Helen. "The Stars and Human Sexuality: Some Medieval Scientific Views." *Isis,* 71 (1980), 127-137.

Lemnius, Levinus. *An herbal for the Bible.* Trans. Thomas Newton. London, 1587.

Ludwig, Allan I. *Graven Images.* Middletown, Conn., 1966.

Lyte, Henry. *A nieuve herball.* London, 1578.

Macht, David I. "Calendula or Marigold in Medical History and in Shakespeare." *Bulletin of the History of Medicine,* XXIX (1955), 491-502.

_____. "Mandrakes in the Bible, Literature, and Pharmacology." *American Druggist* (December 1933), 24-76.

Marvell, Andrew. *The Complete Poems.* Ed. Elizabeth Story Donno. Harmondsworth, 1976.

Mascall, Leonard. *A booke of the arte and maner, how to plant and graffe all sortes of trees.* London, 1572.

_____. *The country-mans new art of planting and graffing.* London, 1652.

Matthioli, Pietro Andrea. *Kreutterbuch.* (durch Camerarium). Franckfurt, 1600.

Meager, Leonard. *The compleat English gardener.* London, 1710.

_____. *The mystery of husbandry.* London, 1649.

_____. *The new art of gardening.* London, 1697.

Meer, F. van der, and Christine Mohrmann. *Atlas of the Early Christian World.* London and Edinburgh, 1958.

Mercklin, Georg Abraham. *Sylloge physico-medicinalium casuum incantationi adscribi solitorum.* Nürnberg, 1698.

Milton, John. *John Milton: Complete Poems and Major Prose.* Ed. Merritt Y. Hughes. New York, 1957.

Mohrmann, C. "Sacramentium dans les plus anciens textes chrétiens." *Études sur le latin des chrétiens.* Rome, 1958.

Mollet, André. *Der lust-garten.* Stockholm, 1651.

_____. *The garden of pleasure.* London, 1670.

Murr, Josef. *Die Pflanzenwelt in der Griechischen Mythologie.* Innsbruck, 1890, Groningen, 1969.

Mylius, Ioannis Danielis. *Antidotarium.* Francofvrti, 1620.

Nourse, Timothy. *Campania foelix.* London, 1700.

Otten, Charlotte F. "Donne's 'Elegie upon the Untimely Death of the Incomparable Prince Henry.' " *Explicator,* 33 (1975), 59.

_____. "Milton's Haemony." *English Literary Renaissance,* V (1975), 81-95.

_____ . "Ophelia's 'Long Purples' or 'Dead Men's Fingers.' " *Shakespeare Quarterly*, 30 (1979), 397-402.

Paracelsus. *His dispensatory and chirurgery*. Trans. W.D. London, 1656.

Parkinson, John. *Paradisi in sole paradisus terrestris*. London, 1629.

_____ . *Theatrum botanicum*. London, 1640.

Pauly, August F. von, and Georg Wissowa. *Pauly's Real-Encyclopädie der Classischen Altertumswissenschaft*. 24 vols. Stuttgart, 1893-1956.

Perkins, William. *A discourse of witchcraft*. Cambridge, 1609.

Petrucci, Gioseffe. *Prodomo apologetico*. Amsterdam, 1677.

Phayre, Thomas. *A treatyse of the pestilence*. London, 1545.

Philo of Carpasia. *Commentary on the Canticles*, 217, Migne, *Patrologia Graeca*, 40, 136B.

Platt, Hugh. *Delights for ladies*. London, 1617.

_____ . *Floraes Paradise*. London, 1608.

Plattes, Gabriel. *A discovery of infinite treasure*. London, 1639.

Pliny. *Natural history*. The Loeb Classical Library. 10 vols. London, 1938-1962.

Plot, Robert. *The natural history of Stafford-shire*. Oxford, 1686.

Rahner, Hugo. *Greek Myths and Christian Mystery*. London, 1963.

Randolph, Charles B. "The Mandragora of the Ancients in Folk-Lore and Medicine." *Proceedings of the American Academy of Arts and Sciences*, 40 (1905), 487-537.

Raven, Charles E. *English Naturalists from Neckham to Ray*. Cambridge, 1947.

_____ . *John Ray*. Cambridge, 1950.

Rea, John. *Flora: seu, de florum cultura*. London, 1665.

Rydén, Mats. *Shakespearean Plant Names*. Stockholm, 1978.

Salmon, William. *Botanologia.* London, 1710.

Schiller, Gertrude. *Iconography of Christian Art.* London, 1972.

Scot, Reginald. *Discoverie of Witchcraft.* Edited by Hugh Ross Williamson. London, 1964.

Shakespeare, William. *The Riverside Shakespeare.* Ed. G. Blakemore Evans, Boston, 1974.

Sharrock, Robert. *The history of the propagation & improvement of vegetables.* Oxford, 1660.

Sinistrari, Luigi Maria. *Demoniality.* English trans. Paris, 1879.

Snow, T. *Apopiroscopy.* London, 1702.

St. Augustine. *Confessions.* Trans. R.S. Pine-Coffin. Baltimore, 1961.

Stevens, Charles and John Liebault. *Maison rustique or the countrie farme.* Trans. Richard Surflet. London, 1600.

Sweert, Emanuel. *Florilegium.* Francofurti, 1612.

Switzer, Stephen. *The nobleman, gentleman, and gardener's recreation.* London, 1715.

Tourneur, Cyril. *The Atheist's Tragedy.* Ed. Irving Ribner. London, 1964.

Toynbee, J.M.C. *Death and Burial in the Roman World.* London, 1971.

Tradescant, John the Younger. *Musaeum Tradescantianum.* London, 1656.

Traherne, Thomas. *Centuries, Poems, and Thanksgivings.* Ed. H.M. Margoliouth. 2 vols. Oxford, 1958.

Turner, Robert. *Botanologia.* London, 1664.

Turner, William. *A new herball.* London, 1551.

_____ . *The first and seconde partes of the herbal of William Turner.* Collen, 1568.

Vaughan, Henry. *The Complete Poetry* Ed. French Fogle. New York, 1964.

Vaughan, William. *Directions for health.* 6th ed. London, 1626.

van der Groen, I. *Den Nederlandtsen hovenier.* Amsterdam, 1669.

Webster, Charles. *The Great Instauration.* London, 1975.

_____ . "Henry More and Descartes: Some New Sources." *British Journal for the History of Science,* 4 (1969), 359-377.

Webster, John. *The Complete Works of John Webster.* Ed. F.L. Lucas. London, 1927.

Westmacott, William. *A Scripture herbal.* London, 1694.

_____ . *Theolobotonologia.* London, 1694.

Wier, Johann. *De praestigiis daemonum.* Basel, 1568.

Willis, Thomas. *Two discourses concerning the soul of brutes.* Trans. S. Pordage. London, 1683.

Woodhouse, A.S.P. and Douglas Bush, ed. *A Variorum Commentary on the Poems of John Milton.* New York, 1972.

Worlidge, John. *Systema agriculturae.* London, 1669, 1677, 1681.

INDEX

Of Names

Of Plants